EXPERIENCING VISUAL STORYWORLDS

THEORY AND INTERPRETATION OF NARRATIVE
James Phelan, Katra Byram, and Faye Halpern, Series Editors

EXPERIENCING VISUAL STORYWORLDS

FOCALIZATION IN COMICS

Silke Horstkotte
and Nancy Pedri

THE OHIO STATE UNIVERSITY PRESS
COLUMBUS

Copyright © 2022 by The Ohio State University.
All rights reserved.

Library of Congress Cataloging-in-Publication Data
Names: Horstkotte, Silke, author. | Pedri, Nancy, author.
Title: Experiencing visual storyworlds : focalization in comics / Silke Horstkotte and Nancy Pedri.
Other titles: Theory and interpretation of narrative series.
Description: Columbus : The Ohio State University Press, [2022] | Series: Theory and interpretation of narrative | Includes bibliographical references and index. | Summary: "Through a series of close readings from a wide range of comics and graphic narratives—including Jason Lutes's *Berlin*, Charles Burns's *Black Hole*, Ellen Forney's *Marbles*, Eric Drooker's *Flood!*, and Craig Thompson's *Habibi*—the authors dissect how comics draw readers into the actions, minds, and worlds of characters"—Provided by publisher.
Identifiers: LCCN 2021057738 | ISBN 9780814215029 (cloth) | ISBN 0814215025 (cloth) | ISBN 9780814282052 (ebook) | ISBN 0814282059 (ebook)
Subjects: LCSH: Comic books, strips, etc.—History and criticism. | Graphic novels—History and criticism. | Storytelling in literature. | Narration (Rhetoric)
Classification: LCC PN6714 .H677 2022 | DDC 741.5/9—dc23/eng/20220202
LC record available at https://lccn.loc.gov/2021057738
Other identifiers: 9780814258293 (paper) | 0814258298 (paper)

Cover design by Nathan Putens
Text composition by Stuart Rodriguez
Type set in Minion Pro

∞ The paper used in this publication meets the minimum requirements of the American National Standard for Information Sciences—Permanence of Paper for Printed Library Materials. ANSI Z39.48-1992.

For our mothers

Eva-Maria Horstkotte & *Mariagrazia Pedri*
14.8.1940–23.12.1997   *22.8.1950–16.4.2009*

CONTENTS

List of Illustrations		ix
Acknowledgments		xiii
PREFACE	Focalization's Action	xvii
CHAPTER 1	Experiencing Visual Storyworlds: Focalization in Comics	1
CHAPTER 2	Focalization, Experience, and What It's Like	28
CHAPTER 3	Graphic Memoir	59
CHAPTER 4	Graphic Historiography	101
CHAPTER 5	Wordlessness	146
CHAPTER 6	Metafictionality	178
CONCLUSION	Putting Focalization in Perspective	217
Bibliography		237
Index		251

ILLUSTRATIONS

FIGURE 0.1	McKean, Dave. 2016. *Cages.* 25th anniversary edition. Dark Horse. p. 240.	xxii
FIGURE 1.1	Lutes, Jason. 2002. *Berlin: City of Stones.* Drawn and Quarterly. p. 179.	19
FIGURE 1.2	Lutes, Jason. 2002. *Berlin: City of Stones.* Drawn and Quarterly. p. 17.	21
FIGURE 2.1	Simmons, Josh. 2008. *Jessica Farm: Volume 1.* Fantagraphics. p. 5.	37
FIGURE 2.2	Simmons, Josh. 2008. *Jessica Farm: Volume 1.* Fantagraphics. p. 5.	37
FIGURE 2.3	Burns, Charles. 2005. *Black Hole.* Pantheon. n.p.	41
FIGURE 2.4	Burns, Charles. 2005. *Black Hole.* Pantheon. n.p.	42
FIGURE 2.5	Burns, Charles. 2005. *Black Hole.* Pantheon. n.p.	43
FIGURE 2.6	Burns, Charles. 2005. *Black Hole.* Pantheon. n.p.	44
FIGURE 2.7	Burns, Charles. 2005. *Black Hole.* Pantheon. n.p.	46
FIGURE 2.8	Ware, Chris. 2000. *Jimmy Corrigan: The Smartest Kid on Earth.* Pantheon. n.p.	51

FIGURE 2.9	Ware, Chris. 2000. *Jimmy Corrigan: The Smartest Kid on Earth.* Pantheon. n.p.	54–55
FIGURE 3.1	Bechdel, Alison. 2006. *Fun Home: A Family Tragicomic.* Mariner. p. 78.	63
FIGURE 3.2	Barry, Lynda. 2002. *One! Hundred! Demons!* Sasquatch Books. n.p.	71
FIGURE 3.3	Forney, Ellen. 2012. *Marbles: Mania, Depression, Michelangelo, and Me.* Gotham. p. 10.	74
FIGURE 3.4	Forney, Ellen. 2012. *Marbles: Mania, Depression, Michelangelo, and Me.* Gotham. p. 102.	75
FIGURE 3.5	Forney, Ellen. 2012. *Marbles: Mania, Depression, Michelangelo, and Me.* Gotham. pp. 50–51.	78–79
FIGURE 3.6	Leavitt, Sarah. 2010. *Tangles: A Story about Alzheimer's, My Mother and Me.* Broadview. p. 37.	84
FIGURE 3.7	Leavitt, Sarah. 2010. *Tangles: A Story about Alzheimer's, My Mother and Me.* Broadview. Title page.	85
FIGURE 3.8	Small, David. 2009. *Stitches: A Memoir.* McClelland and Stewart. p. 63.	87
FIGURE 3.9	Small, David. 2009. *Stitches: A Memoir.* McClelland and Stewart. p. 191.	89
FIGURE 3.10	Small, David. 2009. *Stitches: A Memoir.* McClelland and Stewart. p. 39.	90
FIGURE 3.11	Small, David. 2009. *Stitches: A Memoir.* McClelland and Stewart. p. 147.	91
FIGURE 3.12	B., David. 2005. *Epileptic.* Translated by Kim Thompson. Pantheon. p. 41.	95
FIGURE 3.13	B., David. 2005. *Epileptic.* Translated by Kim Thompson. Pantheon. p. 72.	97
FIGURE 3.14	B., David. 2005. *Epileptic.* Translated by Kim Thompson. Pantheon. p. 202.	98
FIGURE 4.1	Spiegelman, Art. 1991. *Maus: A Survivor's Tale. Part II: And Here My Troubles Began.* Pantheon. p. 50.	110
FIGURE 4.2	Spiegelman, Art. 1991. *Maus: A Survivor's Tale. Part II: And Here My Troubles Began.* Pantheon. p. 41.	114
FIGURE 4.3	Stassen, Jean-Philippe. 2006. *Deogratias: A Tale of Rwanda.* Translated by Alexis Siegel. First Second Books. p. 1.	118

FIGURE 4.4	Stassen, Jean-Philippe. 2006. *Deogratias: A Tale of Rwanda*. Translated by Alexis Siegel. First Second Books. p. 27.	121
FIGURE 4.5	Kunwu, Li and Philippe Ôtié. [2009; 2011] 2012. *A Chinese Life*. Translated by Edward Gauvin. Harry N. Abrams. Chapter 3 title page.	129
FIGURE 4.6	Kunwu, Li and Philippe Ôtié. [2009; 2011] 2012. *A Chinese Life*. Translated by Edward Gauvin. Harry N. Abrams. p. 103.	131
FIGURE 4.7	Kunwu, Li and Philippe Ôtié. [2009; 2011] 2012. *A Chinese Life*. Translated by Edward Gauvin. Harry N. Abrams. p. 489.	133
FIGURE 4.8	Sacco, Joe. 2003. *Palestine*. Jonathan Cape. p. 33.	136
FIGURE 4.9	Sacco, Joe. 2003. *Palestine*. Jonathan Cape. p. 67.	138
FIGURE 4.10	Sacco, Joe. 2003. *Palestine*. Jonathan Cape. p. 2.	139
FIGURE 4.11	Sacco, Joe. 2002. *Safe Area Goražde: The War in Eastern Bosnia 1992–1995*. Fantagraphics. p. 109.	141
FIGURE 4.12	Sacco, Joe. 2009. *Footnotes in Gaza*. Jonathan Cape. p. 265.	143
FIGURE 5.1	Simmons, Josh. 2007. *House*. Fantagraphics. n.p.	156
FIGURE 5.2	Simmons, Josh. 2007. *House*. Fantagraphics. n.p.	157
FIGURE 5.3	Drooker, Eric. 2007. *Flood! A Novel in Pictures*. Dark Horse. n.p.	163
FIGURE 5.4	Drooker, Eric. 2007. *Flood! A Novel in Pictures*. Dark Horse. n.p.	163
FIGURE 5.5	Drooker, Eric. 2007. *Flood! A Novel in Pictures*. Dark Horse. n.p.	166
FIGURE 5.6	Tan, Shaun. 2006. *The Arrival*. Hodder Children's Books. n.p.	171
FIGURE 5.7	Tan, Shaun. 2006. *The Arrival*. Hodder Children's Books. n.p.	173
FIGURE 5.8	Tan, Shaun. 2006. *The Arrival*. Hodder Children's Books. n.p.	175
FIGURE 6.1	Mazzucchelli, David. 2009. *Asterios Polyp*. Pantheon. n.p.	183
FIGURE 6.2	Mazzucchelli, David. 2009. *Asterios Polyp*. Pantheon. n.p.	186
FIGURE 6.3	Mazzucchelli, David. 2009. *Asterios Polyp*. Pantheon. n.p.	188
FIGURE 6.4	Thompson, Craig. 2011. *Habibi*. Faber. p. 39.	196
FIGURE 6.5	Thompson, Craig. 2011. *Habibi*. Faber. p. 9.	198
FIGURE 6.6	Thompson, Craig. 2011. *Habibi*. Faber. p. 13.	200
FIGURE 6.7	Thompson, Craig. 2011. *Habibi*. Faber. pp. 104–5.	203
FIGURE 6.8	Thompson, Craig. 2011. *Habibi*. Faber. p. 47.	209

ACKNOWLEDGMENTS

So many people and places have played a role in the creation of this book. To know where to begin to thank them all is not so simple, and the risk of forgetting some is big.

An obvious place for us to start acknowledging those who have impacted our book is at the Amsterdam School for Cultural Analysis, where we met each other and Mieke Bal. Although we didn't know at the time that we would be spending so much time with the focalization concept, there is little doubt that Mieke's influence and guidance have shaped our thinking. With her, the ASCA research community provided us with a stimulating lived experience that launched us into the world of narratology and into our long history of collaboration. Esther Peeren, who introduced us, and Eloe Kingma, ASCA's longtime managing director, played a large role in making us feel welcome in Amsterdam. To say thank you seems too small a gesture in return for how ASCA and the great people it gathers together have influenced us over the years.

Some years and collaborations after that initial encounter, we had the opportunity to begin work on *Experiencing Visual Storyworlds: Focalization in Comics* in St. John's, Newfoundland. A John G. Diefenbaker Award brought Silke to Nancy's home base, and over that year we traced out an initial idea for the book and wrote a test article, "Focalization in Graphic Narrative," to see if we were on to something. Ideas developed with the support of and exchanges with members of the English Department at Memorial University of Newfoundland, especially Jennifer Lokash, Andrew Loman, and Fiona Polack. That support and encouragement has not faded over time, and we are extremely grateful for that.

Since her academic year in Newfoundland, Silke has worked at the Universities of Leipzig, Tübingen, Cologne, and Warwick, while our collaboration has developed over various long-distance communication channels and several research trips to Leipzig. During this time, the community of scholars in the International Society for the Study of Narrative has provided a home for our work and a wonderful, unpredictable mix of experiences. From the start of this project, the narrative crowd has offered us critical feedback, stimulating conversations, and guidance that have shaped the writing of this book. It has recognized our work on focalization in comics with a 2012 Award for the Best Essay in *Narrative* and an invitation in 2016 to speak at the Contemporary Narrative Theory panel. Throughout the years, the narrative crowd has approached our work with attentive ears and open smiles, but also at times with suspicious eyes that told us to go back to work and think a bit more about focalization and visual narratology. Among our many friends, Emma Kafalenos, Brian McHale, and Jim Phelan were particularly instrumental in getting our work on track. We consider ourselves fortunate to be part of an academic family that laughs and dances, celebrates and mourns, and regularly gathers despite distances and weather and other unforeseeable obstacles. If only our arms were long enough and our voices loud enough to distribute hugs and thank yous to each and every one of you, wherever you may be around the globe!

Several institutions have welcomed us, together or individually, to present our work on focalization in comics. These include the Department of Comparative Literature (University of Toronto), the Department of English (Memorial University of Newfoundland), the Institut des langues et cultures d'Europe, Amérique, Afrique, Asie et Australie (Université Grenoble Alpes), the Humanities Research Group (University of Windsor), the Feminist Research Institute (University of New Mexico), the School of Modern Languages and Cultures (University of Warwick), the Department of English (Bergische Universität Wuppertal), the PathoGraphics Research Group (Freie Universität Berlin), Project Narrative (The Ohio State University), Gesellschaft für Comicforschung (ComFor), Closure (Christian-Albrechts-Universität zu Kiel), and the Institut für Medienkultur und Theater (Universität zu Köln). We are so grateful for the generosity of those who invited us and of those who engaged with our work through open discussions and questions. This dialogue has definitely informed the thinking and writing of this book.

We would also like to thank the readers, editors, and production team at The Ohio State University Press. They have been critical and sharp, but also patient and kind, lending advice and encouragement when needed. *Experiencing Visual Storyworlds: Focalization in Comics* is the book it is also because of them.

Finally, we would like to thank our families, who have seen (or heard) us working on this book, asked about and listened to updates about the book, and shown the appropriate amount of enthusiasm for our book at just the right time. To them, we say thank you tons.

PREFACE

Focalization's Action

Focalization, by which we understand the filtering of a story through the perception and evaluation of a character or noncharacter narrator, is a central category of narrative analysis and crucial to the understanding of narratives. The type of focalization in a given narrative colors the mood and atmosphere of the storyworld, giving it a particular feel. Moreover, by cuing recipients into how the narrative world is understood by its characters, focalization draws them into the experiencing of that world. Especially when it is tied to a focal character, focalization makes it possible for recipients to understand why characters do what they do, even to feel what characters feel and experience what they experience. Focalization encompasses corporeal and affective as well as cognitive and perceptual aspects, and often produces feelings of closeness in recipients. When the filtering of focalization is associated with a noncharacter narrator, however, it can become distanced, evaluative, even ironic, evoking a more intellectual, cognitive mood.

Focalization is at work in every narrative. It can be marked in different ways in different narrative media. In literary fiction, focalization markers include free indirect discourse, reported thought, and what Dorrit Cohn has called "psycho-narration," the "profusion of verbs and nouns of consciousness" that are applied to a central character but rendered in the narrator's voice (32). In film, focalization can be marked through point-of-view shots, perception or projection shots, and other angles of framing (Branigan 79).

In comics, point-of-view images, gaze images, and subjective optical effects have been identified as focalization markers (Mikkonen 2013: 102–3). Other comics storytelling techniques that may cue focalization include color, shading and line work, panel size and framing, layout, lettering, the repetition of identical or similar panels, and the use of visual metaphors, as well as the style and genre of a comic, all of which can operate individually or in conjunction to indicate focalization and direct the mood of a graphic narrative. In fact, because comics are a highly versatile, stylistically diverse storytelling medium, focalization markers are often specific to a particular comic book and its narrative world.

This study is devoted to focalization in comics. We demonstrate how the comics medium requires a substantial revision of the narratological key concept of focalization, and we show how that revised concept enables a deeper understanding of the art of comics and of some especially striking examples of that art. We thereby hope to contribute to the fields of comics studies and of narrative theory, as well as to the critical conversations about the specific narratives they analyze. Comics are a bimodal medium, narrating across visual and verbal tracks simultaneously. Their bimodality allows for a complex distribution of narration and focalization. Comics also communicate on multiple levels, including those of the panel, the sequence, the page layout, and the entire comic book. Their multilayered narrative structure prompts readers to continuously consider several combinations of narrative instances at once, to return to previous moments in the narrative, and to reconfigure their understanding and experiencing of the narrative in relation to newly acquired information.

Comics are stylistically versatile, and they often explicitly connect the hand-drawn quality of their style to the corporeality of the comic artist. To readers, this corporeal quality offers a particular kind of rich sensorial experience. The style of a comic can express the subjective perception of characters, the atmosphere of a narrative world, or the take of a noncharacter narrator on characters and their world. Style is a subtle, highly effective focalization marker, conveying character attitude and emotion and inviting affective responses in readers. However, focalization markers like style or color should not be confused with focalization itself: While style and color are aspects of the text that can be pinpointed in analyses, focalization is not an aspect of the text but an analytical concept that describes the distribution of perception, knowledge, and affect in a narrative based on the identification of textual markers.

Besides color, style, panel size, and so on, focalization in comics is also affected by genre, because distinct comics genres draw on specific combinations of narration and focalization and tend to carry with them specific ways of thinking and feeling. For example, autobiographical comics or graphic memoirs, as they are often called, are typically rendered by an autodiegetic narrator who is also the focal character. The genres of graphic journalism and graphic historiography often rely on a similar combination of homodiegetic narration and character-bound focalization. However, narrators in them are typically outside witnesses to other characters' stories, and their internal focalization frequently embeds the focalization of these others, leading to a more speculative, multilayered focal filtering. *Sans paroles* present an even more ambiguous focalization, often taxing readers' understanding by deliberately veiling the distinction between character bound focalization and narratorial focalization or between a character's "what it's like" and the mood of an entire narrative world. When readers sit down with a comic from a particular genre, they are already primed to experience certain things in a certain way.

Our main argument in this book is that the focalization of a narrative gives readers a particular kind of access to experiences within the storyworld, enabling them to have experiences in their own turn. In our study of how focalization can be productively engaged in concrete analyses of individual comics, we emphasize that focalization's greatest action is not to provide an angle of vision on a particular object or narrative agent. Rather, its main narrative work is to cue readers as to how the narrative world is understood by those who occupy it and, by doing so, draw readers into the mental and physical experiencing of those inhabitants and their world. By talking about the experiences inside a narrative, we adopt a phenomenologically inspired approach to comics narratology in order to investigate how the distribution of information and knowledge and the physical, cognitive, and emotional experiences of characters impact readers. Phenomenology addresses lived experience, that is, our conscious experience of the world (the way we exist in the world as selves) and how that experience makes the world appear a certain way. A phenomenological concept of experience also emphasizes how consciousness and the world it experiences are reciprocally related and mutually dependent. A phenomenologically inspired approach to focalization allows us to assess how the subjective experiences inside the narrative world of a comic—the seeing, acting, and judging of that world—are not confined to the narrative world, but can be accessed, even shared, by readers.

Our investigation of focalization in comics develops ideas that we first outlined in an article entitled "Focalization in Graphic Narrative" (S. Horstkotte and Pedri 2011). In it, we articulated the need to adjust focalization theories to account for the storytelling strategies of comics. We emphasized that despite the strong visual component of graphic narrative, focalization as an analytical concept cannot be used in a narrow optical sense. In this book, too, we treat optical perspective in comics as an important technique that cues focalization, but by no means the only or principal one. *Experiencing Visual Storyworlds: Focalization in Comics* participates in the endeavor to take closer account of the intricacy of comics narration, a goal that we share with comics scholars like Karin Kukkonen (2011a, 2013a, 2013b) and Kai Mikkonen (2008, 2011, 2013, 2017) on whose work we build. Within that larger undertaking, we place special emphasis on aesthetically ambitious graphic narratives to show how focalization can be a valuable concept for studying the relation between a narrator's reporting, characters' processing, and their embedding within a graphic narrative world, but also readers' response to and engagement with the narrative world.

With this endeavor, we share in the recent highlighting of mind and subjectivity in narratives across media (Palmer 2004, 2010; Reinerth and Thon; Zunshine 2006), and we show what the focalization concept can contribute to debates that have been raised by cognitive narratology and cognitive poetics (Aldama 2010; Stockwell 2002; Zunshine 2010). *Experiencing Visual Storyworlds: Focalization in Comics* ties in with new research that considers narrative "from the vantage point of the experience involved, rather than as set texts" (Brosch 2007: 143), and follows post-classical narratologists such as Renate Brosch (2007, 2008), Monika Fludernik (1996, 2001, 2009), and Manfred Jahn (1996, 1997, 1999, 2005) in conceiving of focalization as a "site of interaction between textual strategy and reader response" (Brosch 2007: 144). David Herman's description of the "what-it's-like dimension of experiencing minds" as a common focus of narratives in all media is particularly important to our concept of focalization (2009a: 147).

Our analyses connect these discussions about mind, subjectivity, and experientiality to concerns with visuality, especially with visual style. Because focalization, as we understand it, accounts for how mediation manipulates information and experience in a way that draws readers into or hinders their access to a particular narrative experience, it is necessarily bound up with larger questions of style. This is particularly apparent in comics, a highly malleable medium where the story is communicated across a verbal and a visual track that also gain in meaning across the combination of a large selection of stylistic choices, including page composition, panel layout, font selection, balloon placement, color design, and visual design. All representation depends on framing, but the comics medium is unique in visually manifesting the frame—or its absence: It directs attention to what is shown inside the frame of a panel, to what remains outside of it, and to what comes into meaning through sequencing and arrangement. Indeed, to study focalization in comics is to highlight the means by which graphic narratives make experience accessible to their readers and to the conditions under which this access becomes possible—to the dynamics of style.

Comics are a versatile medium, and so how they make experience accessible and the specific cues that are used to mark focalization are versatile, too. Even page arrangements that employ a conventional nine-panel grid can be used to great effect to evoke the cognitive and emotional complexity of an experiencing-I that engages in and with a particular narrative world. Consider, for instance, a page from Dave McKean's *Cages* (2016: 240; figure 0.1). Artist Leo Sabarsky is at a jazz club (the Katakumbe Club) and has just met Karen, whom he has sketched without her knowledge while spying on her from his apartment window. In this scene, Karen has asked Leo if he is "working on anything major" and, for the first time since they met (seven pages earlier!), he participates full-heartedly, confidently, and articulately in the discussion. He smiles and is otherwise animated as he explains how in his current project he's "trying to pull a face out of deliberately abstract marks." As Leo ponders his artistic goals, Karen leans into the table, grows more silent, and supports her chin first with her left hand and then her right. When Leo asks, "You really want to know?," Karen, whose head is now tilted to one side, asserts her interest with a simple "Sure." In the page's long closing panel, Leo and Karen recede into the background as Leo, hand extended forward, enthusiastically states, "Okay. God, I could talk all night about my painting. . . ." Three elderly characters sitting at a table in the foreground frame Karen and Leo; two of them are completely disengaged with their surroundings, their eyes distinctly closed.

This long closing panel reminds readers of the context in which the conversation between the protagonists unfolds and thus echoes the two establishing shots at the beginning of the encounter scene. It also serves another important narrative function: It is charged with emotional information that spills over into the previous panels and thus impacts how readers interpret Karen's mental state and her attitude toward the conversation and, perhaps, Leo. The group of three elderly characters in the panel sit apart from Karen and Leo, do not engage in their discussion, or even take note of them. However, despite the physical disjunction between the characters in the foreground and Karen and Leo in the background, several cues come together in this final panel to draw a link between the anonymous characters and Karen: Like Karen, the anonymous characters face toward the right of the panel; the profile of the woman in the foreground whose eyes are closed is similar in shape to Karen's profile in the background; that woman's head overlaps with Leo's large speech balloon; and, as in the previous two rows, Karen occupies the large panel's central position, her face highlighted by dark shadows. Karen is

FIGURE 0.1. McKean, Dave. 2016. *Cages*. 25th anniversary edition. Dark Horse. p. 240.

thus signaled out for consideration, as is her emotional connection to the disengaged anonymous characters. Together, these visual cues mark a character-bound focalization not through optical perspectivation, but rather across the complex interplay of panels. They join the verbal text to suggest that emotionally, the anonymous characters reflect Karen's feeling of ennui.

By communicating this shared experience to readers, these stylistic features point readers toward Karen as the main experiencing agent in the sequence and ultimately bring them to reconsider Karen's attitude toward Leo and what he is saying as being not of interest and attentiveness (as they may have thought), but rather of growing boredom and distraction. The bored facial expressions and closed eyes of the secondary characters that frame the conversation unfolding between the protagonists thus semantically complete Karen's drooped eyelids as pictured in the previous panel. In light of this closing panel, Karen's "Sure" stands in contradiction to what is now interpreted as a weary stance that betrays her lack of interest. Indeed, by drawing out Karen's lack of emotional investment, the closing panel asks readers to return to the page's first six panels and read Karen's expression as more nuanced than first imagined.

The focalization in this sequence is marked not through individual narrative devices, but through a complex interplay of narrative and stylistic features over the course of the sequence. The final larger panel in particular marks focalization within the context of the entire page layout. The page's design draws notice to the large closing panel, whose size and slight variation to the nine-panel grid design used in the first pages of the encounter scene mark a change in the conversation's rhythm. Significantly more static than the establishing shots or panoramas at the beginning of the encounter scene and the large sketch-like panels that follow the page under discussion, the page's large closing panel invites readers to pause and identify the scene's emotional nuances. The style of this comics page—panel shape and distribution, framing and focusing techniques, facial expressions and body gestures, angle and dialogue—thus grants readers access to Karen's mind, but also to the *feel* or mood of the encounter scene and of the narrative world in general. In this sense, stylistic features come together to create what Frederick Aldama calls "emotion blueprints for the reader to follow, gap-fill, and feel" (2013), and what we refer to as the "what it's like" of a narrative, following David Herman's *Basic Elements of Narrative* (2009a). Together, these features give readers access to Karen's being-in-the-world, to what it is like to be her and to experience the world from her point of view.

The trajectory of this book moves from a theoretical engagement with focalization theory and phenomenology through a consideration of focalization in different comics genres. We begin with a theoretical overview of the focalization concept, addressing its importance for the study of literary narratives before considering its application in the study of comics. Chapter 1 goes back to the origins of focalization theory to account for the similarities and differences between comics focalization and focalization in literature. Through a close reading of key passages from Jason Lutes's *Berlin: City of Stones* (2001), we draw a distinction between character-bound (or internal) and narratorial (or external) focalization in comics, but we also show how comics narrative often troubles that distinction by embedding instances of character-bound focalization in intersubjective networks of looking, and by evoking deliberate ambiguity about the deictic center of a narrative. In chapter 2, we outline the phenomenological basis of our focalization concept, and explain the connection between focalization and what it's like. We analyze three graphic novels that present unusual kinds of what it's like: Josh Simmons's *Jessica Farm: Volume 1* (2008), Charles Burns's *Black Hole* (2005), and Chris Ware's *Jimmy Corrigan: The Smartest Kid on Earth* (2000).

Chapter 3 is devoted to graphic memoir, one of the best-known and most popular comics genres. Analyses of Ellen Forney's *Marbles: Mania, Depression, Michelangelo, and Me* (2012), Sarah Leavitt's *Tangles: A Story about Alzheimer's, My Mother and Me* (2010), David Small's *Stitches: A Memoir* (2009), and David B.'s *Epileptic* (2005) focus on the central role of corporeality and embodiment that characterizes focalization in graphic memoir. We argue that embodiment in graphic memoir necessarily intersects with concerns about style, especially the creative crafting of one's physical body that speaks to the self-conscious exploration of subjectivity so central to the genre's truth claims.

The accentuation of a truthful take on a realistic narrative world is also central to graphic historiography, a genre category under which we subsume graphic journalism and nonfictional comics that represent historical events. Chapter 4 examines the complex interplay between internal and external focalization in Art Spiegelman's *Maus: A Survivor's Tale* (1986, 1991) and J. P. Stassen's *Deogratias: A Tale of Rwanda* (2006), the focalization of collective experience in Li Kunwu and Philippe Ôtié's *A Chinese Life* (2012), and the use of multiple focalization in Jo Sacco's *Palestine* (2003), *Footnotes in Gaza* (2009), and *Safe Area Goražde: The War in Eastern Bosnia 1992–1995* (2002). The different focalization strategies in these comics not only grant readers access to the what it's like of historical events but also engage them in the interpretative process—in the very experience—of trying to assign meaning to the narrative world.

In chapters 5 and 6, we turn to the fictional comics genres of *sans paroles*, or wordless comics, and to metafictional graphic novels. Wordless comics, as we emphasize in chapter 5, engage readers through visual storytelling practices that mark an ambiguous focalization at the same time as they activate an intensification of emotional experience that thrusts readers into the complex psychological realities of characters and their world. We examine several of these visual storytelling practices in Josh Simmons's *House* (2007), Eric

Drooker's *Flood! A Novel in Pictures* (2007a), and Shaun Tan's *The Arrival* (2006). Chapter 6, devoted to two metafictional graphic novels, David Mazzucchelli's *Asterios Polyp* (2009) and Craig Thompson's *Habibi* (2011), draws on several of the conclusions reached in the previous chapters to assess how the self-reflexivity of comics narrative impacts readers' understanding of focalization cues and hence their ability to engage with experiences inside the narrative.

Due to its outward-moving trajectory, our book can be read in several ways. Readers with a general curiosity about comics, about narratology, or both may follow our journey of discovery from first definitions in chapter 1 through a process of growing insight into the complexity of focalization strategies and focalization markers in different comics genres to the conclusion chapter at the end of this book. Readers with a particular interest in one of the genres we discuss may, however, also simply focus on a single chapter. And readers who don't like long stories but prefer a spoiler: Start with the conclusion and then move back to any chapter that also interests you!

CHAPTER 1

Experiencing Visual Storyworlds

Focalization in Comics

Focalization is a central concept of narrative theory. First proposed by Gérard Genette as a replacement for the older concepts "point of view" and "perspective" (1980, 1988), focalization describes the distribution of knowledge and experience within a narrative, referring to the "mood" of a narrative as opposed to the "voice" of its narrator. Although most narrative theorists find the focalization concept useful and use it widely, focalization is also a contested topic. Debates concern, among other things, the scope of the concept (Does focalization refer primarily to perception or to cognition and knowledge, or does it include both?), its differentiation from narration (Is focalization subordinate to narration or independent from it?), and its application to narrative media other than literary fiction (Is focalization in film and comics basically the same as focalization in literature, or should the concept be reformulated to account for the affordances of nonliterary media?).

In this book, we define focalization as the filtering of a story through the experiencing consciousness of a character or noncharacter narrator (see S. Horstkotte and Pedri 2011). As we will show through our analyses, this filtering includes perceptual, cognitive, affective, and corporeal aspects. Presenting readers with one or several experiential angles on the events of a narrative, focalization regulates what and how much we get to know and experience about the storyworld. It operates in narratives with a character narrator as well as in ones where the narrator is not a character, and always creates some distance between experiences within the diegesis on the one hand, and the representation of those experiences on the other. The degree of that distance, however, varies considerably between individual narratives. Narration and focalization can be grounded in the same character, or lie outside of any character, but they can also be associated with different characters, or they can be divided between a noncharacter narrator and a focalizing character.

In all of these instances, the thoughts, emotions, and perceptions of focalizing characters cannot be neatly separated out of the narrative since they only become accessible through the narratorial mediation. Depending on the specific distribution of narration and focalization in a narrative, focalization can create closeness and foster empathy with characters, particularly in cases of internal (character-bound) focalization. However, the focalization of a narrative can also inhibit or even hinder readers' emotional engagement with characters and events, especially when external focalization is bound up with an ironic narration.

Focalization is marked by textual cues through which a subjective angle is articulated and through which subjective experience becomes available to recipients. Identifying focalization markers allows readers to weigh different aspects under which a storyworld—the mental representation that readers build of a narrative world (D. Herman 2009a: 106)—can be experienced: that of a narrator against that of a character or that of one character against that of another character. Vis-à-vis the more general claim that narratives are concerned with the subjective "what it's like" of a narrative world (D. Herman 2009a), studying a narrative in terms of its focalization makes the point that this what it's like has its origin in some instance inside the narrative, and that readers thus experience narrative worlds through a particular angle of subjectivity. Because the experientiality of narrative creates opportunities for readers to have their own experiences in immersive readings, however, that angle is not necessarily restricted to one option.[1] Empirical studies conducted by Marisa Bortolussi and Peter Dixon show that the identification of focalization in a text "is subject to much idiosyncratic interpretation" (168), and the extensive narratological debates about focalization point toward the same conclusion.

This is a book about focalization in comics, a bimodal medium. Like narratives in other media, comics do not only tell stories about a fictional or nonfictional world; they also communicate to their readers what that world is *like*—how it feels to the characters who experience it and with whose expe-

---

1. On experientiality as a defining feature of narrative, see Fludernik (1996), as well as chapter 2 of this book.

rience readers engage. Unlike literary narrative, however, comics narration typically unfolds across two channels or semiotic modes, a visual and a verbal one (although both can also exist in isolation). The availability of two semiotic modes has significant consequences for the way narration and focalization operate in graphic narrative, as narration and focalization can become split or distributed between modes, leading to a high degree of narrative complexity that integrates multiple experiential angles on the world and events of a narrative. Thus, the bimodality of comics warrants a revisiting of the focalization concept, both concerning the visual expression of focalization and the kinds of focalization markers used in a comics environment, as well as the relation between narration and focalization as these play out across words and images.

In this chapter, we outline the most important contributions to focalization theory and explain our own understanding of focalization. We begin with a brief look at focalization in literature, identifying some of the focalization markers that set the frame for how readers experience literary narrative. We then consider how the distinct medial affordances of comics storytelling challenge established understandings of focalization. In the second half of this chapter, we analyze Jason Lutes's graphic novel *Berlin: City of Stones* (2001) to elucidate how focalization in comics is in some ways similar to and in other ways different from focalization in literature. We have chosen this example, the first part of Lutes's trilogy, because it embeds two intradiegetic narratives, one visual and one verbal, thereby presenting a particularly nuanced and self-reflexive take on how words and images provide different kinds of experiential angles on a narrative world. While it is often productive to analyze focalization in comics in terms of optical perspectivation—what is at times referred to as ocularization (Badman; Jost; Mikkonen 2013; Schlickers; see Pedri)—our close reading of *Berlin* demonstrates that focalization in comics has cognitive and stylistic as well as perceptual implications.

Indeed, an important goal of our analyses is to show how comics, with their bimodal narration and their outward, visual expression of subjectivity, call for a medium-specific understanding of focalization. Thus, although we find it useful to adhere to structuralist concepts of narrative for the sake of mutual understanding, we contend that some concepts are more salient in some media than in others, based on the affordances of each medium, and that concepts introduced for the study of literary narrative need to be tweaked to fit different media. For instance, the distinction between story and plot, *syuzhet* and *fabula,* that underlies all ideas of a medium-independent narrative becomes highly problematic in the context of graphic narrative, where content is inseparably bound up in individual styles, forms, and layouts. When we talk about focalization in comics, we therefore build on an established understanding of focalization in literature but we also challenge that understanding through our focus on experience and on the medium's visual and multimodal expression of experience.

Focalization and Narration

It has long been known that novels, novellas, and short stories have a narrator who appears to utter the words on the page, and that those words are also presented from a certain perspective or point of view. However, Genette appears to have been the first narrative theorist to recognize that "perspective" and "point of view" tend to conflate two things that might be better thought of apart in the analysis of a literary narrative: the "voice" of the narrator and the "mood" of a narrative (1972, 1980). In his seminal study *Narrative Discourse*, Genette coined the new term "focalization" to distinguish between these two aspects of narrative (1972, 1980). When analyzing the voice of a narrative, he explained, scholars should pose the question "Who speaks?" Determining mood, on the other hand, means asking "Who sees?" or "Who perceives?" (1980: 186). Genette thereby emphasized that perceptions, evaluations, and judgments inside a narrative world do not have to originate with the narrator but can also be anchored in non-narratorial characters. Thus, narratorial discourse can embed a second narrative focus or orientation that ought to be analyzed separately from narration.

When Genette set out to outline his understanding of focalization more clearly, however, it became obvious that focalization cannot be as rigorously detached from narration as he had first suggested. Genette distinguished between three types of focalization based on the degree of knowledge separating a narrator from the characters of a narrative (1980: 189–90). In narratives with *zero focalization*, the narrator knows and perceives more than any one character and lets readers participate in this knowledge by communicating the perceptions, thoughts, and feelings of all characters. By contrast, in *internal focalization*, the narrator perceives and knows only what the narrative's central consciousness perceives and knows, making it seem to readers as if they are in the mind of that character. In *external focalization*, finally, the narrator knows less than the central consciousness or protagonist. In this typology, focalization is not clearly separated out from narration; rather, it is embedded within or subordinate to narration and can only be determined in relation to narration.

That Genette did not consider focalization and narration as wholly separate categories but as relational terms became even more evident when he replied to some of the criticism that had been leveled against *Narrative Discourse* in his follow-up book, *Narrative Discourse Revisited* (1983, 1988). Although Genette reiterated his typology once more, he now also argued that focalization does not have to be anchored in a character: "The narrator's voice is indeed always conveyed as the voice of a person, even if anonymous, but the focal position, when there is one, is not always identified with a person" (1988: 64). The question "Who sees" or "Who perceives," Genette explained, should therefore be reformulated as "Where is the focus of perception," which "may or may not . . . be embodied in a character" (1988: 64). This specification was partly in response to Mieke Bal, who had sought to refine Genette's model by introducing an autonomous narrative agent tasked with focalization whom she called the "focalizor" (1977; see Bal 1997). Genette, in his rebuttal, insisted that focalization, unlike narration, did not come with its own instance or agent. On the contrary, he insisted that "the person who focalizes the narrative" is no one else but the narrator, "or, if one wanted to go outside the conventions of fiction, the author himself" (1988: 73).

Although often praised for its clarity, Genette's concept of focalization is in fact highly contradictory. On the one hand, Genette persistently argues that focalization is a necessary concept for understanding the contribution of characters to narrative world knowledge and mood. On the other hand, however, he associates focalization with narration and even with authorship. Not least because of Genette's wavering between separating voice and mood, on the one hand, and his emphasis on the interrelatedness of narration and focalization, on the other, focalization quickly became one of the most intensely fought over concepts of narrative theory. Besides focalization's relation to narration, debates about the concept continue to concern its differentiation from previous concepts of point of view and perspective, its internal typological distinctions, and its uneasy hitching to the optical domain.[2]

In this study, we follow Manfred Jahn and Shlomith Rimmon-Kenan, who propose a broad definition of focalization that includes not only perceptual activity and mentation but also the spatial orientation, ideological and epistemic positioning, emotional stance, and dispositions and attitudes of focal characters and narrators (Jahn 1996; Rimmon-Kenan 71).[3] Our analyses will show that this range of aspects best accounts for the wide variety of focalization in graphic narrative. We also adapt Jahn's and Bal's distinction between character-bound (or internal) and narratorial (external) focalization as a base heuristic because it offers a clear way of describing where the focal center

---

2. See, for instance, Fludernik (2001); L. Herman and Vervaeck; Hühn, Schmid, and Schönert; Jahn (1996, 1999); Margolin (2009); Niederhoff; Phelan; Schmid (2005, 2010).

3. See also D. Herman (2002, 2009b); Jahn (1997, 1999); Margolin (2009); Schlickers.

of a comic lies (Jahn 1996; Bal 2009: 150–52). As we will argue in our analyses, the focalization of a given narrative can be closely aligned with its narrative instance, or be distinct from it. Moreover, a narratorial focalization can also embed instances of character-bound focalization. Indeed, cases of mutually embedded, variable, or ambiguous focalization (where the narrative can be read both in terms of character-bound and of narratorial focalization, or where focalization may be attributed to one of several characters) abound in graphic narrative, making for a rich and reflective but sometimes also taxing reading experience.

By connecting focalization to reader response, we build on the work of Monika Fludernik, who was one of the first narratologists to move away from formal narratology and into pragmatics and reception theory. In her groundbreaking study, *Towards a "Natural" Narratology,* Fludernik defines narrativity as "mediated experientiality," arguing that "the representation of human experience is the central aim of narrative, and it can be achieved both by means of the low-level narrativity of action report and by a variety of telling, viewing and experiencing patterns in sophisticated combination" (1996: 37). We extend this understanding of narrative further into the direction of reception theory and the phenomenology of reading by asking how narrative experience is shared between characters and readers. Focalization, as we understand it, encompasses knowledge about as well as engagement with a narrative world's agents and mood. By filtering a narrative world and its events through the perceptual, cognitive, and evaluative angle of a character or noncharacter narrator, focalization provides access to specific experiential qualities, and it offers readers the opportunity to vicariously experience those qualities. Analyzing the focalization of a narrative thus leads from pinpointing textual features and formal properties that mark a subjective angle to questions of style and genre, to authorial world building, and to reader responses to narrative.

It is one of our central points that although every narrative is focalized, focalization works in many different ways, and *how* a narrative is focalized is crucial for the interpretive building of a storyworld by readers. We therefore place great emphasis on close readings, describing the focalization markers in individual graphic narratives and the way in which they work together with as much detail as possible. Storyworlds, according to David Herman, are "global mental representations enabling interpreters to frame inferences about the situations, characters, and occurrences either explicitly mentioned in or implied by a narrative text or discourse" (2009a: 106). They are interpretations of a narrative that build on textual cues, such as descriptions of locations and characters, on the way that characters speak and act, and also on the tone and mood of a narrative based on a text's style and poetics (2009a: 107).

Other theorists address the experiential dimension of reading by describing the construction of a storyworld as an imaginative "transportation" (Gerrig), a "recentering" (Ryan 2001), or a "deictic shift" of the reader on to the scene of a narrative's action (Segal). This experientiality of reading depends not only on what a narrator tells readers about a setting, characters, and their actions; it also depends on how these elements of a story are reflected through the experience of characters. Stories are not transparent windows offering a panoramic view onto a complete world. Represented through language, images, or both, and distorted to a greater or smaller degree by the voice, views, and opinions of narrators and characters, stories are always partial and incomplete. Reading a narrative is thus a creative exercise whereby gaps and indeterminacies have to be filled in creatively (Iser).

Focalization is crucial to this filling-in process. This is a point that Manfred Jahn makes in his seminal article, "Windows of Focalization." Jahn argues that the "house of fiction" (a metaphor Henry James introduced in his preface to *Portrait of a Lady*) has "a million windows of all sizes and shapes, but not a single exit . . . for the narrators to get out or for the characters to get in" (1996: 252). The same story, that is, can be presented from an infinite variety of angles, out of which any narrative mediation picks at least two: The narrator's window is "perched aloft," while the window of a "special story-internal character" may be located "within the human scene itself" (252). Under this conception, focalization theory describes the "gradient of possibilities of a text's windows on story events and existents," taking into account both the "narratorial origo" and the "deictic center" of the focalization windows through which readers look into a story (256).[4] How a narrative world appears to its readers, then, depends on the kinds of windows it provides—and on how closely these windows work in conjunction with each other. In the next section of this chapter, we will explain this experiential understanding of focalization in relation to some literary examples.

Focalization in Literature

Focalization in literature provides a crucial point of access for readers necessary for their immersion in the world of a narrative; it provides a juncture between the aesthetic representation of a narrative and the response of readers to it. How the window of focalization appears, and what specific kind of access a narrative provides for its readers, is therefore bound up with the dis-

---

4. On narrative and deixis, see Banfield.

tribution of narrative agency and knowledge in a narrative but also with the language and style of a narrative. Although this allows for an infinite variety of permutations of focalization and narration, we limit ourselves to only three examples in this section.

The first comes from James Joyce's "The Dead" (1914), the final story in his *Dubliners* collection and an oft-cited example of heterodiegetic narration with internal focalization: "Lily, the caretaker's daughter, was literally run off her feet" (Joyce 1992: 175). In this first sentence, the narratorial origo is impersonal and impossible to locate precisely, whereas the narrative's deixis is associated with Lily, the central character of the first few paragraphs. In Jahn's terms, this house of fiction has two windows, the narrator's and Lily's. When readers look into the narrative world of "The Dead," they can make use of both of these windows, seeing characters and events inside that world refracted through two lenses simultaneously. But the window metaphor with its optical implications emphasizes only one of several aspects of focalization in literature. Another aspect concerns the use of language and style to express a character-bound take on the world. Lily is not only the narrative's deictic center, anchoring thinking and perceiving in time and place. Her vocabulary ("literally") also inflects the narrative, giving it a distinctively lower-class Dublin accent. It is almost as if there were two voices in this sentence, although only one of them speaks to us directly, while Lily's voice is ventriloquized through that of the narrator. The technical term for this peculiar and highly artificial expression of subjectivity is free indirect discourse. In free indirect discourse, the thoughts, perceptions, and feelings are those of a non-narrating character but they are expressed by the narrator ("indirect") and without explicit attribution ("free") (see Cohn; McHale 1978). First developed in nineteenth-century prose fiction, free indirect discourse constitutes one of the strongest focalization markers in literature.

Several general insights into the workings of focalization can be drawn from our first example. Focalization in literature, Joyce's sentence clearly shows, is at work in the subjective coloring that the representation of events and actions and the description of characters and settings in the narrative world receives from the narrator, who mediates the narrative world through their words but who operates in conjunction with a non-narratorial character with whom knowledge and perception, as well as some of the language in the story, originate. In this context, the focalization concept refers to a subjective representation in the sense that *every* representation has a subjective tinge to it (this is how Lily the caretaker's daughter feels about the evening), but it is not necessarily identical with the representation of subjectivity as it can also color seemingly objective statements (Lily really has been running around a lot).[5] Focalization in literature is often associated with the representation of consciousness; however, a character's consciousness can be represented directly, through narratorial statements, as well as through reported thought or, even more indirectly, through free indirect discourse. It follows that focalization can be associated with a deictic center but does not have to be. While many novels anchor focalization in the embodied experiences and perceptions of characters, there also exist impersonal vantage points and experiential angles with no deictic reference (Genette's external focalization or Banfield's empty center; Genette 1980; Banfield).

As a contrast to Joyce, consider our second example, Franz Kafka's *Der Process* (*The Trial*) (1925), beginning with another famous first sentence: "Jemand mußte Josef K. verleumdet haben, denn ohne daß er etwas Böses getan hätte, wurde er eines Morgens verhaftet" ("Someone must have been telling lies about Josef K., for without having done anything wrong he was arrested one morning") (1990: 7; 1984: 1). Although he lived and wrote on the margins of the German-speaking world, Kafka wrote in a peculiarly neutral, unaccented German. There is no trace of dialect or personal idiom in *Der Process*, and yet the narrative voice is clearly bound up with the focalization of a character, Josef K. We can discern this in the predicate "mußte" ("must have been"). Unlike the narrator, who could just tell us that Josef K. has been denounced and by whom, Josef K. has to guess at the events leading up to his arrest. However, readers are not made to feel with Josef K. to the same extent that we enter the mind of Lily the caretaker's daughter; even the first sentence's linkage with Josef K. is somewhat tentative. The unsettling effect of Kafka's novels derives, in part, from the way in which almost all perceptions, sensations, thoughts, feelings, and judgments seem to originate with the protagonist (or *can* be constructed to do so), yet the narrative voice contains ironic undertones that make readers distrust this point of origin. Kafka's sentence thus plays two focalizations off against each other—that of Josef K. and that of the narrator, within which the character-bound focalization is embedded.

Narration and focalization have different points of origin in Joyce and Kafka, but they can also originate in one and the same person in novels with a character narrator. Our third example, Margaret Atwood's *The Handmaid's Tale* (1986), is related by the protagonist, who has been renamed Offred (literally "belonging to Fred") in the novel's dystopian future set in a newly estab-

---

5. On the distinction between subjective representation and the representation of subjectivity, see Reinerth and Thon.

lished totalitarian theocracy in New England. At the beginning of the second chapter, Offred (whose original name we never learn) describes her room like this: "A chair, a table, a lamp. Above, on the white ceiling, a relief ornament in the shape of a wreath, and in the centre of it a blank space, plastered over, like the place in a face where the eye has been taken out. There must have been a chandelier, once. They've removed anything you could tie a rope to" (7). The voice here, as throughout the novel, is Offred's. The focalization mediated by that voice, which evokes the felt experience out of which narration arises, is hers as well. Offred sees objects and decorations, but she also sees *through* them and judges them by her use of simile ("like the place in a face where the eye has been taken out"), deduces that there "must have been a chandelier," and arrives at the conclusion that the goal of the ugly ceiling renovation is suicide prevention.

Thus, readers learn not only what her room looks like, but more particularly how it feels to Offred and about her state of mind more generally (she may well be contemplating suicide if she is scanning the ceiling for hooks, or she is judging the new regime under which taking her own life seems like an obvious choice, and perhaps the only one she can make). Offred's subjectivity is refracted through the space around her, through her environment, constituting an ambient focalization that originates in Offred but that also takes into account other characters and their decisions as well as past and hypothetical experiential angles.[6] Even though Offred is at once *The Handmaid's Tale*'s narrator and focal character, it is still important to distinguish between narration and focalization because Offred's thoughts, perceptions, and evaluations are anchored in different points of time that do not always correspond with the point from which she is narrating. Thus, focalization is often associated with the experiencing-I rather than with the narrating-I. Descriptions of Offred's new life are interspersed with memories of the past, and both temporal layers infect each other when the past is nostalgically evoked from a present perspective or when the present is judged on the basis of past experiences. Offred may be one character (or is she still the same character after her enforced name change?), but she understands herself and her life from multiple and changing angles.

Together, these three examples show that literary texts make use of language and style to mark focalization in their specific contexts, and thus indicate the need for close stylistic analysis in ascertaining the focalization of a literary text. Given the importance of style for focalization, it is high time to

---

6. On ambient focalization, see Jahn (1999); on hypothetical focalization, see D. Herman (2002).

move away from the dogmatic debates over definitions and terminology that have dominated focalization theory in the past decades. Attention needs to move toward close readings that give rise to a more nuanced understanding of the many different forms and functions of focalization. This shift in attention is particularly important in a comics context because of the formal versatility and vast variety of visual styles in graphic narrative.

Focalization in Comics

Graphic narratives, like literary fiction, provide readers with different kinds of access to their narrative worlds. Like literary novels, comics are frequently preoccupied not only with what happens in the narrative world but also with the experiencing of world events by characters and with the representation of that experience by narratorial agents. Because of their multimodality and dominant visuality, however, the means by which that access is granted and the kind of access graphic narratives offer differ in crucial ways from the established mechanics of focalization in literature.

Comics are an inherently segmented medium that often breaks storylines down into distinct panels separated by gaps or gutters (Hatfield 2005; Gardner 2011). As a consequence, meaning in comics may be generated inside individual panels but also by patterns of panels and page layouts that extend across the entire book and by the overall composition (Miller and Beaty 116). Thus, focalization in comics can be marked through isolated instances of perspectivation inside panels but also by the interaction between panels and page layout, as well as by larger patterns of repetition, variation, and omission. Comics theorist Thierry Groensteen, in his influential *The System of Comics*, distinguishes between two basic relations between images in a comic: *découpage*, the operation of "breaking down" or "gridding" that puts in place the sequential syntagm, and *tressage*, or "braiding," which constitutes "a more elaborated level of integration between the narrative flux . . . and the spatiotemporal operation" of a comic book (2007: 22). Whereas gridding accounts for the division of space on the individual page that partitions narrative material into distinct panels, braiding describes the structuration of comics beyond the single page. This rich texture needs to be considered in its entirety when determining focalization and how it works in graphic narrative.

Generally speaking, cues for world building in comics, as Karin Kukkonen points out, can be "verbal, visual, or based on the sequence of panels and their arrangement on the page. Panels can be read out of order and in order, thereby prefiguring inferences or reminding readers of double meanings" (2013a: 35).

Focalization in comics, too, can be marked visually as well as verbally. Kukkonen, who defines focalization in comics as the "horizon of knowledge and emotional involvement, from which the sequence in the panels is told," cites the representation of facial expressions and of bodily postures, the use of shot/reverse-shot narration, and the drawing of different kinds of frames among the techniques that mark such a horizon (2013a: 48, 50). Kai Mikkonen names a similar range of techniques, to which he adds metaphoric images and forms of spatial articulation, all of which provide access to the minds of characters (2011, 2017). As our analyses in this book will show, the style and genre of a comic can also impact focalization. Indeed, it is one of our central arguments that individual focalization markers in comics need to be identified and interpreted in relation to, and in light of, more global aspects such as style and genre that direct the overall mood of a graphic narrative.

Comics contain many possibilities for cross-referencing or interplay between visual and verbal focalization markers because they narrate on two modal levels simultaneously. Deixis becomes complicated when readers have to integrate experiential information from different semiotic channels that can present in a complementary or contrasting relationship. This interplay also conditions the relation between narration and focalization. In the absence of verbal narratorial discourse, the origin of visual images often remains uncertain, and where verbal narrative is included in captions or text boxes, words and images may exist in a strained, ambiguous, or fractured relationship. Since comics frequently do not make use of an overt narrator, narrative emphasis often falls on the experience of characters.

Perspectivation of images, color, style, shading and line work, panel size and framing, layout, ordering, and lettering—all of these various aspects can operate in conjunction to indicate whose perspective, thinking, and emotions ground the what it's like of a graphic narrative. However, they may also work against each other, creating a multilayered reading experience that grants readers considerable room for interpretation. How readers understand pictorial and other nonverbal material in comics, Janina Wildfeuer points out, "often involves not only the actual data available in the respective panels of the comic, thus in the visual data themselves but also the information provided by the context in further panels and by the relationships between panels" (217). Meaning in comics is "often not as overtly provided as in verbal texts," and this multimodal complexity, which also includes "intersemiotic interplay of color, framing, or line thickness," grants a much more active role to readers' meaning-making (217, 219).

Comics that integrate a verbal narrative in captions or text boxes add another level of complexity to this already rich expressivity. As in literary narrative, the verbal narrator of a comic book may be a character or an impersonal instance, operating in conjunction with or in disjunction from other sources and angles of experience within the narrative. However, in comics, this relation between narration and focalization has to be judged against the visual images that narrate alongside the verbal narrative. Even though text and image may be joined together in composite panels, the visual component is not necessarily associated with the same deictic origin or with the same perceptual and emotional orientation. Often, there is no clear indication where the images come from, leaving readers to search for clues as to their relation with the verbal text. Meanwhile, in comics that do not have an explicit narratorial "voice," there is no single instance that corresponds to the narrator of a literary narrative (Thon).

In both instances—comics with and without captions or text box narration—the analogy with film, another multimodal medium, may be more helpful than that with literature. Films, like comics, most commonly do not present an explicit origin for their narration. Instead, film narration comes into being through the combination of visuals and sound, as well as through montage, editing, and other filmic techniques. Film narratologist Markus Kuhn therefore argues that "there is no primary relationship of dominance between visual and verbal instances in film," emphasizing that focalization, too, "can only be determined through the *interplay* of edited shots," rather than in relation to individual means of expression (2009: 264, 262, our italics). In addition to a composite or cinematic narrator (Chatman 135), some films include a second potential narrative origin by means of voice-over narration that may operate in conjunction with other narrative components but that may also diverge from or even contradict what the camera shows (Kozloff). In fact, voice-over in film is often a source of unreliability, and that should warn us against too easily conflating verbal text and visuals in comics that similarly combine two narrative tracks.

Comics, with their hand-drawn quality and flexibility of page layout, are an extremely versatile storytelling medium. This versatility means that there are no hard-and-fast rules for what can and cannot constitute a focalization marker in graphic narrative. As a consequence, focalization in comics needs to be assessed in relation to the specific givens of a particular text. The presence of a narratorial voice on the verbal track may help to pinpoint focalization, but only if it coincides with what the visual images show, which is not always the case and sometimes a matter of interpretation. Moreover, comics are a highly self-reflexive medium in which the visual and verbal representation of character, place, and action is often enriched by a visual engagement with cartooning as a way of seeing, understanding, and experiencing the narrative world.

When metafictional scenes and devices foreground the visual construction, world building, and narrative mediation of graphic narrative, they often also contain powerful focalization markers that invite readers to adopt a particular angle or posture toward characters and events, while simultaneously drawing attention to the writing and drawing process and to the aesthetic choices that comic artists make. Due to this frequent doubling-up, graphic narrative can be a highly meta-experiential medium that reflects on basic questions concerning focalization even as it exposes the many creative ways in which words and images make experience accessible.

In the context of comics, a dominantly visual medium, it may seem tempting to closely identify focalization with the visual. Indeed, many comics narratologists emphasize such a link. Thus, David Herman suggests focusing on optical aspects such as "shifting figure-ground alignments, changes in the vantage-point or location of the perspective point within the referent scene, and alterations in perspective mode and direction of viewing" when analyzing the focalization of a graphic narrative (2009b: 135). For Kai Mikkonen, "it seems imperative that we try to take the question of the perceptual and, more precisely, optical dimension of focalization in comics to its outer limit" before even beginning to think about other, non-optical aspects of focalization (2013: 107). However, an overemphasis on optical aspects of focalization can often be misleading. Even when what we see in a comic is visual, where that points may be mental. Indeed, visual focalization markers such as panel size, perspectival angle, color, or style are frequently used in graphic narrative to indicate the cognitive processing, emotional involvement, or ideological stance of characters. The analysis of comics therefore invites a reconsideration of the unresolved question whether focalization should include optical as well as mental aspects or whether different concepts ought to be used for perceptual matters and for the representation of consciousness.

This brings us to our final point in this section. Another way in which graphic narrative differs from literature concerns the presentation and understanding of subjectivity in both media, and this too has important implications for the interpretative process, especially concerning focalization. As Maike Reinerth and Jan-Noël Thon point out, there exists a "close interrelation between the question of how recipients *comprehend* subjectivity as part of their everyday world knowledge and the question of how media *represent* subjectivity within the limitations and affordances that their specific mediality provides" (1). When analyzing media in relation to subjectivity, a heuristic distinction may be made between "representations of subjectivity," which "rely on cultural knowledge *about* subjectivity," and "subjective representations," or the imitation of subjective experience through medial representation that grants recipients access to characters' ways of perceiving the world (5).

However, these are two sides of the same coin: Ideas about subjectivity that are transported through a medial representation depend on the affordances of the medium in question, that is, on how specific media express subjectivity and subjective takes on the world. In the words of Reinerth and Thon, "media representations of subjectivity are . . . subjective in the sense that they constitute instances of media attempting to represent experiences that are necessarily exclusive to the inner realms of a character (or person), and they are representational because they attempt to medially transform the complex interactions of subjective intentional states into intersubjectively comprehensible external forms of representation" (3). In communicating the experientiality of characters, media representations of subjectivity necessarily mediate and, consequently, transform that experientiality. In graphic narrative, however, narratorial choice is notoriously difficult to disentangle from the perception and subjective stances of characters, and subjective representation often blends into the representation of subjectivity as there is no clear equivalent of the first-person pronoun in the visual track. The medial affordances of graphic narrative thus have important consequences for our understanding of focalization in comics.

The visual presentation of characters in graphic narrative and the often self-reflexive emphasis on the particular style of a narrative and on the drawing hand of the artist lead to a focus on embodied selves in addition to an inner sense of self (El Refaie 2012; S. Horstkotte and Pedri 2017). Experience in graphic narrative is not confined to an inner processing of consciousness; rather, it also encompasses a variety of outer, physical, and material aspects of being in the narrative world. Moreover, as our analyses will show, many graphic narratives focus on non-normative (diseased or queer) selves and on social rather than individual forms of subjectivity. Often, graphic narratives expose split or multiform selves, instead of narrating the development of a unified self. The visual techniques used for expressing such counter-canonical forms of selfhood derive from (self-)portraiture and artist sketchbooks as well as from literary conventions of consciousness representation. For narratologists working in all media, this poses the question of whether we need a wider understanding of focalization that better accounts for aspects of embodied selfhood beyond the individual mind. At the same time, comics also work against a mind-body split and thus against the exclusively mental association of focalization as consciousness representation that has been suggested by some narratologists who argue against the optical connotations of focalization (see Niederhoff). In this way, the semiotic structure of graphic narrative makes it difficult, if not impossible, to separate a thinking and judging mind from physical, material, and corporeal experience and, consequently, the subjective representation of experience from the representation of subjectivity.

In the next, final section of this chapter, we analyze Jason Lutes's *Berlin: City of Stones* to show that the visual presentation of perspectival angling is not necessarily an exclusively optical matter. Perspectival techniques can also be expressive of narrative authority, or else they can expose claims toward authority as false. The malleability of visual storytelling techniques in graphic narrative means that the same technique can be used to communicate features of plot or character development, to establish different moods, or to impact tone. The perspectival orientation of a comics panel can be simultaneously expressive of a character's visual perception and of their mental and emotional experience even when the perspective of the image does not necessarily relate to a character's experience. We show how the open nature of visual techniques that relate to character subjectivity in graphic narrative seriously complicates the distinction between thinking, experiencing, and seeing, and thus between focalization and perspective. Through our analysis, we conclude that when studying comics, it is highly problematic to attempt to either reduce focalization to the optical or to separate optical perspectivation from cognitive focalization.

Words and Images: Jason Lutes, *Berlin*

Originally published as a series of twenty-two comic magazines, Jason Lutes's *Berlin* chronicles the Weimar Republic's descent into fascism in the years between 1928 and 1933. As has become common in the comics industry, issues 1 to 8 of the series were subsequently published as a graphic novel entitled *Berlin: City of Stones*, issues 9 to 16 as *Berlin: City of Smoke*, and issues 17 to 22 as *Berlin: City of Light* (2001, 2008, 2018). Rendered in a classical ink-drawing style, this serial graphic novel relates the story of a nation in turmoil through alternating narrative strands that focus on a number of characters from different strata of society: the working-class Braun family, the Jewish schoolboy David Schwartz, the Cocoa Kids Jazz band, and the aristocratic Margarethe von Falkensee. The main focus of the narrative, however, is on its two protagonists: art student Marthe Müller and her lover Kurt Severing, a journalist writing for the cosmopolitan left-wing magazine *Die Weltbühne*.

The choice of an artist and a writer as protagonists mirrors the bimodality of the comics medium through which these stories are related. Both

Marthe and Kurt keep journals, extracts of which are shown at key moments in the narrative. Thus, both serve as second-order narrators whose narration sometimes adds to and sometimes contradicts the narration of others and the first-order narration that embeds them. While Kurt's diary is a typewritten account, Marthe's journaling combines handwriting and sketching. Taken together, their notebooks introduce a meta-medial as well as a metanarrative reflection to the series, as it is out of the combination of word and image, writing and drawing that the comics form arises.

Comics theorist Charles Hatfield has described comics as an art of tensions between panels and gutters and between words and images (2005, 2009). He argues that it is by negotiating the tension between what is shown and what is not shown and between the two semiotic modes that readers of comics can make meaning. Jared Gardner, too, points out that the reader of comics is called upon to construe a coherent plot out of the gaps between panels that only ever frame relatively small action kernels (2011). The *Berlin* series exploits frame-by-frame narration and makes significant interpretative demands on readers by alternating quickly between characters, scenes, places, memories, diaries, and optical perceptions. The narrative also exposes the manifold connections that exist between characters, often without their awareness, through juxtaposition as well as through forms of continuity editing. Often, the interlocking narrative in *Berlin: City of Stones* works like a relay race, passing the baton by moving from character to character in one continuous swipe of chance encounters (see esp. 29–48).

In this section, we focus on the first trilogy volume, *Berlin: City of Stones*, to show how the self-conscious introduction of visual and verbal modes of representing the world and the use of different voices and experiential angles create a subtle, nuanced bimodal narrative. We read *Berlin: City of Stones* as a meta-perspectival text that reflects on the potential of comics to refract culturally shaped assumptions about seeing, perspectivation, and optics. Apart from the dates and times given at the beginning of some chapters, there is no explicit indication of a narratorial origin in *Berlin: City of Stones*. Yet the pacing of frames, their placement on the page, and the perspectival orientation within individual panels reveal the kind of organizing consciousness that literary theorists ascribe to an impersonal or heterodiegetic narrator. For the most part, focalization appears to be tied to this organizing instance, but it can also diverge from it when alternative, character-bound ways of experiencing the world are introduced.

An obvious instance of character-bound focalization occurs in chapter 7, toward the end of *Berlin: City of Stones*, when Marthe and Kurt meet in a small park in the center of Berlin. While the main part of this four-page sequence makes it perfectly clear that the lovers are fully clothed and respectable-looking, an isolated panel in the middle of the page that closes the sequence shows them embracing naked, in an idyllic setting devoid of city context and before an empty backdrop (179; figure 1.1). The six panels framing this surprising view zoom in on some of the setting's nature details—a tree branch, clouds, some tufts of grass—that can be discerned in previous views of the park, but without indicating any context. The three panels at the bottom of the previous page that lead into the sequence's symmetric arrangement indicate where the source of this otherworldly scene and its obvious break with realistic representation lie. They contain close-ups of Marthe whispering into Kurt's ear, "I love you," of Kurt's still eye looking straight ahead, and finally, zooming slightly out, of Kurt's gaze turning toward Marthe.

This three-panel sequence adapts the film convention of the point-of-view shot, which constitutes one of the main markers for character focalization in film (see Branigan; Kuhn 2011: 140–41; Verstraeten 96–124). Point-of-view shots show what a character is seeing by including the looking character in the image by means of an over-the-shoulder shot or cutting back and forth between the looking character and that which is seen in a shot/reverse-shot pattern. The close-up of Kurt's eye is particularly suggestive of a character-bound focalization and, as such, invites readers to view the subsequent panel arrangement with its echoes of the enclosed garden trope as a representation of Kurt's emotional reaction to Marthe's declaration of love. Seen in this way, the central panel shows the pair not as they appear to uninvolved bystanders or to an objective narrator but as they appear to themselves. Hence, despite the optical reference of the preceding point-of-view sequence, the central panel depicts not what the characters see, in an optical sense, but how they feel. The erotic attraction it presents is indicative of Kurt and Marthe's emotional processing of the situation, rather than of visual perception.

In this way, the central panel shows visually what is not itself visual, and it does so from an optical perspective that is external to the two characters even though the image is associated with their feelings and with their imagination. While the preceding sequence follows the convention of the point-of-view shot, the following page with the framed central panel adapts a wider array of subjective camera techniques, where visual means such as color and change of scene or the communication of sound and music differentiate a sequence from the surrounding film aesthetic in such a way as to indicate the subjective experience of a character (Flueckiger). Just as film focalization "can only be determined through the interplay of edited shots" (Kuhn 2009: 262; see Schlickers 244), focalization in this sequence of panels is marked not so much by individual instances of optical perspective or ocularization (the

FIGURE 1.1. Lutes, Jason. 2002. *Berlin: City of Stones*. Drawn and Quarterly. p. 179.

evocation of visual perception; see Jost) but by the interplay between panels; by their rhythm of repetition, variation, and alternation; and by unexpected shifts of setting and perspective.

Throughout the three volumes of *Berlin*, boxed-off quotations from Marthe's and Kurt's journals as well as Marthe's drawings serve a similar purpose of marking a character-bound focalization by expressing the subjective experience of characters, while panels drawn in soft pencil may also represent Kurt's myopic gaze—another adaptation of subjective camera techniques (Lutes 2001: 136–37). Focalization, however, does not only operate in these isolated instances; it also directs the mood and feel of the narrative world on a larger scale. Through the embedding of second-order narratives and its first-order polyperspectival narration, the *Berlin* series explores different viewpoints on the tumultuous political events of 1920s Germany, especially the 1929 May Day demonstration at which the factory worker Gudrun Braun is shot while Kurt and Marthe merely witness the demonstration as passersby. Such polyperspectivalism directs the overall composition of the series as well as individual passages that often shift rapidly between perspectival angles and subjective ways of seeing, but also experiencing the world, without easily identifying one with the other.

Indeed, optical perspectivation (or seeing) and focalization (the combined effect of seeing and other modes of perception, epistemic positioning, value attribution, and emotional stance) are quite often slightly out of step with each other in *Berlin*. This becomes obvious in the passage chronicling Marthe's arrival in Berlin, which combines visual snippets of Berlin city life with Marthe's handwritten commentary in her notebook, taken down later that day in her lodgings (16). Although the images show Marthe's experiences preceding her journal entries, the optical perspective in them is not hers. Instead, the montage of images and text boxes in these composite panels functions like voice-over in unreliable film narration, where the second-order voice-over narrative can also diverge from or even contradict the images (Kozloff). For instance, the final panel on the sequence's second page sets three text boxes containing Marthe's handwritten remarks, "Through the rush of traffic I hear music—is it Chopin?—," "as if being played deep underwater," and "I am losing myself," against an Olympic view of a Berlin street corner (17; figure 1.2). Whereas the preceding panels on the page relied on point-of-view conventions to represent what Marthe sees on her first walk through the city, the final panel steps out of the established pattern of perspectivation by drawing attention to Marthe's sense of hearing, which cannot be directly represented in graphic narrative, and to her immaterial sense of self.

The concluding statement, "I am losing myself," may be taken to indicate that the panel's elevated view serves a metaphorical purpose. Just as readers are losing sight of Marthe among the tiny characters in this view, she too loses sight of herself and feels lost in the city. At the same time, this panel marks a switching point between the following-units of the narrative—sequences in which readers get the sense of "following a character from action to action and scene to scene" (Altman 15). The next sequence of panels identifies the elevated view with the optical perspective of the traffic officer policing Potsdamer Platz in central Berlin (18–19). Thus, the panel exposes not only the tension between Marthe's experience of the city as a chaotic, continuous motion of

FIGURE 1.2. Lutes, Jason. 2002. *Berlin: City of Stones*. Drawn and Quarterly. p. 17.

"flow," "river," or "rush of traffic" on the one hand, and her dissipating sense of self on the other, but also that between Marthe's on-the-ground perception and the elevated view of the traffic officer. The visual overlay of two distinct sets of experience enables the narrative to move from Marthe to the traffic officer as the central experiencing consciousness of the next sequence.

In this subsequent passage, readers see the city traffic no longer with Marthe's eyes but with the traffic officer's. However, the switch also has a second, metaphorical level of meaning. While a whole-page view (18) plays with reader expectations that the elevated eye not only commands a privileged position and can perceive more details but also possesses more knowledge and power than other angles of vision, the following sequence exposes the traffic officer as a helpless watcher who sees the cars on the ground as "fat black beetle[s]" or "cattle" he would like to step on while being unable to do anything about the traffic chaos other than punching traffic light buttons (21). His main interest, in any case, lies in discovering what lunch his wife has packed for him.

Kurt, in looking up at the traffic officer, imagines how "that poor fellow up there [is] trying to make sense of it all" (19), but that assumption turns out to be false: The officer has no interest in making sense of the chaos. Optical perspectivation here may be associated with the traffic officer, but the focalization in this sequence is more complex since it embeds the officer's actual perception in Kurt's imagination of what this perception might be like, and also connects this imagination to Marthe's dissipating sense of self, which provided the springboard for the upward turn in optical perspective.

We now turn our attention to this higher-order focalization, in which individual instances of looking, judging, imagining, and feeling are embedded and which may be associated with a narratorial consciousness rather than with individual characters. Although events in *Berlin* are often seen from above, however, this is often not an indicator of omniscience but rather of its shortcomings, as these elevated perspectives do not necessarily offer more insight than the more partial perspectives of characters. Instead, they often function as a kind of relay that switches from one strand of the narrative to another, making readers take account of how many things happen in a city without characters being aware of each other or of nearby happenings. This can be read as a commentary on a modernity where there is simply too much going on at once for anyone to have an overview of their world. It could also be approached as an invitation to readers to adopt a different, more grounded and more empathic perspective that gives up claims to lofty overviews and takes in the gritty details of individual lives in the city.

Another way in which the narrative makes readers aware of connections that are not known to any of the characters is by having narrative world details move through a sequence of panels. Often, these are sounds traveling through panels that show different parts of the city, as for instance the "ch-ch" of the train on which Marthe arrives, or when Kurt's clicking typewriter keys sound out across all of Berlin (7, 78–80). These sound effects serve a double purpose. They can indicate the subjective perception of characters and thus mark character focalization, but they can also connect characters who are not aware of each other and thus mark a non-character-bound, narratorial focalization. For instance, while Kurt's typewriter noise introduces his imagination of other journalists typing their articles at the same time and of the stacks of newspaper issues that will result from all this furious typing, the many local trains and trams moving through the panels and pages of *Berlin* are not usually bound to any one character's perception. Instead, narrow panels showing trains are often used to bisect pages and to cut from one following-unit to another.

Together, these details that travel across panels and pages build a rhythm of repetition and variation that structures the narrative. This pattern can be understood through Thierry Groensteen's concept of *tressage*, or braiding, which addresses how panels relate to each other across a page, a spread, or an entire comic book by way of similarity, contiguity, and repetition, but also through opposition, contradiction, or discrepancy (2007: 144–47). Since these connections have to be made by readers, braiding always operates on two levels simultaneously: synchronically through the co-presence of panels on a page or across a comic book and diachronically through a reading that "recognizes in each new term of a [panel] series a recollection or an echo of an anterior term" (147). Through the creative and interpretive operations of braiding, a single comics image gains meaning on several levels: alongside its immediate neighbors with which it stands in relation but also across a wider arc of narration. Across these different spatial frames of reference, images can complement and perpetuate each other, their meanings intersecting and adjusting one in relation to the other. They can appear as a flow of images that captures the attention of readers and vectorizes their eye movement. In this sense, the contiguity of braided images can be understood as a configuration that needs to be interpreted as a larger form of a still image or, using an analogy from music, as a rhythm to be followed (Groensteen 2013: 34). In these different ways, braiding "overdetermines the panel by equipping coordinates that we can qualify as *hyper-topical,* indicating their belonging to one or several notable series, and the place that it occupies," producing a significant "enrichment and densification of the 'text' of the comic" (Groensteen 2007: 147).

In *Berlin: City of Stones,* the recurrent panels of public transport traveling across a comics page or of characters traveling on public transportation constitute a crucial instrument of braiding. They structure the narrative, separate following-units from each other, and function as relays from one unit into the next. Through braiding, they connect sequences in an almost random fashion, establishing a snowball system of storytelling with sometimes surprising cuts between storylines. Thus, recurring images of public transportation indicate a balance of value between narrative threads about, for instance, the working-class Braun family with its Nazi father and communist mother and the Schwartzes, a mixed family of observant Jews, antiques dealers, and small-time peddlers in stolen goods. At the same time, public transport cars and the streets through which they move represent a common if precarious ground between these different people and thus stand in for the diversity of Berlin's inhabitants prior to 1933.

Considered within the framework of focalization theory, these switches between following-units introduce serious complications into the relation between perspectivation and focalization, and between character-bound and higher-order modes of perception, epistemic and emotional positioning, and value attribution. The narrative often makes it difficult to pinpoint the exact source of thoughts and perceptions, especially in sequences that explore the same series of events as they affect different sets of characters. For example, toward the middle of the book, Frau Faber, the wife of a wealthy industrialist who owns a number of factories involved in the building and furnishing of Zeppelin airships, throws a lavish dinner party (71–72). During the party, guests listen to a live radio broadcast about a Zeppelin journey. At the same time, the Braun family is also listening to the broadcast in their apartment, while a broadcasting van moves through the city in intermittent panels (73–74). But even though everyone listens to the same broadcast, each group of listeners has a distinct level of knowledge related to the Zeppelin.

Thus, Frau Braun works in one of the factories that have furnished the Zeppelin, but unlike the Fabers and their guests, she does not yet know that the factory is about to close, that this is the last Zeppelin that will be built, and that she will soon lose her job. Moreover, neither of the two families knows anything about the other. Only readers are made aware of their connection through the narrative's cross-cutting between the two parallel plotlines. Sometimes, such narrative omniscience is associated with an elevated or Olympic perspective, such as when a bird's-eye view in the middle of a page that is part of this scene shows the broadcast sound traveling from the dinner party to the working-class neighborhood (73). As in the earlier passage with the traffic officer, however, here too the association of elevation with omniscience becomes complicated since the Olympic perspective may also be connected with the Zeppelin traveling across the sky and with its barely visible passengers who are not aware of any of the broadcast listeners.

The braiding structure of following-units connected in a snowball system is put to effective use in the finale of *Berlin: City of Stones,* which tells of the brutal police suppression of the communist May Day rally. It is introduced by a wordless three-by-two panel page showing six different bed scenes, all drawn from the same angle and distance and showing, from top left to bottom right, the Jewish boy David Schwartz, who was the protagonist of the previous following-unit; Marthe and Kurt, holding each other tightly; Otto Braun with his youngest son cuddled against his chest; Gudrun Braun, who has separated from her husband, holding her two daughters; Anna, Marthe's fellow art student; and, finally, an unknown woman smoking a cigarette and watching a man get out of bed (183). On the next page, readers discover that the unknown woman is a prostitute and that her customer is one of the armed officers ordered to shoot down the May Day rally. Yet although they are united by time and setting and by the pattern of composition, none of the characters in this sequence know about the others.

The *Berlin* trilogy often puts different ways of experiencing the same situation side by side, but in this instance, the bed page also sets the pattern for the narrative build-up closing the first volume, which links different experiences of the rally through a short cuts pattern structured by an accelerating rhythm of clock times and culminating in the shooting of Gudrun Braun. At this point, the narrative slows down again, closing with a double page of frameless panels of Gudrun Braun and her new partner, the communist Otto, sitting naked in an idyllic nature setting (208–9). Both the sudden break with realistic representation codes and the remarkable similarity with the love scene between Marthe and Kurt clearly mark this sequence as imaginary. Moreover, the preceding sequence, in which Gudrun discovers that she has been shot, sits down on the pavement, and rolls over to her side, clearly indicates that what follows is her death vision (207). In the bottom four panels on this page, seen from Gudrun's sideways perspective, the conventional panel frame used throughout the graphic novel slowly disappears, one panel side at a time.

Berlin: City of Stones frequently experiments with film editing techniques such as cinematic continuity, tracking shots, or eye-of-God shots that represent an impersonal, disembodied perspective. It also indexes the drawing hand of the artist through the physicality and materiality of the line, foregrounding this embodied deixis by including Marthe's hand-drawn secondary narrative to present a personal and grounded perspective. These two options are presented as optical matters but also refer to broader questions of world knowledge and engagement. Indeed, the *Berlin* trilogy often self-consciously reflects on the relation between optical perspectivation, world knowledge, and power. When Marthe takes drawing lessons at the art academy, the commentary of her teachers and the discussion with fellow students add a reflective dimension to the representation of different perspectives and experiential angles in *Berlin*, while the students' drawings echo the graphic novel's construction of panels and pages. Thus, a blackboard drawing mirrors the way train panels often bisect page layouts in *Berlin,* and the teacher's accompanying commentary may be taken to ironically comment on comics composition and on the different attitudes toward vision and representation and their relation to knowledge in *Berlin*: "As the horizontal, mm, defines the extent of our vision in the world, so the horizon line defines the extent of the draughtsman's vision in his representation of the world on the page" (101).

As Herr Schenck, the teacher, goes on to explain, such representation is always partial and relative, and this might be taken as a warning against trusting any one single viewpoint: "The observer's location is what really determines the placement of a vanishing point; a drawing from life is as much about the subject as the exact position of the artist's head and eyes in relation to it" (101). Marthe, however, reacts against this lesson in perspectival construction, arguing that it is not an adequate way of seeing the world: "I don't *want* to see the world converging towards a vanishing point! I don't *want* to understand people in terms of their skeletal structure or the muscle group that controls their ability to smile. I can't reconcile those things with what I see" (124). She thus makes a point the *Berlin* trilogy as a whole supports through its emphasis on intersubjectivity: No one character alone can master all that there is to see and experience in a narrative world. It is only out of the composition of many different optical and experiential views of the world that an adequate image of 1920s Berlin can even begin to emerge.

•

Although our analysis of *Berlin* has drawn on the distinction between a narratorial and a character-bound focalization as a base heuristic, we have also shown how the *Berlin* trilogy challenges that distinction by working toward an intersubjective or collective focalization in three ways: (1) by embedding instances of subjective representation that expresses character focalization in intersubjective networks of looking and feeling; (2) by evoking deliberate ambiguity about the deictic center of a narrative so as to make readers consider the depicted scenes and events from multiple perspectives; and (3) by creating rhythms of repetition and variation that serve to expose different aspects under which the same or similar events can be experienced. These observations strongly suggest that the disputed distinction between focalization and perspectivation needs to be rendered more complex, more nuanced, and more interesting and rewarding for close readings of individual texts. Our analyses in the next chapters will continue to move against the grain of focalization theories that seek to draw a sharp line between focalization (the mental processing of characters and narrators) and optical perspectivation or ocularization (the visual rendering of perception). We argue that this distinction, first developed in the context of film studies and later adapted for comics narratology, is attractive only in certain instances, namely, when the visual narrative is focalized in ways that are consistent with a character's mental process but presented visually through an optical perspective external to that character.

In our analysis of *Berlin*, we have also made the point that a character's subjective experience can be shown not only through optical perspectivation but also through panel size, shape, and placement as well as through sequencing and variation. Again, these means of access are common to many graphic narratives. An analysis of focalization in comics therefore needs to consider a great variety of comics storytelling techniques, including the use of blank or empty panels, the presence or absence of captions, the inclusion or exclusion of background detail, and the use of visual metaphors. The broad variety of focalization markers that are used in comics suggests that focalization and perspective are not interchangeable but also are not strong, necessary distinctions in graphic narrative. As our analyses will show, the presentation of visual perception cannot be neatly separated out of a fuller picture of felt experience that includes dispositions, attitudes, and emotions; spatial orientation; perceptual processing; and ideological conviction. A working model of focalization in comics needs to consider *all* kinds of perspectivation (optical, cognitive, ideological, emotional, and so forth) under the broad heading of focalization, regardless of whether or not this perspectivation unfolds on the verbal or the visual track.

CHAPTER 2

Focalization, Experience, and What It's Like

Focalization in comics becomes particularly noticeable whenever readers are confronted with the subjectively felt quality of experiences, perceptions, and events. In *Berlin: City of Stones,* the enclosed garden panel that shows Marthe and Kurt embracing naked before an empty backdrop expresses emotional intensity and intimacy, a mutual focus of the two lovers that excludes the exterior world, and an imaginary sexual anticipation (Lutes 2001: 179). The image's break with realistic representation conventions, as well as its introduction through a sequence of point-of-view panels zeroing in on Kurt's gaze, indicate a character-bound focalization. Together, these focalization markers draw attention to what being in love feels like for Marthe and Kurt. The felt quality of what it's like constitutes an important and integral aspect of real-life experience. In the fields of psychology, the cognitive sciences, and philosophy of mind, it is also referred to as the *qualia* of felt experience (S. Gallagher and Zahavi; Nagel; O'Regan, Myin, and Noë). Qualia are individual qualities of subjective experience that account for why different people perceive the same experience differently. While the enclosed garden panel in *Berlin: City of Stones* presents a key moment of insight for the two characters, qualia also characterize more mundane, everyday experiences.

Narratives in all media are potent qualia machines, presenting an infinite spectrum of subjective experiences (D. Herman 2009a; Reinerth and Thon). Indeed, this is an important factor in what makes narrative attractive to readers. Narratives make it possible for readers to vicariously experience a story and the world in which it is set as well as the thoughts and feelings that characters have about the world, its events, and each other. Alan Palmer calls this experiential quality of a narrative world its "aspectuality," adapting Mieke Bal's definition of focalization to state that "whenever events occur in the storyworld, they are always experienced from within a certain vision" (2004: 51–52). With this emphasis on the experience of characters, Palmer builds on the experiential turn in narratology that argues that experience, and not plot, drives narratives (Fludernik 1996; D. Herman 2009a). Over against the more global emphasis that Fludernik and Herman place on the role of experience in narrative, Palmer makes the specific point that a narrative world can be considered under different experiential aspects: the aspect of the narrator but also the aspects of one or several characters who are not the narrator. Each of these aspects will carry particular experiential qualities.

As our analysis of *Berlin: City of Stones* in chapter 1 suggests, comics are particularly apt at evoking a plurality of aspects due to their segmented structure. Placing distinct ways of experiencing the world bound to different characters side by side in panels and sequences, *Berlin: City of Stones* offers a multilayered reading experience. Rather than showing a world that simply *is*, the accelerating rhythm of short cuts, the adoption of shot/counter-shot techniques, and the multimodal counterpoint between words and images emphasize the different ways in which the world appears to different narrative agents. In some instances, the subjective angle through which experience becomes available to readers is anchored in a character. In others, a character's experience is made accessible through the focal filtering of a narratorial consciousness, across the thoughts and perceptions of another character, or both, as in the traffic sequence in which Kurt's assumptions about the traffic officer in his observation tower become refocalized first via the officer's own thoughts and then via a narratorial, Olympic viewpoint. Through this complex layering of focalization, *Berlin: City of Stones* communicates the what it's like of its characters while simultaneously highlighting the intersubjective web of perceptions and judgments in which individual experiences are embedded.

In this chapter, we go further in exploring the experiential dimension of focalization. We draw on a phenomenological understanding of experience, and we explain what phenomenology can contribute to the study of focalization. Phenomenology, in a nutshell, is a philosophical approach dedicated to "particular experiential structures of perception . . . as they relate to the world in which the perceiver is situated" (S. Gallagher and Zahavi 9). Pushing aside all metaphysical questions, the phenomenological method concerns itself with concrete experiences. By means of a careful description of experience, phenomenology attempts to say what that experience is like (S. Gallagher and Zahavi 7). This does not mean, however, that experience is considered in isolation. On the contrary! Experience, in phenomenology, is thought to have an *intentional* or directed structure; it is something that happens between a subject and its world. Perception, a type of experience that is of particular interest to phenomenologists, is similarly understood as a transaction, a sharing of a situation with what you perceive (Noë 2012).

When applied to the study of narrative, a phenomenological approach assumes that experience and experiential structures do not refer to a static object that is either embedded in a text or occurs within the subject in response to a text. Rather, experience invokes a "field of relations that surround the experiencer" (Caracciolo 2014: 54). In other words, experience does not reside exclusively inside a narrative but is constituted in the interaction between reader and text. While some narratologists associate experientiality mainly with the experiences of characters within the fictional world (Margolin 2000; Palmer 2004), we side with those who argue that experientiality is also integral to the reading process, as readers too undergo experiences in interaction with narrative texts (Caracciolo 2014; Kutsch and Strasen).

The emphasis on subjective experience in a lived space, the conceptualization of that experience as relational, and the call for a close description of experiential structures make phenomenology an attractive methodology for the study of focalization. In this chapter, we analyze three fictional graphic novels that draw attention to experientiality by introducing their readers to strange or unfamiliar qualia: Josh Simmons's *Jessica Farm* (2008), a surreal tale that fuses mind, experience, and world; Charles Burns's *Black Hole* (2005), an uncanny story focalized through several teenage characters, who are infected with a disfiguring and highly contagious bug; and Chris Ware's *Jimmy Corrigan: The Smartest Kid on Earth* (2000), which confronts character-bound with non-character-bound types of focalization and challenges readers' engagement through the exploration of different viewpoints on the same character's life. We identify media-specific cues of graphic narrative that evoke qualia, enabling readers to engage with forms of experience in these graphic narratives. We also discuss how different narrative strategies contribute toward empathetic closeness or distance between a graphic narrative and its readers. Through our analyses, we show how a phenomenological concept of experience can enrich the narratological study of focalization when focalization is viewed as a point of connectivity between text-internal experience and the sense-making of readers who bring their own real-life experiences to bear on the narrative (see Caracciolo 2012: 182).

Comics and Phenomenology

Narratives in all media make it possible for their audiences to participate in the experience of others. Novel reading, in particular, is often described as an intensely immersive experience whose fictional world "acquires the presence of an autonomous, language-independent reality populated with live human beings" (Ryan 2001: 14). David Herman argues that "narrative as a mode of representation uniquely allows for the comparison of versions of what it was like to experience particular situations and events," concluding that "stories capture and sustain our interest because of how their structure maps on to the mind's own engagement with the world" (2009a: 152, 157). Empirical studies show that readers of a novel "typically adapt their point of view to one or another of a story's characters, usually the protagonist, and make their way through the narrative by tracking that character's actions" (Vermeule 41). Characters who require a lot of mind reading are particularly appealing because their extraordinary complexity challenges readers' theory of mind in interesting ways (Vermeule 52).

The sharing of experience that makes reading such a pleasurable activity does not stop at a purely mental engagement. Recent phenomenologically inflected contributions to cognitive literary studies have highlighted that cognition involves all the senses, the entire body, and the emotions (Caracciolo 2014). They show that narratives have the potential to change the perceptive, imaginative, and affective environment of their audience, inviting participation and provoking reciprocal acts of imagination (Cave). The imaginative transfer that occurs in immersive reading entices imitative experience through the production of multimodal imagery—a simulation (Oatley 1999b)—as well as nonimitative activity, in which readers use their own bodily processes to enhance the experience of reading, for instance by fast or shallow breathing (Esrock 2004). Reading experience encompasses conceptual as well as physical sensations like laughter, shivering, or arousal, all "clear physical manifestations of emotions and feelings that are immediate and direct" (Stockwell 2009: 56). Such physical sensations are not distinct from, but rather continuous with the conceptual sensations that trained readers are usually more aware of. Both are connected at the point of texture (the way a text's style and aesthetics make experience available to readers), as richness of texture can be directly correlated to a sense of readerly involvement (Stockwell 2009: 63). Reading may create sympathy, a compassionate feeling for characters in the fictional world, or evoke empathy, a feeling with characters through the spontaneous, vicarious sharing of affect, although the extent to which this occurs depends on audience dispositions and on textual features (Keen 2007, 2008, 2011).

The quality of what it's like is essential to this sharing of experience, both in relation to the resonance that a narrative creates through its tone and atmosphere and in relation to the possibility of engaging with the aspectuality of a specific character or other agent in the narrative. This quality was first theorized by the philosopher Thomas Nagel in his 1974 article "What Is It Like to Be a Bat?," which has since become a landmark study in subjectivity. In this article, Nagel engaged with debates about the nature of consciousness by asking what it is like to have a consciousness—not for researchers who theorize about consciousness but for the organism having that consciousness. Rather than trying to formulate a full-scale theory of consciousness as such, Nagel emphasized the phenomenal quality of experience, which is irreducible to physical fact, as well as the subjectivity of experience, which is connected with a specific point of view (442). To test his assumptions, Nagel introduced the bat as an extreme case that can help explore the limits of what we can say about the mind. On the one hand, the bat is a mammal, closely enough related to humans to support the belief that it possesses conscious experience. On the other hand, however, the bat has a different enough sensory apparatus for that experience to appear fundamentally alien to us. From this thought experiment, Nagel concluded that we may be able to imagine what it would be like for us to be a bat, but we can never know what it is like for the bat to be a bat since its sensory apparatus produces facts that are inaccessible to human concepts.

More recent studies that integrate a phenomenological approach with insights gained from cognitive science correct this view of subjectivity as essentially inaccessible to others. They point out that consciousness is not something that merely exists in the private isolation of the mind but is actively produced between embodied subjects and their world (O'Regan, Myin, and Noë). In this view, qualia are a product of the perceiver's exploratory activity, of his or her "being-engaged-in-the-process of manipulating the sensory input" (373), and perception occurs through a direct embodied involvement with the world that is set in motion by the subject's activity in dynamic interplay with others (S. Gallagher and Zahavi 104, 109; see Merleau-Ponty 1963: 377; Noë 2004: 1).

To the theory of narrative, phenomenology offers the twin insight that experience is always marked by subjectivity and that others are able to access that subjective quality because we all have experiences in a shared world. This has important consequences for the study of focalization, particularly of focalization in comics. As we pointed out above, narrative is credited with providing access to the experience of others. Out of an entanglement of experience, it is able to imagine and render imaginable what it's like to be an entity or person with strange qualia (D. Herman 2009a). This imagination, however, remains vicarious if it does not proceed from a feeling for the other's otherness that acknowledges its encounter with something irreducible and different that is often inaccessible through an empathetic vision (J. Bennett).

Engaging another's qualia is founded on a construction of difference, since my second-person perception of the other can never be the same as their own first-person experience. Indeed, this difference between me and the other is constitutive of experience as such. In real-world experience, qualia are the product of the perceiver's exploratory activity in a situation shared with others. The world of a narrative, however, cannot be processed through the recipient's senses alone; it comes to us already experienced and mediated by characters and narrators. It follows that qualia "form a basis or rather condition for narrative" (D. Herman 2009a: 143) but also its end product in the reading experience of recipients. It is in this field of tensions that focalization markers cue the qualia of characters and in which they gain meaning for readers, thereby giving rise to readers' own experiences.

Many of the comics that we analyze in this book grant their readers access to alien forms of experience, thereby challenging the borders of readers' imagination and empathy. In chapter 4, we show how graphic journalist Joe Sacco draws on the conventions of travel narratives to openly address the difficulty of understanding what it's like to live through conflicts in the Middle East. Similarly, *A Chinese Life*, a collaboration between the French writer Philippe Ôtié and the Chinese artist Li Kunwu, constructs a self-consciously subaltern, non-Western view of twentieth-century Chinese history. J. P. Stassen's *Deogratias* approaches the hard-to-imagine experience of a child participant in the Rwandan genocide through the metaphor of becoming animal, while graphic memoirists Ellen Forney, Sarah Leavitt, and David Small, whose work we discuss in chapter 3, present what it's like to be ill or disabled. These and other comics make the subjective experience of others available based on distinct narrative structures and medial affordances, including a specific use of focalization in graphic narrative.

Another way in which a phenomenologically inflected concept of focalization can become productive is by directing attention to embodiment in comics and to the corporeal experience of readers. As we have pointed out, comics rely heavily on the body in their presentation of subjectivity, and this also leads to a distinct conception of perception as an activity that is anchored in the body. When comics readers consider the bodily activities of characters, they can "get a sense of how [these characters] perceive the storyworld around them, without having to read about their mental states in thought bubbles and without having to see the storyworld from their point of view" (Kukkonen 2013b: 51). It is then likely that "readers of comics, too, experience bodily echoes of the motions and actions they observe" (53), and this embodied response "involves a substantial degree of perspective-taking" (56). Indeed, it is a long-held assumption in the phenomenology of art that "visual art, especially painting, has a particular power to bring us into contact with the world that we study and in which we study because it can convey what the world itself gives us to perceive" (Parry and Wrathall 2). In contrast to the written word, "a painting doesn't merely represent reality. It duplicates, re-stages the meanings that make up and structure our most basic experience as human perceivers in the world in which we find ourselves" (Parry and Wrathall 3; see Merleau-Ponty 2004: 293). When spectators view art, they too can immerse themselves in the picture by "visually exploring the object, imaginatively touching it" and thereby bringing to consciousness an unconscious sensorimotor image that includes the feel of objects inside the painting or even the sensation of reaching into the image and acting within it (Esrock 2010: 226).

Comics, like other visual arts, invite perception with all the senses and an embodied engagement with the narrative world. While the texture of a narrative—its "experiential quality of textuality" (Stockwell 2009: 14)—often goes unnoticed in the silent reading of literature, comics make such an experiential quality noticeable, thereby introducing a meta-phenomenological dimension to the act of reading. Due to the infinite variety of graphic styles, each graphic narrative evokes not only a storyline but also a complete narrative universe with a highly distinctive feel. Pascal Lefèvre even argues that "a graphic style creates the fictive world, giving a certain perspective on the diegesis" (2011: 16). At the same time, the strongly stylized, hand-drawn quality of cartooning serves to highlight the discursive qualities of the narrative representation, rather than emphasizing a story-level similarity to the actual world.

The foregrounding of different drawing styles in graphic narrative and the endless variety of ways panels can speak to each other requires close attention to individual choices in style and patterning and how they encourage active reading (S. Horstkotte 2013). Through braiding, every panel in a graphic narrative addresses readers on multiple levels of increasing complexity, and this media-specific structure increases the likelihood of a nonlinear, roaming reading pattern. In relation to focalization, comics often beg the question of where the deictic center of a sequence lies and through what agent the what it's like of a narrative becomes accessible. If texts in general, as Peter Stockwell suggests, function as "tools by which the human sensorium can be extended" (2009: 58), then comics are particularly efficient tools because their multimodal address leads to a sensorially rich, embodied reading experience. In the following sections of this chapter, we explore the texture of comics and its potential for engaging readers through a close reading of Josh Simmons's *Jessica Farm*, Charles Burns's *Black Hole*, and Chris Ware's *Jimmy Corrigan: The Smartest Kid on Earth*.

Focalization and World Building: Josh Simmons, *Jessica Farm*

Narratives in all media present aspects of one or several worlds that readers flesh out into coherent storyworlds. We refer to this aspect of narrative as its "world building" to emphasize the active and dynamic dimension of how text and reader collude. Because storyworlds are interpretations of a narrative, no two readers experience a narrative world in exactly the same way. Still, identifying textual features provides common ground that makes it possible to distinguish between more and less realistic worlds, as well as between narratives that present a vantage point external to the storyworld (narratorial focalization) and those that are closely aligned with the subjective experience of one or several of its characters (character-bound focalization). Moreover, world building as such can be foregrounded to a greater or lesser extent in a given narrative. While realistic narratives often treat their world as a self-evident given and direct no particular attention toward it, fantastic, science fiction, and other experimental forms of narrative often go to great lengths to explore how their worlds differ from the background expectation of readers.

This is certainly the case in *Jessica Farm*, which evokes qualia that are utterly strange and unfamiliar to readers but provides little help for readers in assessing those qualia in relation to a shared world. *Jessica Farm: Volume 1* marks the beginning of an ambitious project that began in January 2000, when cartoonist Josh Simmons announced his intention to draw one page a month until December 2049, releasing a 96-page comic every eight years (Simmons 2008: 98). To the theory of focalization, *Jessica Farm* offers an interesting case study because it presents a world that is inseparable from the mind of its protagonist, Jessica—even though Jessica is not the narrator. Readers are presented with a bizarre world in which realistic plot elements—like Jessica getting out of bed on Christmas morning; being greeted by her father, who tells her that "you have some really super presents waiting for you under the tree, hon" (5); and taking a shower—blend into a surreal story in which Jessica converses with a band of miniature musicians, finds a room full of grotesquely distorted infants in the landing cupboard, and is paired off by her grandparents with the naked, androgynous Mr. Sugarcock. Since this surreal world is filtered almost entirely through the protagonist's perception, readers have no access to a vantage point from which they might reliably assess whether Jessica lives in a strange world, or whether it is her aspectuality that provides a strange filter to an otherwise unremarkable world.

The comic book contains some dialogue, but apart from the very first panel ("On the farm, Christmas day"), there are no captions that would indicate a narratorial perspective. Many of its panels and pages are entirely wordless. The responsibility of expressing this world's what it's like, and of associating that what it's like with a specific vantage point, therefore lies primarily with the visuals. These are ink drawings that use darkness and light as well as different degrees of detail to express the atmosphere of each room that Jessica enters: the light inside her bedroom and bathroom, the gloom of hallways and cupboards, and the near-darkness of the mysterious interior spaces where Jessica climbs endless flights of stairs or falls down chutes and tunnels.

In a number of ways, the images indicate that these atmospheric changes are associated with the perception, feelings, and imagination of the protagonist. *Jessica Farm* is not a very sophisticated comic book, relying heavily on established optical devices adapted from classical Hollywood film to indicate a character-bound focalization. Apart from the very first panel, which establishes the narrative's setting, Jessica is the focus of all panels. The images either look *at* her (she is at the center of the image) or they look *with* her by means of over-the-shoulder shots or images that are seen with her eyes. A transition from looking at Jessica to looking with Jessica is achieved through images that show her gazing at something, as is indicated through eyes that are drawn larger than usual and that look away from the center of the image (figure 2.1). In this manner, *Jessica Farm* draws on established cues—especially on point-of-view images—that are often used to mark character focalization in film and that have been adapted by comics relying on Hollywood conventions (see Kuhn 2009). By focusing again and again on Jessica's visual perception, the comic indicates that everything that is seen is filtered through Jessica's subjectivity.

A second way in which Jessica's subjective experience is marked lies in the surreal dream quality of her encounters with diminutive, overly large, or inappropriately (un)clothed characters and with animated objects that unexpectedly materialize in enclosed spaces. These encounters violate the realistic background of expectation that is set up by the outside view of the farmhouse in the first panel. In his review of *Jessica Farm*, Robert Martin calls these episodes a form of "Snoopy Syndrome," referring to the active fantasy life of the beagle Snoopy from Charles Schulz's *Peanuts*, which is similarly marked through its contrast with a realistic context. Often, surreal episodes in *Jessica Farm* are initiated by the protagonist looking at something or physically moving into a space. However, their surrealism is not so much a matter of optical perspective as one of context and contrast. Both the interplay of semiotic resources within individual panels and the contrast and contiguity between panels mark these episodes as infused with Jessica's qualia.

Other focalization markers in *Jessica Farm* include the use of light and darkness, which expresses not only atmosphere in a general sense but more

FIGURE 2.1. Simmons, Josh. 2008. *Jessica Farm: Volume 1*. Fantagraphics. p. 5.

FIGURE 2.2. Simmons, Josh. 2008. *Jessica Farm: Volume 1*. Fantagraphics. p. 5.

specifically the mood or feeling of a situation as it appears to Jessica. Again, this is mediated through Jessica's perception as, for instance, when she sees her father as a black shadowy figure with white Mickey Mouse gloves (figure 2.2). The unreality of the gloves and their obvious reference to a pop cultural trope, combined with a panel at the bottom of the page that shows Jessica staring up at her father with huge round eyes, suggest that the image does not present a realistic portrayal of Mr. Farm but rather visualizes Jessica's subjective take on him.

The inherent solipsism of this narrative construction has consequences for the reading experience that may be partly responsible for the negative reviews that *Jessica Farm* has received (Martin). Through its exclusive use of character-bound focalization, the comic makes readers experience its world entirely in terms of Jessica's what it's like. For a better understanding of what this exclusive access entails for readers' ability to engage with the narrative, Peter Stockwell's distinction between three levels of experience provides a useful matrix. Generally, intense sensations of reading depend on a sense of richness, the "feeling of a richly textured literary work" that can be directly correlated with a "sense of readerly involvement" (2009: 63). A number of factors are at work between text and reader to facilitate this sense of richness, including loading, when textual features "match the disposition of the reader to generate satisfactory meanings or effects," and granularity, a feature of the text that creates a "wilful intensification of attention" (63, 65). In *Jessica Farm*, the atmospheric use of light and darkness is an example of granularity, leading to immediate reading sensations that Stockwell defines as a feeling *of* the text.

While reading sensations react to textual effects in a general manner, they also provide the basis for more reflective experiences of sympathy, feeling *for* a character, and empathy, feeling *with* a character (feeling what the character feels), that engage with the experience and perception of characters in a more targeted manner. While *Jessica Farm* may create resonance in readers through the tone and atmosphere of its surreal panels, however, a sympathetic or empathetic engagement with the protagonist's aspectuality is thwarted both by the lack of insight into Jessica's thoughts and emotions and by the unavailability of an alternative viewpoint, bound either to another character or to a narratorial consciousness, from which readers might evaluate the trustworthiness of Jessica's focalization and orient themselves in relation to the storyworld. Despite its emphasis on character, then, *Jessica Farm*'s combination of strict internal focalization with a surreal world forecloses a reflective reading experience that would enable readers to feel *with* or *for* Jessica since it leaves no room for alternative interpretations of the narrative world. In effect, *Jessica Farm* evokes alien qualia, but its closed-off focalization appears designed to repel rather than engage readers in the protagonist's what it's like.

Unnatural and Uncanny: Charles Burns, *Black Hole*

A more engaged reading experience may be reached when a narrative offers a variety of perspectives on its world, the experience of characters in it, and the intersubjectivity of that experience. This can happen in a number of different ways as the experiential dimension of narrative is tied up in its world building (the *what* of a narrative world) and narrative mediation (the *how* of its presentation) and is made accessible through focalization. Each of these three aspects can be foregrounded to a greater or lesser degree in any given graphic narrative, and they can also combine in various ways. A particularly complex experientiality emerges when a narrative integrates more than one origin for its narrative presentation, for its focalization, or for both.

To address this intersubjectivity of experience, we turn to Charles Burns's *Black Hole*, a gothic tale of adolescent angst that places particular demands on readers' attempts to disentangle the facts of its world from the characters' experience of it. Its surrealism bears some similarity with that of *Jessica Farm*, but unlike *Jessica Farm*, the what it's like of *Black Hole* is not that of one but of several characters. Presented through an intricately layered narrative with many visual echoes between spatially distant panels and sequences, and narrated through a mix of flash-forwards and flashbacks, *Black Hole* confronts readers with a web of experiences, perceptions, and emotions binding the qualia of individual characters together with the what it's like of a weird world. Readers have to judge between perspectives and make connections between enigmatic images that are initially presented out of context and reoccur in later passages. A variety of perceptions of events and characters are provided through the voices of its teenage protagonists Keith and Chris and through the book's stark, clean inked images. Parts of the narrative, especially those passages that are verbally narrated by Keith or Chris in captions, are tied to the subjective experience of characters. Other panels or entire passages, however, bear no discernible subjective index, even though the world of *Black Hole* consistently follows the dream logic of nightmares and drug-induced hallucinations. This begs the question of whose dreams these are.

Black Hole's storyline opens as a teen romance set in 1970s Seattle, with the predictable themes of awakening sexuality, drug and alcohol experimentation, and the formation of peer groups. However, genre expectations are quickly dashed when characters start showing symptoms of an unexplained sexually transmitted bug that leads to different kinds of disfigurement, such as the sudden appearance of slits and wounds on the body, the growth of a tail, facial boils, or rotting limbs. While some characters can hide their symptoms and pass as healthy, others, whose disfigurements are more severe, hide out in an encampment in the forest where they subsist on scavenged food and on donations from their peers. Chris and Keith and their love interests Rob and Eliza are at first able to pass. However, when Chris goes skinny-dipping one night, her friends discover her infected back, and she and Rob move into the woods, where Rob is subsequently murdered. While the identity of the killer is revealed in the end, the fate of the surviving characters—Chris, Keith, and Eliza—remains uncertain.

Withholding closure is consistent with a narrative whose main emphasis is not on explanation but on following the dark, confounding logic of its symbolism. The plot of *Black Hole* centers entirely on its protagonists, who live in an exclusively teenage world. Neither parents nor other authority figures play a part in the characters' struggle to survive, and no adult figure attempts to explain or medically treat the bug. A centering on adolescent experience also directs the narrative structure of *Black Hole,* although it does so with notable exceptions. Where Keith and Chris function as character narrators in text captions, the visual panels that accompany their narration often express the same orientation, using point-of-view images to mark a character-bound focalization. At other times, however, the visual track betrays more than the narrating characters know. Such a split between a focalization bound to character narrators on the verbal track and an external focalization on the visual track appears when Chris becomes infected with the bug, causing a large wound to appear in the middle of her back. In the last panel of the chapter "Racing Towards Something," this wound is dramatically exposed to readers, who now understand why Chris's friends have been staring at her as she undresses (figure 2.3). Chris, however, remains unaware of her infection, musing in thought balloons that her friends "can be such jerks sometimes . . . it's probably nothing." This disjunction between the visual information of the image and the knowledge of the protagonist-narrator provides subtle, ironic commentary on the lack of self-knowledge and limited or belated insight that characterizes the focalization through *Black Hole*'s teenage characters.

Other ways *Black Hole* splits or complicates the origin of perceptions include jumping back and forth in time, juxtaposing panels and sequences that may or may not be connected in the minds of characters, and splicing together half-panels that show the memories of characters with conversations in the present in which these memories are raised. Often, different panel borders indicate the reality level of panels or signal their anchoring in the past or present. When Keith drives out to buy some marijuana with his friend Todd in the chapter "Bag Action," for example, the borders of the narrow page-height panels that extend across two pages are split into straight-edged bottom halves that show Keith conversing in the car and wavy-edged top halves that illustrate his simultaneous fantasies about Chris. In this instance, a connection is made between the two halves through Keith's verbal commentary, in inlaid text captions, explaining, "The only thing I could think about was Chris. My mind was stuck on her and I was hurting" (figure 2.4).

Here, the difference in panel borders indicates that the images in the top and bottom halves of the panels have a radically different status in relation to the world they depict. While the bottom halves relate information about plot, setting, and characters that is intersubjectively reliable because shared between several characters, the top halves depict the interior fantasy life of

FIGURE 2.3. Burns, Charles. 2005. *Black Hole*. Pantheon. n.p.

only one of the characters—Keith. The use of different kinds of borders has been identified as a frequently used focalization marker in comics (Kukkonen 2013a; Mikkonen 2013). In *Black Hole*, however, the handling of different border shapes or types is not always consistent, and can therefore be confusing to readers as they attempt to identify the sources of thoughts and perceptions. Later in "Bag Action," a second series of long split panels is framed by wavy lines at the top and straight edges on the bottom (figure 2.5). The bottom halves show Keith smoking a joint as he listens to his friend Todd. The top wavy-framed portion of the panel contains Keith's narrative voice explaining that he wants "to be deep in the woods, leaning up against a tree." The images in these half-panels zoom in through leaves and branches on to a girl lying naked on her back in a small clearing. When she turns her head, the girl turns out to be Chris. If the panels' wavy bordered top half cues an interior vision, this sequence may indicate that Chris is once more in Keith's thoughts—possibly at a subconscious level that is detached from the conscious thought about always wanting "to be somewhere else" expressed in the caption.

But the top images also contain visual premonitions of a third split-panel sequence in which Chris is replaced by Eliza as the object of Keith's desire (figure 2.6). Here, the V-shaped opening in the trees through which Chris is first glimpsed has transformed into Eliza's opening thighs, while the sugges-

FIGURE 2.4. Burns, Charles. 2005. *Black Hole*. Pantheon. n.p.

tively vulva-shaped dark center of the undergrowth behind Chris is replaced by Eliza's tail, her bug symptom and a constant point of sexual fascination for Keith. In the top half of this last split-panel series, Eliza is positioned between Keith and Chris, establishing a provocative visual reference to a key point in *Black Hole*'s plot.

FIGURE 2.5. Burns, Charles. 2005. *Black Hole*. Pantheon. n.p.

The melding of a character's internal and external worlds across three different series of panels puts in place a complex interaction between distinct types of focalization that is bound to confuse readers. At first, all of the images in the three series appear to derive from Keith. The bottom images portray what unfolds in the real world, while the top halves represent Keith's

FIGURE 2.6. Burns, Charles. 2005. *Black Hole*. Pantheon. n.p.

thoughts at that moment in time. As the three series progress, however, their panels become increasingly infected with a more knowledgeable aspectuality that appears to be unbound to any single character, as Keith's memories begin to blend with imagery that extends beyond his range of experience or knowledge. This blending becomes particularly noticeable in the third series where the top wavy-lined portion of the panel border echoes the bottom solid-lined portion that shows Eliza behind Keith, her hands on his shoulders while encouraging him to admit that he liked her tail. Other details similarly imply that the top panel halves contain a greater degree of knowledge and insight than that of any one character and are therefore better understood in terms of an external focalization. Both the second and third sequences end with the desired girl—Chris in the second, Eliza in the third—revealing herself to Keith. In both instances, the girls' facial features and hairstyle closely resemble those of Keith in the accompanying bottom half. This similarity may suggest that Keith sees both girls as an extension of his own self-image, that they are, for him, projections of his desires.

This intricate perspective structure becomes even more complicated when the three series are considered in the larger context of *Black Hole*'s recurrent use of symbolism. Both the open thighs and the displacement of desire from Chris to Eliza are first introduced in another fantasy sequence associated with Keith at the beginning of "Biology 101." The setting of this expository chapter is a biology class in which Keith and Chris have been assigned to each other as lab partners for dissecting a frog. As Keith makes the first incision, he feels a sudden "premonition . . . like I was looking into the future . . . and the future looked really messed up." On the following two pages, this premonition is illustrated across a 180-degree-rotated layout comprised of panels showing the upper part of Keith's face, especially his eyes, and two composite images of four long, narrow panels that are linked to the panels showing Keith's eyes by a long text box. Framed by the images of Keith's eyes, first focusing downward and then upward, the two composite images introduce a number of themes, symbols, and objects that have no obvious reference at this point in the narrative but become meaningful later (figure 2.7).

The first composite panel juxtaposes four narrow frames, each with a kind of slit, cut, or wound at its center: the cut Keith has just made in the frog's abdomen, a small wound under someone's foot, a large slit down a woman's back from which skin is peeling away, and finally a female vulva covered with a hand. Although the objects in these images are distinct from each other, the slits at their center are connected through their formal similarity as well as through a shared background of white rings and black waves that invites readers to interpret them as one meaningful whole. The second composite panel makes this connection even more obvious, since the white rings now move into the foreground in a pattern of concentric circles. Through this foregrounding, the rings break up the four images, interrupting their congruity almost beyond recognition by introducing sections of debris, flames, a snake, tadpoles, and, ominously, a handgun. Fragments of familiar, unfamiliar, and

FIGURE 2.7. Burns, Charles. 2005. *Black Hole*. Pantheon. n.p.

soon-to-become familiar images are caught in a confusing pattern of vertical and circular panels at once separated and united by gutters.

Out of the four images of slits or cuts, only the frog has an obvious reference in the context of "Biology 101." At this early stage, their combination is therefore bound to baffle readers. This was particularly true for early readers, who followed the original serial publication of *Black Hole* across twelve issues from 1993 until 2005, and who had to wait several years to discover the reference of these images. When the twelve issues or chapters are read in sequence, however, it becomes apparent that *Black Hole* contains many repetitions of similar or identical panels and images that are framed in different ways by their context, but that refer to each other across the length of the book as the narrative jumps back and forth in time, connecting different temporal levels by means of braiding. As these connections are not known to any of the characters, braiding in *Black Hole* appears to mark a narratorial focalization in which instances of character-bound focalization are embedded. Thus, the cut foot foreshadows a similar image preceding the title page of "Cut," the chapter that tells of Chris cutting her foot on a piece of glass as she gets dressed after her swim in the lake. In that chapter, Keith spies on Chris as she gets dressed; it is only when she cuts her foot that Keith reveals himself to her. Three panels in that chapter portray Chris's wounded, bleeding foot as Keith tends to it. Although the reference to the foot image is not at first associated with any character's point of view, a version of it may also lie in Keith's memory. It at once introduces a view that no one in the narrative could have seen and suggests a lingering trace of what Keith experienced.

The image showing the wounded back has a more direct reference: It is a detail of a panel in "SSSSSSSSSS," a chapter in which Chris dreams of seeing a group of naked men with snake-like penises beside a swimming hole. As she walks toward them, Chris cuts her foot on glass and, with the glass, pulls out of her wound a scroll depicting a water snake. Her dream, which ends with her holding the scroll, gives way to one of Keith's dreams in which he holds a similarly shaped drawing of a water snake in a heavily polluted lagoon where a large cave-shaped rock juts out of the water. Following upon the two dreams with their clear marking of a character-bound focalization, the next panel, which exposes Chris's back with its open wound, exposes an external focalization by showing something that is not seen or imagined by any character in the narrative.

The fourth image, showing a hand covering a female vulva, draws readers back into Keith's experience. It foreshadows a panel in "Bag Action," the chapter in which Keith meets Eliza. Although the bracelet and black pubic hair are the same in both images, however, the position of the hand and legs does not match. Changes to images that are placed in different contexts impact focalization as they invite readers to consider what is seen, how it is being seen, and how that seeing is framed differently in different contexts. In the composite panel, two externally focalized images contrast with two internally focalized ones, as Keith sees both the frog and the covered vulva. Significantly, the vulva image, with its suggestive evocation of a title-giving "black hole," refers to the chapter "Bag Action," whose split-panel sequences also combine internal and external focalization. Although the images in the wavy part of the frame can be attributed to Keith, the information they reveal is not always available to him. The text caption accompanying an image of Eliza's back and tail reads: "She *knew* something. She knew more than I did." At the same time, the symbolism that is used to express this limitation is itself a product of Keith's hallucination. Indeed, Keith's retrospective narration in "Biology 101" may suggest that the entire novel consists of his extended plunge into the black hole he sees opening up during his biology class.

Evoked through an intricate, often confusing web of images, *Black Hole*'s fictional world appears far removed from ordinary experience. Yet Elizabeth Stone notes the highly charged impact that Burns's *Black Hole* series has had on many readers, highlighting its "astonishing ability to produce an affective response." This response may in fact be due to *Black Hole*'s intricate use of focalization. The graphic narrative is characterized by a distribution of experience across characters and narrative levels. Its continually shifting viewpoint opens the theme of sexual awakening and the associated troubling of the male-female and of the human-nonhuman binary to a variety of interpretations. As Laura Perna argues, *Black Hole*'s multiple and ambiguous focalization may be associated with building deep psychological resonances with readers by operating "through a logic of the uncanny, suspending the reader between familiarity and unfamiliarity, primarily via visual means (doublings of characters, events and images by alternating points of view, shuffling time sequence, and portraying characters' visions)" (9). The dreams and visions characters experience as well as the book's narrative structure and plot trigger a sense of uncertainty in readers. But it is *Black Hole*'s dynamic interplay between alternating, substitutive, and shared subjectivities that ultimately draws readers into its uncanny world. Readers are invited to consider and reconsider events in light of newly acquired information and according to the what it's like of different characters. Thus, the book's intricate use of braiding calls for a reflective reading that we argue produces an empathetic response, as readers repeatedly reassess what it was like for characters to experience situations and events.

Focalization at a Distance: Chris Ware, *Jimmy Corrigan: The Smartest Kid on Earth*

Whereas the multiple focalization in *Black Hole* makes the surreal appear normal and creates empathy with its protagonists, our third text in this chapter,

Chris Ware's *Jimmy Corrigan: The Smartest Kid on Earth*, appears designed to subvert reader attempts to engage with its protagonist. Introduced in 1993 as a weekly strip in a Chicago newspaper and later assembled into an attractively bound book, Ware's comic combines four parallel storylines around its central character, Jimmy Corrigan. The primary narrative introduces Jimmy as a lonely and awkward man with an overbearing mother, a boring office job, and no social life. Jimmy agrees to meet his father, who abandoned him as an infant, but their get-together is inconsequential and the two have little to say to each other. While some episodes in this storyline may be read in terms of character focalization, the majority of focalization markers point toward a narratorial focalization.

A second storyline, set in the past, narrates the prequel to this dreary story. Here, readers encounter Jimmy as a lonely child with a rich fantasy life. This storyline contains clear markers of character-bound focalization, but its combination with the other three storylines produces many contrasts with a narratorial focalization that often ironizes Jimmy's what it's like. The third storyline is interwoven with this two-tier biographical narrative. It tells the story of Jimmy's grandfather, who is confusingly also named Jimmy and was abandoned by his father while visiting Chicago's 1893 Columbian Exposition. At a first glance, this story appears to be unknown to the protagonist. However, the rear endpaper of the book suggests a link with the first two storylines. There, "exposition" is defined in a large rectangular panel of the Columbian Exposition buildings as "(ĕt'spa-zĭsh'an) n. the main body of a work, esp. that which explicates a main theme, or introduces a fundamental motif." Abandonment, which is a central motif of *Jimmy Corrigan*, links Jimmy's story to that of his grandfather via his father.

This linkage is complicated through the fourth storyline, which consists of a series of mini-narratives in which Jimmy seeks imaginary escape from his unhappy life by fantasizing about being the smartest kid on earth—even though (or because?) he is constantly reminded that the opposite holds true. Like the second storyline, the fourth one contains many markers of a character-bound focalization. When read in light of this exposure of Jimmy's fantasy world, the grandfather's story, too, may be taken to constitute a product of Jimmy's vivid imagination, rather than a factual account. As we will show, *Jimmy Corrigan*'s combination of storylines, with its embedding of character-bound and narratorial instances of focalization, is designed to produce ambivalence about the origin of perceptions and judgments and may give rise to contradictory readings. In particular, readers will have to decide whether to process the grandfather's story as one that actually happened (despite the ironic narrative voice and the use of different fonts within the same drawing style) or as one of Jimmy's fantasies about events he could not have actually experienced, from vantage points he could never have shared.

In terms of Peter Stockwell's three levels of experiencing narrative, the focus on an individual's life at first seems to invite readers' sympathy with that character. Indeed, the narrative goes to great lengths to explain why Jimmy is the way he is. At the same time, however, both the flat drawing style and tight narrative construction of *Jimmy Corrigan* are designed to generate dissatisfactory effects, discourage readerly involvement, and impede identification with the protagonist. In interviews, Ware emphasizes that *Jimmy Corrigan* is drawn in a "harsh," "mechanical," "banal" cartooning style with little background detail (qtd. in Sattler 208). Different sizes of square or rectangular panels are framed with a thick black border. At times, panels are arranged in different directions across a page, inviting readers to turn the book around. Many of the book's panel arrangements can be read in a variety of ways, making it difficult to determine what the correct or more plausible sequencing is and ultimately suggesting that different meanings are simultaneously possible and plausible. This relentless experimentation with the aesthetics of comics taxes readers with the unsettling knowledge that they may have missed potentially important details.

Several critics have commented that *Jimmy Corrigan* foregrounds narrative composition, interrogating "the relationships between the architecture of the narrative and the narrative itself" (Bredehoft 870). With its architectural style, the book demands a slow reading, one that constantly requires readers to determine where to place attention and in which direction to proceed (Hagelstein 15). When asked about the reading of comics, Ware explains:

> In comics you make the strip come alive by reading it, by experiencing it beat by beat as you would playing music. So that's one way to aesthetically experience comics. Another way is to pull back and consider the composition all at once, as you would the façade of a building. You can look at a comic as you would look at a structure that you could turn around in your mind and see all sides of it at once. (qtd. in Raeburn 25)

With *Jimmy Corrigan*, Ware shows readers that all elements of graphic textuality—composition and style; the arrangement of panels across a page; the repetition of color patterns, page layouts, and images; and the size and *feel* of the book—contribute to the reading experience and thus impact interpretation. This complex architectural design, however, often generates a distancing effect in readers and "propagates [a] feeling of frustration and difficulty" (Mauro).

FOCALIZATION, EXPERIENCE, AND WHAT IT'S LIKE • 51

FIGURE 2.8. Ware, Chris. 2000. *Jimmy Corrigan: The Smartest Kid on Earth*. Pantheon. n.p.

As in *Jessica Farm* and *Black Hole*, the multimodality of comics narration is exploited in *Jimmy Corrigan* to disorient readers as to the reality status of what they see, as visual details migrate between narrative levels, and sudden spatiotemporal shifts produce further ambiguity as to where readers stand in relation to the protagonist. In one passage, Jimmy sits with his father in a hospital room when a red sound balloon signals a phone ringing in the corridor (figure 2.8). The page's top row of panels includes three images of Jimmy holding a handkerchief to his bleeding nose: on the top left, as a framed medium close-up, sitting on a hospital gurney; on the bottom right, as a smaller framed close-up picturing only Jimmy's head; and on the bottom left, as an identical, but unframed head shot. In the bottom half of the page, a bordered panel extends this latter image by adding Jimmy's torso but not his legs. Instead, Jimmy's body appears grounded in a second reiteration of the red sound balloon. This time, the balloon initiates a narrative sequence in which Jimmy's mother phones him—presumably, a memory that is called up by the hospital's ringing phone. The following panels of a roasted turkey, a dinner plate, and a framed photograph of Jimmy as a boy holding his mother's hand on a flight of stairs, however, are more enigmatic. At the bottom of the page, a series of monochrome panels shows Jimmy and his mother in a car driving through the night until the last panel in the page's bottom right corner returns to the top row's color pattern and to Jimmy's father holding forth on family vacations and turkey dinners.

Through a pattern of repetitions and variations, the page combines at least three narrative layers: (1) a realistic one with Jimmy and his father sitting in the hospital room, (2) one in which Jimmy reacts both to the ring tone and to his father's speech with memories of ringing phones and of family vacations, and (3) one representing in a seemingly objective fashion Jimmy's family eating a turkey dinner. Even in this condensed space, each layer is characterized by a distinct type of focalization. While the second layer appears anchored in Jimmy's subjectivity and marked as an instance of character-bound focalization through the overlaying of Jimmy's body with the ring-tone balloon, the first layer is not connected with Jimmy's aspectuality in an obvious fashion and contains no clues as to the deictic center of the images, suggesting a narratorial focalization. The third layer, meanwhile, may represent Jimmy's visualization of his father's speech. As in many passages throughout *Jimmy Corrigan*, however, it is left to readers to draw inferences concerning the temporal and causal connections between distinct panels and the aspectual orientation of the images.

The pattern continues on the next page with two additional repetitions of the red ring-tone balloon. The combination of a seemingly realistic narrative with intruding visual elements, with memory or fantasy sequences, and with material that seems unrelated to Jimmy's aspectuality is characteristic of the narrative as a whole. *Jimmy Corrigan* blends multiple narratives into one through contrasting patterns of words and pictures or instances "in which the perceived experience is colored by intellectual action" (Kannenberg 183). The effect of this particular type of braiding is ambivalent. On the one hand, the combination of narrative layers invites readers to assume Jimmy's experience of self and world through his dreams, fantasies, memories, and daily activities. On the other hand, the open-endedness of these combinations and the lack of explicit commentary make it extremely difficult for readers to arrive at a plausible and satisfactory interpretation. Reading *Jimmy Corrigan* and trying to gauge the protagonist's what it's like can thus become a frustrating experience.

The narrative construction of *Jimmy Corrigan* is designed to produce such frustration since it embeds Jimmy's character-bound focalization within a highly ironic narratorial focalization that constantly belittles Jimmy's thoughts and perceptions. Readers are thus simultaneously presented with two contradictory takes on the protagonist, one that creates empathy by expressing Jimmy's qualia and one that negates empathy when Jimmy's qualia are held up to ridicule—for instance, when a narratorial caption describes Jimmy as a "decidedly un-magnetic protagonist" and a "lonely, emotionally-impaired human castaway." Despite a sustained focus on Jimmy, it is therefore difficult for readers to overcome the distance that the narrative creates toward its protagonist.

Other indications that Jimmy's focalization is embedded within that of an ironic impersonal narrator include metanarrative commentary on the comics form, authorial intrusions that address readers, and the introduction of cutouts. Self-reflexive commentary on the comics form begins with the book's cover and continues on the front paper, comprised of five sections of framed small typed script that resemble turn-of-the-century newspaper columns and are arranged both horizontally and vertically across the page: 1. Introduction, 2. Ease of Use, 3. Role, 4. Technical Explanation of the Language, Developing Skills, 5. Exam. The "Introduction" describes comics as part of "today's 'cutting-edge culture'" and predicts that the medium's "artistic dominance shall be shortly realized and remain so, indeed, for centuries to come." However, this praise of the comics form is immediately rebutted in "2. Ease of Use," which explains that the book has been packaged to avoid embarrassment when read in public.

The ironic assault on the comic book and its form continues throughout this introductory material. The talent needed for reading the book is described as "essentially intuitive," and a faux-scientific article on "new pictorial language" sarcastically describes the language of comics as "good for showing stuff, leaving out big words" in the subtitle. To underscore this point, the article refers to growing illiteracy rates and a "dive in the general intelligence of the populace" as reasons for the rise of comics. The ironic stance continues on the next page with a list of quotes from popular presses that followed the book's hardcover release. Selected "as an aid to purchasing confidence," the quotes are said to be "included as a shameless and offensive last-minute effort to fill up this space (which reproduces an uncomfortably-sized, yet indispensable, Appendix originally included with the hardcover editions of this book) with something." The commentary not only ridicules the attention paid to each comics page within this and other graphic narratives but also pokes fun at the decision of readers to devote time to reading *Jimmy Corrigan* and, by extension, any other graphic narrative.

PAGES 206-207. — It should be readily apparent to even the most casual reader of this novella that supplied with it are a handful of piquant and diverting "cut out" reference guides, though such "paper activities" are sometimes dismissed as "child's play" or frivolous "hokum," of no value to the serious student of literature, it is hoped that these uncultured negative preconceptions – which really do serve no other purpose than to truncate one's experience of an evocative work – shall be disspelt by the dainties' masterful esthetic and artistic qualities. Besides, the increasing commonplace of such "paper toys" in respectable books, plays, and corporate presentations is enough to muzzle even the most vocal detractor towards the cause. Though admittedly printed too small to be constructed with any degree of satisfaction or pluck, pantographic or electrostatic enlargement of all primary shapes and careful study of the construction principia will potentially reward the concerted craftsman with models of relative usefulness. An outfit of water-color paints, a sharp knife, and limited background in human romantic contact are, of course, key.

It is, needless to say, not entirely necessary to complete these tasks to fully appreciate the story in question, though those who do attempt the feat will find themselves more acquainted with the rivulets and tributaries of its grander scope, and will besides have nice little miniatures to display to friends and family once the fantasy is nothing more than a swamp of misremembered trifles. However, given the relative intelligence and mathematical skills of this textbook's author, all culpability regarding measurement of parts, tabs, and joinery is hereby forfeit, and no submitted claims to the contrary shall be honored.

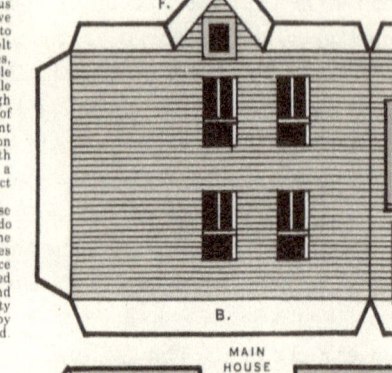

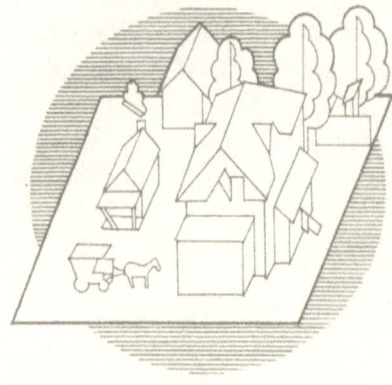

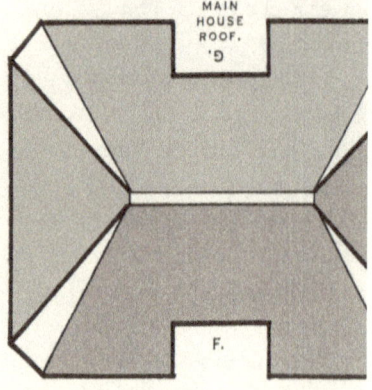

NOTE. — Any student of the history of the neighborhood in question will note that the reconstruction presented here is not without its inconsistencies; based, as it is, upon reminiscence and fragmentary recollection, some details reproduced may possibly contradict and/or overlap one another. Additionally, care should be taken when projecting any of this aid's details temporally forward or backward, as some street names have changed, vegetation has developed, and those personalities concerned with the area have either moved away, perished, or their relative sense of the scale of the world has changed. Regardless, and as elucidated above, those wishing a more fully-developed sense of the events related within these pages may find some diversion by crafting the attached, as it allows a simulated maneuverability about the spaces described, and may, at the very least, prove a lightening influence upon a Sunday afternoon's weakened heart.

INSTRUCTIONS. — Given the generally intuitive level of the task, no detailed directions are provided; it is believed that the matching numerals, letters, and diagrams will be guidance enough to carry the intelligent reader through to completion of the chore. Follow all folds and outlines carefully, and avoid spreading of excess adhesive on exposed elements, as it will spoil the model and prevent attainment of the desired "finished" quality. As well, please take time to allow independent elements to thoroughly dry before committing final assembly; do not "test" parts, as this may compromise sensitive joinery. Those who suffer difficulty should abandon the enterprise immediately.

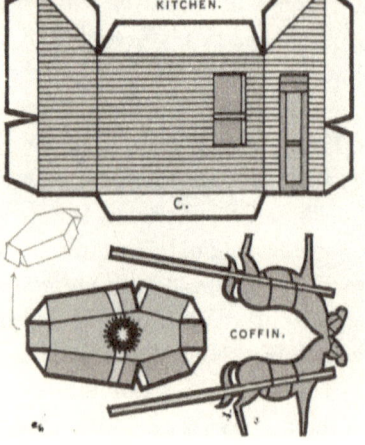

FIGURE 2.9. Ware, Chris. 2000. *Jimmy Corrigan: The Smartest Kid on Earth*. Pantheon. n.p (above and facing).

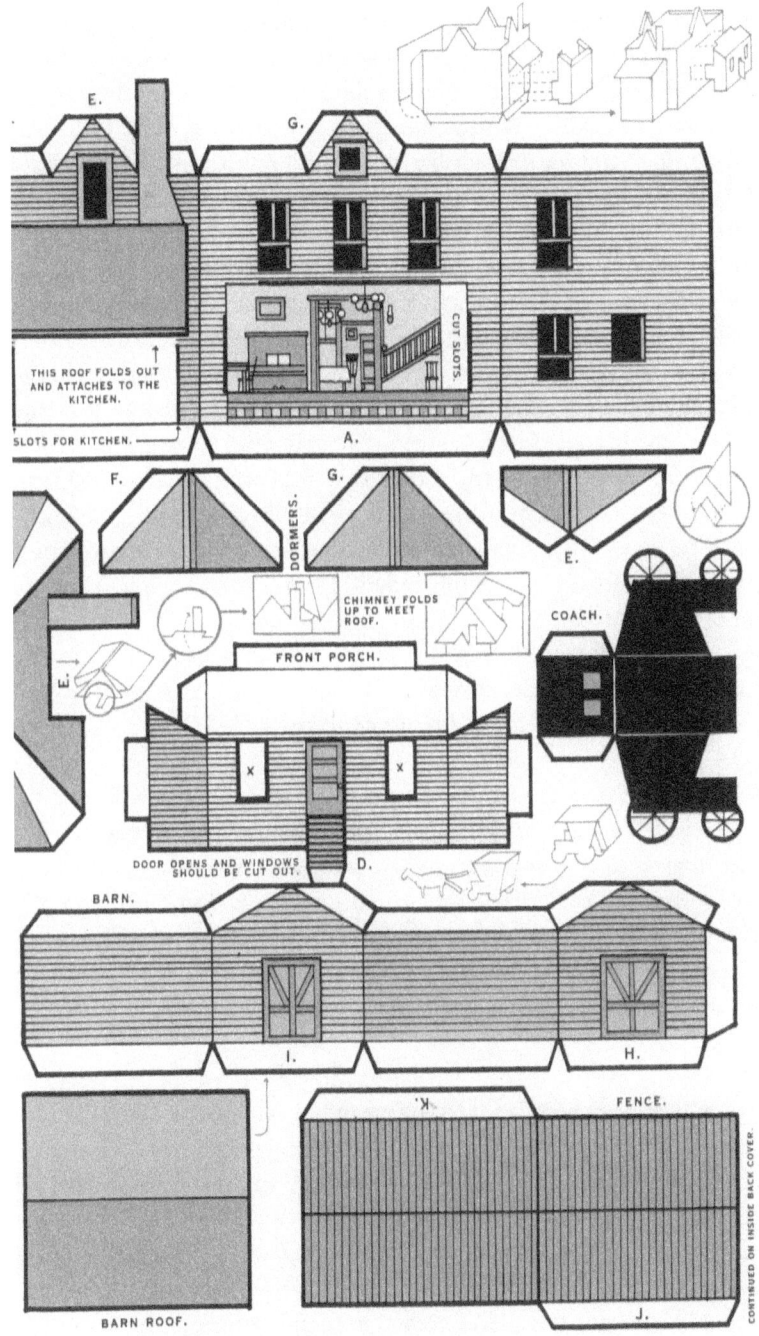

Throughout the book, paratextual material is instrumental in producing a distancing effect between readers and the narrative they are reading. For instance, many of the book's potential title pages introduced throughout *Jimmy Corrigan* emphasize the book's shortcomings and the absurdity of wasting one's time reading it. One title page describes the book as "essentially indefensible" and warns readers that "no great revelation is likely to yield from its consumption, though we did try." This commentary complements the irony expressed through the use of logo-style intertitles that draw on superhero comic conventions by announcing Jimmy as "the smartest kid on earth" (when he is neither a kid nor smart). The ironic assault on readers and their efforts extends up to the book's closing "Corrigenda," which imply that readers of *Jimmy Corrigan* are as simple as its main character, who is also a reader of comics. In its dictionary definition of "simpleton," the example given to clarify the word is "Billy is a simpleton; he reads comic books." Once again, readers are ridiculed for the book they are reading. Whereas paratextual transactions, which "have been prominent in American serial narration since at least the nineteenth century," usually serve as "productive contact zones between producers and consumers, authors and readers" (Stein 160), in *Jimmy Corrigan* the opposite holds true.

The cut-outs included throughout *Jimmy Corrigan* also impact reader involvement by creating a distancing effect (figure 2.9). One cut-out of Jimmy's grandparents' house begins with this address:

> It should be apparent to even the most casual reader of this novella that supplied with it are a handful of piquant and diverting "cut out" reference guides; though such "paper activities" are sometimes dismissed as "child's play" or frivolous "hokum" of no value to the serious student of literature, it is hoped that these uncultured negative preconceptions—which really do serve no other purpose than to truncate one's experience of an evocative work—shall be disspelt by the dainties' masterful esthetic and artistic qualities.

Although readers are encouraged to engage in the assembly activity, they are also informed that "it is, needless to say, not entirely necessary to complete these tasks to fully appreciate the story in question," though those who decide to assemble the "paper toy" may gain "a more fully-developed sense of the events related in these pages" and "may, at the very least, prove a lightening influence upon a Sunday afternoon's weakened heart." In any case, the assembly is impossible because the pieces needed to complete the exercise are reproduced on both sides of the same page, and thus cutting out individual parts necessarily leads to the destruction of equally important parts.

Arguably, the distance that readers of *Jimmy Corrigan* are made to feel reflects the distance Jimmy feels toward himself and his world, as the graphic narrative's intricate patterning of panels, temporal layers, and reality levels produces a disorientation that is analogous to the protagonist's confused experience. Through a broad range of expressive resources, the book's narratorial focalization stages Jimmy's inadequate grasp of his place in the world. Moreover, the contrast between narrative layers frequently provides readers with information about Jimmy and his family to which Jimmy has no access, such as the fact that his great-grandfather, William Corrigan, glazed the windows of the house Jimmy now lives in or that his great-great-grandfather was a doctor. However, by embedding Jimmy's focalization within that of an ironic impersonal narrator, *Jimmy Corrigan* makes readers acutely aware that they, like the protagonist, will never grasp the full picture. They cannot understand fully the "pure density of information" the narrative provides no matter how slowly and carefully they read (Goldberg 206).

•

Taken together, the three analyses in this chapter further support our argument that focalization in graphic narrative can be signaled in a wide range of ways. Potential focalization markers include the size, layout, perspective, angle, color, and framing of individual panels as well as patterns of repetition and variation and the style of a particular graphic narrative. These expressive resources operate in conjunction with each other and need to be assessed in context. They also invite reception with all the senses and the entire body, as for instance when being made to turn the comic book around or when flipping back and forth between distant sections in order to make connections. *Black Hole,* in particular, also invites an embodied engagement with the storyworld through the visual overload of its hallucinatory panels and through visceral reactions to its depiction of disfigurement. It follows that focalization in comics cannot be reduced to purely mental aspects. Instead, analyzing focalization in graphic narrative calls for a phenomenological concept of experience as embodied, enactive, affective, and grounded in intersubjectivity.

The embodied engagement to which focalization in graphic narrative gives rise may produce sympathy (a feeling for characters) or even empathy (a feeling with characters). At the same time, the frequent foregrounding of style in graphic narrative encourages active reading and brings focalization up to notice, and this foregrounding may also produce distance or frustration, especially when evoking strange or unusual qualia. The multimodality of comics, with its high potential for mutually embedding several levels of focalization, often begs the question through what particular character or narrative agent a particular sequence or narrative is focalized. In *Black Hole,* focalization is never just tied to any one character, and thus every section of the narrative can be interpreted in a number of ways, giving rise to distinct experiences depending on the choices that readers make in identifying the source of perceptions and emotions inside the diegesis. The narrative of *Jimmy Corrigan,* meanwhile, sets the character-bound focalization of its antihero off against an ironic narratorial focalization that consistently ridicules and belittles Jimmy, while the inclusion of paratextual material produces an even higher degree of distancing between readers and the graphic narrative that they are reading. Even in *Jessica Farm,* which is presented exclusively through the interior focalization of its protagonist, the surrealism of the representation invites readers to search for alternative vantage points on the narrative world, although none are ever explicitly expressed. In chapter 3, we will follow up on this inquiry into single-focus narratives by discussing focalization in graphic memoir, a comics genre with a strongly subjective single-person focus.

CHAPTER 3

Graphic Memoir

The rise of the aesthetically ambitious graphic novel is intimately linked with the autobiographical genre. Many best-selling graphic narratives, from Art Spiegelman's *Maus* to Alison Bechdel's *Fun Home*, from Marjane Satrapi's *Persepolis* to Lynda Barry's *One! Hundred! Demons!*, are autobiographical in content, and university courses, academic articles, and full-length books are devoted to the study of graphic memoir (Chaney 2011; Chute 2010; El Refaie 2012, 2019; Køhlert; Kunka).[1] Graphic memoir is creative, aesthetically rich, and stylistically innovative. Its experimentation with the comics form foregrounds expressiveness as an important way of fashioning an identity, as well as offering access to the what it's like of that identity.

In the previous chapter, we argued that narratives in all media can make qualia, or subjective qualities of experience, accessible through their structure of focalization, but that they can also produce distance toward those qualia depending on the distribution of focalization and narration within a given narrative. In this chapter, we consider how genre conventions regulate focalization both in the production and in the reception of autobiographical comics. With John Frow, we define genre as a set of "conventional and highly

---

1. Graphic memoir is also referred to as "autographics" by Whitlock, "autobiographical graphic novels" by Chaney (2016), "autography" by Gardner (2008), "autographic memoir" by Watson (2011), and "autobiocomics" or "autobioBD" by Miller and Pratt. Moreover, graphic memoir also partakes in the spectrum of outlaw genres of autobiography proposed by Kaplan.

organized constraints on the production and interpretation of meaning" (10). Genre conventions shape the formal features, thematic structure, situation of address, and rhetoric, and readers draw on them as they interpret a narrative. Far from merely guiding the choice of formal or stylistic devices, genre conventions actively generate knowledge and shape how we understand the narrative world (Frow 2). They determine what kind of access an individual comic book provides to the experience of its characters and to the general mood and atmosphere of its narrative world.

For this reason, we consider genre to have a strong impact both on the expression and on the interpretation of focalization. Distinct comics genres draw on combinations of focalization and narration that carry with them specific ways of thinking and feeling. When readers open a comic book, they are therefore already primed to experience certain things. In this chapter, we explain how this priming works through a close analysis of key texts in the graphic memoir genre. Graphic memoirs are typically rendered by an autodiegetic narrator who is also the focal character and who is moreover closely aligned with the graphic artist who authored the book. Whereas the fictional graphic novels we have considered thus far in chapters 1 and 2 employ variable combinations of internal and external focalization, sometimes within the same panel, the nonfictional genre of graphic memoir is almost invariably internally focalized by a character narrator. Graphic memoirs emphasize this singular focus by dwelling on the memoirist's self-perception, often expressed through repeated visual portrayal, and by developing highly individual drawing styles to evoke the memoirist's subjective experience. The hand-drawn quality of comics style is explicitly connected to the corporeality of the memoirist and their being-in-the-world. To readers, the style of a graphic memoir offers a rich sensorial experience, enabling a nuanced access to the memoirist's what it's like. At the same time, however, graphic memoirs also expand genre-bound expectations regarding focalization by embedding a character-bound focalization in social networks of feeling and perception.

Focalization in graphic memoir invokes all the senses and the entire body. Through close readings of Ellen Forney's *Marbles* (2012), Sarah Leavitt's *Tangles* (2010), David Small's *Stitches* (2009), and David B.'s *Epileptic* (2005), we show how graphic memoir often bends the conventions of autobiographic narrative, which place a strong emphasis on one subject and on that subject's experience and on couching that experience in a language of authenticity. Graphic memoir engages experimental forms of autobiographical narration to propose alternative presentations of selfhood. We argue that the expanded understanding of the self in graphic memoir requires a reformulated concept of focalization. In particular, rather than presenting a disembodied inner sense of self, graphic memoirs focus on embodied selves and on social and entangled rather than individual formations of selfhood.

Frequently reflecting on the very nature of experience, on the self having and representing experiences, and on the relation between subject, object, and other subjects in experience, graphic memoir can justifiably be described as a meta-phenomenological genre. The focalization through which readers can imaginatively participate in graphic memoir's exploration of experience is marked through embodied practices that are expressed stylistically. Style, in the simplest sense of how to draw a story, is always to some extent foregrounded in graphic narrative. Nevertheless, it receives particular attention when characters ponder self-reflexively how to draw something, or when different styles clash. Thierry Groensteen (2013) points out that since style can be used to persuade the reader of a point of view, it is linked to the overall rhetoric of a narrative. Lukas Etter agrees that stylistic variation may be associated "with a specific character's subjective perspective," but adds that, more importantly, "through stylistic markers, we also believe we establish at least a vague connection to the person who authored the comics" (93). Because style can be more or less effective, a main question guiding us in this chapter concerns the extent to which drawing style, which in comics has no fixed norms, can be used to encourage the reader's adoption of a particular perspective through self-portraiture. However, before turning to our close readings, the following sections of this chapter explain in more detail how graphic memoirs express subjectivity and mark focalization, how their narrative structure implicates readers, and how their focus on embodied and social selves expands the genre conventions of autobiographical storytelling.

Subjectivity from the Inside

Graphic memoirs show subjectivity from the inside. The realism of their world presentation relies on the subjectively experienced world of an individual—hence, on internal focalization. Many graphic memoirs emphasize this subjectivity by showing the graphic artist at work as they draw their life and self, ponder different modes of self-representation, and fashion a style that corresponds to their sense of being in the world. Visual self-reflexivity thus abounds in graphic memoir, from images of the protagonist engaged in the act of crafting the book we are reading to cartoon hands holding the comics page we are holding.

To name just one example, Alison Bechdel's *Fun Home: A Family Tragicomic* (2006) contains many self-reflexive panels. The graphic memoir relates the story of Alison's complicated relationship with her father, a closeted homosexual who most likely committed suicide. Alison's coming to terms with her own homosexuality leads to inevitable comparisons between father and daughter that are often expressed through the scrutiny of written documents and photographs. In the middle of the book, a double-page spread shows a larger-than-life-sized left hand holding a square photograph of a naked boy, identified in a caption as "our yardwork assistant/babysitter, Roy" (100–101). A series of eight text boxes superimposed on the photograph contain Alison's reflections on the picture: her memories of the summer the photo was taken, her impression of its aesthetic quality ("the blurriness of the photo gives it an ethereal, painterly quality"), and her interpretation of what the photo conveys about her father ("in an act of prestidigitation typical of the way my father juggled his public appearance and private reality, the evidence is simultaneously hidden and revealed"). Represented through a highly detailed ink drawing that is quite unlike the cartoon style used throughout the book, the photograph's rendering as a faux facsimile is similar to that of other photographs and handwritten documents included in *Fun Home*.

This spread provides a striking example of embodied focalization in graphic memoir. By picturing Alison's hand as she holds the photograph and adopting an angle of vision that corresponds to where her eyes would be, the memoirist beckons readers to imagine themselves inside her body and to adopt her gaze as we are reading her thoughts in the text boxes. That this is the only spread in *Fun Home* adds to its importance, while simultaneously highlighting the process of scrutiny that Alison performs on the photographic image and to which we are also invited. These embodied gestures prompt readers to feel what it's like to be Alison at that particular moment in time when she discovers the photograph in a box of family photos. Visual and verbal markers of Alison's surprise and understanding, bafflement and self-questioning come together in this two-page spread to draw readers into her mental and emotional experience.

Other self-reflexive panels portray Alison in the activities of reading, writing, drawing, and doodling. Panels frequently adopt the angle of a cinematic point-of-view shot, but connect this perspectival technique with the memoirist's embodied experience by showing her hands holding pen and page. In one of these instances, Alison has cut herself with her Swiss army knife and confesses that she "smeared the blood into my journal, pleased by the opportunity to transmit my anguish to the page so literally" (78). The half-page panel below shows Alison's hands, an adhesive bandage wrapped around her right index finger, as she writes in her journal with a black fountain pen (figure 3.1). Seven streaks of blood are smeared across the journal's opposite page

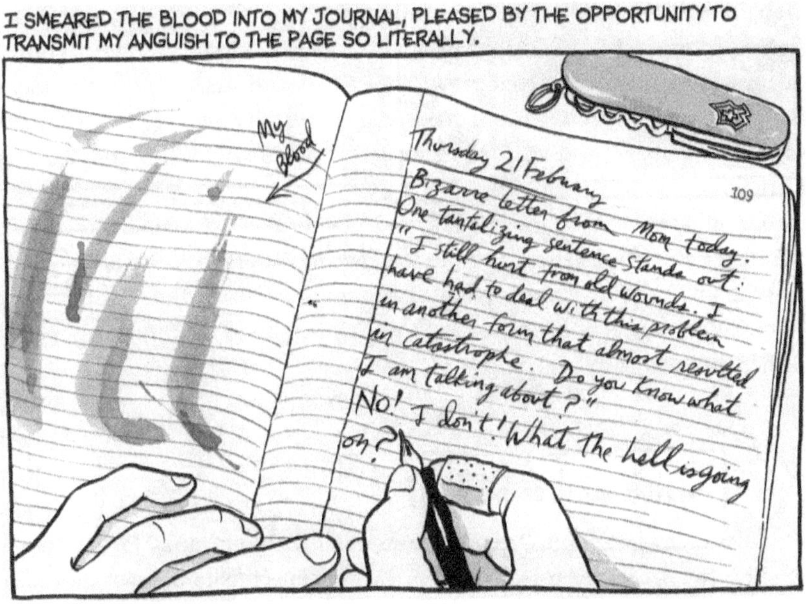

> I SMEARED THE BLOOD INTO MY JOURNAL, PLEASED BY THE OPPORTUNITY TO TRANSMIT MY ANGUISH TO THE PAGE SO LITERALLY.

FIGURE 3.1. Bechdel, Alison. 2006. *Fun Home: A Family Tragicomic.* Mariner. p. 78.

and labeled "My blood," while the offending army knife rests in the panel's top right corner, behind the open journal. The panel offers a potent commentary on journaling and on the crafting of the graphic memoir that grew out of the journal: These are embodied practices, and they should be read as the material traces of a living body (see Warhol; Watson 2011b).

Such instances of reflexivity in graphic memoir draw attention to the duality of the autobiographical self by accentuating the importance of self-portraiture for rendering visible the complex relationship between the narrating-I and the experiencing-I. This rendering of the story of a subject in a subjective style that self-consciously points to its maker renders graphic memoir uniquely suited to expressing subjectivity. As Bechdel admits in an interview, "I always felt like there was something inherently autobiographical about cartooning . . . I still believe that. I haven't exactly worked out my theory of why, but it does feel like it almost demands people to write autobiographies" (2007). Yet the splitting of subjectivity across two tracks, the combination of narrative autobiography and visual self-portraiture, and the focus on the body in graphic memoir also complicates assumptions about the self and its representation (see S. Horstkotte and Pedri 2017).

According to Paul John Eakin, the pronoun "I" in literary autobiographies transports a sense of being in full command of itself and its stories (25). In graphic memoir, there is no such strong pronoun, at least not on the visual track, and so the self often appears split or divided. This splitting has consequences not only for the concept of self expressed through graphic memoir, but also for the possibilities that graphic memoirs offer their readers to empathize with that self, and thus for the genre's structure of focalization. Charles Hatfield argues that "while the written text in a comic may confide in the reader much like unaccompanied, first-person prose, the graphic presence of the image at once distances and inflects the autobiographer's voice. Whereas first-person prose invites complicity, cartooning invites scrutiny" (2005: 117). In the following section, we discuss how this invitation to scrutiny addresses readers of graphic memoir.

A Meeting of Minds?

Autobiography is a popular genre: Memoirs of well-known public figures are practically guaranteed to sell. But in the current climate of what has been dubbed "generation self," the life writing of lesser-known people is also widely read. All sorts of autobiographical narratives are felt to forge an intimate connection between readers and the individuals whose lives they tell. People, to put it bluntly, are interested in other people, and autobiography feeds that interest. Many novels, too, follow the life, thoughts, and feelings of individuals. In the eyes of many readers, however, autobiographies have the additional benefit of being true, authentic representations of a real person's actual private life, and this creates a particularly strong reader bond.

In her study of narrative empathy, Suzanne Keen concludes that "novels inviting empathy do better in the marketplace" because empathy is, for many readers, a "sought-after experience—tantamount to a precondition for success with a large segment of the book-buying and novel-reading public" (2007: 104–5). Many influential narrative theorists, including Wayne C. Booth, Dorrit Cohn, and Franz Stanzel, have argued that the use of first-person narration, the interior representation of characters' consciousness, and the depiction of emotional states are core techniques contributing to character identification and to empathetic reading experiences (see Keen 2007: x, 96–97). Although Keen emphasizes that no strong experimental data exists to support this hypothesis, the prevalence of its intuitive theorizing as well as the commercial success of autobiographical narratives suggest that the close aligning of a narrative with the subjective perspective and experience of one character often promotes character identification and engages the empathy of readers.

If empathetic reading is a sought-after experience, it comes as no surprise that graphic memoir is a popular comics genre not only with academics but also with the publishing industry and a wider reading public, often serving as a gateway drug into the comics universe for first-time comics readers. But how exactly do graphic memoirs invite readers to empathize with their protagonists, and how effective is this invitation? In chapter 2, we explained that narrative affects readers because it offers access to the experience, perception, and cognition of others. According to Fritz Breithaupt, we understand other people (and ourselves) by implicating them in imaginary mini-narratives that calculate the scope of action for that person (10). Actual narratives may train their readers in this vicarious sharing of affect (Keen 2007). However, as we pointed out in chapter 2, this sharing of affect is often far from a simple process of identification. The experience that is made accessible in graphic narrative can derive from one or several characters; it can also lie in between characters, and it can have a social or intersubjective mode. The texts that we examined to make this point were fictional graphic narratives with complex relationships between authorship, narration/graphiation, and the processing of characters.

In graphic memoir, these relations appear more straightforward since author, narrator/graphiator, and protagonist are the same person—or are assumed to be the same person by readers who take part in an "autobiographical pact" by which a number of textual and paratextual signals, including the identical name of author, narrator/graphiator, and protagonist, are taken to indicate the truthfulness of a life story (Lejeune). According to this influential understanding of autobiography, graphic memoir's suggestion of realism would more or less automatically produce in readers a sense of intimacy with the memoirist, as long as readers correctly decode signals of authenticity and do not read against the grain. Many comics theorists subscribe to this view, stressing that graphic memoir, by focusing on an individual's life story and aligning the narrative parameters into a single speaking, seeing, and experiencing agent, strongly invites readers to empathize with its protagonist, triggering affiliation between readers and characters (see, e.g., Versaci 38). According to Keith Oatley, life writing can go so far as to achieve a "meeting of minds" between characters and readers, creating "a species of empathy, in which we do not merely sympathize with a person, we become that person" (1999a: 440, 446).

However, as we have pointed out in the previous section, not only is graphic memoir experimental in relation to style, but its bimodal narration offers many possibilities for a complex, multilayered approach to the self whose life story it narrates. At once narrating and portraying the self, graphic memoir moves the body as a decisive dimension of selfhood into focus. In its presentation of a cartoon avatar of the artist's self, graphic memoir represents the body visually while also directing attention toward the drawing hand that produced the imaged body. The cartoon avatar views the events that make up the comics universe through its personal perspective, but it is also on view, drawn into the text as an embodied entity rendered in a particular style and presented to look a certain way. In addition, the cartoon self is often engaged in creating the story of which it is the major character, and this visual self-reflexivity challenges genre-bound assumptions about authenticity and truthfulness.

The temporal structure of autobiographical storytelling adds to this complexity of access. Focalization in autobiographical narratives becomes complicated when it is divided between a more mature narrating-I and a younger experiencing-I. In graphic memoir, this duality of the autobiographical self is rendered tangible since both narration and focalization operate on two modal tracks simultaneously. As Kai Mikkonen (2011) reminds us, the question of perceptual origin—Genette's "who sees" or "who perceives"—is relevant both in relation to the words and to the images of comics narration, thereby opening up many possibilities for cross-referencing and interplay between visual and verbal focalization markers. In all comics genres, the narrating and processing of information occurs at once on the verbal and on the visual track so that switches between character-bound and narratorial focalization are often ambiguous at best. In graphic memoir, however, this complication concerns different dimensions of the same subject; it thus conditions ideas about the subject, about subjectivity, and about subjective experience. Graphic memoir does not simply show the world, but simultaneously renders an internal world and reflects on the perceptual, emotional, and cognitive processing of both the external and internal world by its protagonist. In this sense, it is a meta-phenomenological exploration.

Given the prominence of the visual and embodied aspects of the self that is created in graphic memoir, we argue that graphic memoir is best understood as a hybrid of autobiography and self-portraiture. This hybridity further complicates the sense of self communicated through graphic memoirs as well as the realism of its representation. Although the self-portrait is often approached as a visual cousin to autobiography, and both have been closely linked in the cultural history of subjectivity, the practice of portraiture is actually the older one. It can be traced to Egyptian mummy portraits from the Roman era, dating back to the first century BC, and may have influenced the literary construction of the self in autobiographies from late antiquity onward. While the self-portrait is naturalistic and concerned with the individual, it is also playful and self-reflexive, an aspect that is highlighted in the common subgenre of the portraitist in their studio. Far from supporting likeness and accuracy, the frequent use of mirrors in artists' self-portraits induces unique levels of uncertainty in the viewer (Hall). Is the artist looking at us, at themselves, or at the mirror? Are they creating a persona or painting from memory? In twentieth-century self-portraiture, there is a thin line between self-portraiture and caricature, while self-portraits prior to the late modern period often emphasize conventional and collective, rather than individual, aspects of the self and its attitude. Thus, the self-portrait stands at an uneasy crossroads between likeness and self-fashioning. Its emphasis on staging and posing reveals it to be not so much a representation of a prior self as an active agent in constructing identity, including gender identity, and in linking identity, status, and subjectivity (Pointon).

In many graphic memoirs, the exploratory and self-conscious use of self-portraits counteracts the modern cult of the artist, while the repetition of the portrayal of self over the course of a book challenges the idea of a unified self by presenting many variations of the self across time and space. Pictures of the memoirist at work, which abound in graphic memoir, draw notice to the duality of the autobiographical self and accentuate self-portraiture's "implicit purpose" to reveal and interpret "a specific, delimited human identity" (Lubin 3). Besides resemblance and recognition, self-portraiture's fashioning of self strives to achieve a manifestation of an intangible sense of personality and inner life. Yet the portrayal of self in graphic memoir is multiple and often oscillates between various iterations of the autobiographical subject (Groensteen 2013: 108). As Julia Watson points out, graphic memoir's repeated portrayal of self "offers multiple possibilities for interpreting experience, reworking memory, and staging self-reflection" (2011: 124–25). Crafting the body to reflect different physical and mental experiences, the graphic memoirist is able to fashion embodiment on their own terms and also amplify, expound, and ultimately complicate their visual self-representation "with variation, embellishment and interpretation" (Mitchell 257).

Besides the self-conscious repetition and modification of self-portraits, the frequent use of visual metaphors is yet another way in which graphic memoirs cue the subjectivity and creativity but also the intricacy of their focalization, as that focalization is split or distributed between a drawing and narrating self and an experiencing-I, between words and images. In comics, a visual metaphor is a visual element whose incongruence with its surrounding context signals a shift of semantic field (Pedri and Staveley). The comprehension of linguistic, visual, and multimodal metaphors involves similar mental procedures: "Although the perception of images differs from linguistic decoding, reaching an interpretation of metaphors entails similar adjustments of conceptual information of texts and images and multimodal combinations, regardless of the modal quality of the input" (Yus 147). Just like their linguistic counterparts, visual metaphors can express "memories, emotions, or sensations occurring within characters in the world of the story but undetectable by the senses" (Duncan and Smith 155) but also have a more enigmatic horizon of meaning that is not associated with a character. Especially "bold" or "living" metaphors tax our understanding because they paradoxically seem to say one thing, but mean something else entirely (Ricoeur).

Multiple metaphors for the self coexist, clash, and otherwise interact in *Cancer Vixen* (2006), a graphic memoir by Marisa Acocella Marchetto that tells the story of her struggle with breast cancer. Portraying herself as an emotionally overdetermined person, Marisa's otherwise fashionable self transforms into a street rat (45), a woman armored with a steel pail head cover (54, 100), a red super-muscled ninja lady (56), a minuscule version of herself held in the palm of her fiancé's hand (67), a breast-eyed face (156), a gray matter globby head (165), and a cyclops (201, 208). The drastic changes in Marisa's body join other visual techniques, such as exaggeration and caricature, to express a multifaceted subjectivity that readjusts with changing experiences. Instances of animal symbolism that recur in many graphic memoirs, including David B.'s *Epileptic*, Marjane Satrapi's *Persepolis*, and Art Spiegelman's *Maus*, are another example of the many self-reflexive narrative strategies adopted by graphic memoir to make the perceptive, emotive, and cognitive processing of the memoirist accessible. As with more realistic self-portraiture, in metaphorical iterations of the self, physical and mental realities meet across the body.

The sustained visual self-portraiture that characterizes graphic memoir draws attention not only to different, possibly changing, and multiple perceptions of self but equally importantly to the mediated and fabricated quality of that very self. Graphic memoirs openly address processes of self-fashioning, frequently drawing notice to the memoirist's hand and mind engaged in the process of self-representation. Their investment in the presentation and performance of a particularized, embodied, and material self troubles any illusion of referentiality, whereas the emphasis on drawing as a process highlights identity formation not as something that finishes with a product, but rather as a lifelong process of making selves. The rendering of subjectivity in graphic memoir puts forward an integrated, dynamic view of the self. In it, visual self-portrayal and self-reflexive strategies draw notice to how "we are all becoming different persons all the time, we are not what we are; self and memory are emergent, in process, constantly evolving, and both are grounded in the body and the body image" (Eakin ix).

Lives and Bodies

When American underground comics artists began producing graphic memoirs in the late 1960s, their subversive, often sexually explicit stories drew attention to new groups of people and aspects of subjectivity that had not predominantly factored into autobiographical writing before (El Refaie 2012). This particularly concerned the embodied aspects of identity and the sociocultural models underpinning body image, which were also being highlighted in other genres and across different media. Within the memoir boom of the past decades, so-called nobody memoirs, written by people who were not famous before publication, have often been "about what it's like to have or to be, to live in or as, a particular body—indeed, a body that is usually odd or anomalous" (Couser 2009: 2). For Thomas Couser, a specialist in illness and disability narratives, the rise of memoirs written by people with non-normative bodies marks a "significant shift in the demographics and body politics of American life writing" (2009: 3).

Many graphic memoirs fall into the category of nobody memoirs, portraying ill and differently abled bodies and addressing diseases such as Alzheimer's (*Tangles*), Asperger's (*Something Different about My Dad*), bipolar disorder (*Marbles, Rock Steady*), cancer (*Stitches, Cancer Vixen, The Story of My Tits*), deafness (*El Deafo*), depression (*Hyperbole and a Half, It's All Absolutely Fine*), eating disorders (*Inside Out*), epilepsy (*Epileptic*), mental illness (*Bitter Medicine, Lighter than My Shadow, Psychiatric Tales*), and spina bifida (*Spiral Cage*). Their presentation of corporeal, non-normative, and social selves goes hand in hand with a changed understanding of autobiography's treatment of subjectivity and with a growing attention to embodiment in phenomenology. While classical theories of autobiography such as Philippe Lejeune's assumed an authenticity of subjective experience in autobiographical narratives, or at least the successful narrative presentation of an authentic subjectivity, more recent studies have reversed the relation of truthfulness and subjectivity in autobiography, arguing that the illusion of truth in autobiographical narration is premised on its invitation of intimacy, and not vice versa (Warner 93–99).

According to this more recent view, autobiographical narration is not grounded in a world of reference beyond the text, but based in an act of constructing the self with the goal of presenting a specific understanding of self and the self's life story. Thus, Paul John Eakin points out that we are every one of us constantly making ourselves by constructing stories that present our current understanding of who we are. Similarly, Ben Yagoda emphasizes that the act of autobiographical writing is one where the account of self—the events, emotions, and people that shape self—is informed by "one's interpretation of one's life" (110). Questions of self-representation and expression thus tightly intertwine with questions of how the self understands itself as a textual subject: Who I am is not a fact that precedes my telling of my story, but I make my self and what it is by telling my story to myself and to others.

This constructive and performative view of the self and of self-narration has received support through readings of autobiography based in gender theory, queer theory, and most recently in disease and disability studies (Bell and Yalom; Couser 1997; Watson and Smith 1992, 2002). The growing number of life narratives by marginalized groups since the 1980s has raised awareness that subjectivity and identity cannot be treated as natural or given and thus beyond explanation. On the contrary, the representation of the self questions what identity means and how subjectivity can be defined (Benstock). Responding to traditional misrepresentations in Western culture, autobiographies by members of marginalized groups raise important ethical and political questions about visibility and representation that go far beyond reader-character alignment (Couser 2013: 457).

On a fundamental level, the representation of non-normative bodies in illness and disability memoirs challenges a normative understanding of the self as an immaterial inner site distinct from its surroundings. Foregrounding the embodied and social dimension of the self, they emphasize that "we have our being in the world, and act upon it, through our bodies and only through them" (Couser 1999: 164). These new forms of life writing thus bring into focus a more phenomenological view of the self as embodied and engaged in a shared world of subjects and objects, a world in which the self interacts with others.

In graphic memoir, where words and images come together to tell one's story, individual minds and perceptions necessarily intersect with the body. The visual portrayal of the graphic memoirist's body underscores "the important role of the body in giving us a sense of our own existence and identity" (El Refaie 2012: 50). Grounding the self in physicality while at the same time drawing attention to the creativity and artistry of that grounding through repeated representation, graphic memoirs undermine the alternative between an authenticating and a constructionist understanding of the self in life writing. This alternative has long divided scholars of autobiography, life writing, and "autofiction," which understands the autobiographical self as radically fictitious (see Doubrovsky). On one side of the spectrum of autobiography theories, autobiography is seen as a genre premised on the authenticity of the I telling the story of him- or herself (Lejeune), while on the other side, feminist scholars have voiced reservations about the reliability of the autobiographical text, focusing instead on the cultural and political norms that dictate what can and cannot be represented (Gilmore; Smith). But many graphic

FIGURE 3.2. Barry, Lynda. 2002. *One! Hundred! Demons!* Sasquatch Books. n.p.

memoirs implicitly and explicitly make the point that a tentative life narrative presenting a physical and social self is not necessarily inauthentic, untruthful, or fictitious. Instead, the notion of autobiographic truth itself needs to be reconsidered.

One! Hundred! Demons! (2002), a collection of seventeen "autobifictionalography" short stories by Lynda Barry about her troubled adolescence, opens with a two-panel page portraying the artist sitting at her desk, brush in hand, questioning her role as memoirist and pondering her cartoon self as at once true to what she knows of herself and not true to her knowledge of self (figure 3.2). The second panel of the two-panel page shows Barry reflecting on her completed drawing, which is an image of the very panel readers are scrutinizing. Like a signature, this image of Barry at work on the graphic memoir that we are reading serves as a guarantee of self-presence, albeit one that is tied to the activity that produced it, rather than to a stable essence. To render conspicuous the textualization of self, then, sends a double signal, announcing the interjection of a subjective mind that directs the graphic memoir's visual (and verbal) telling *and* the cartoonist's authorial role in the building of her own textual self. Many graphic memoirs foreground this process of constructing both self and story with cartoonists representing their physical identities "in ways that reflect their own innermost sense of self, often by using a range of symbolic elements and rhetorical tropes to add further layers of meaning to their self-portraits" (El Refaie 2012: 51; see Mitchell).

Focalization is often associated with consciousness representation and with a disembodied processing of information. The genre conventions of graphic memoir challenge that understanding. Graphic memoir is concerned with the body as a central site of subjectivity, showing a self that is grounded in embodiment. Focalization in graphic memoir is thus marked through visual representations of the body and through stylistic shifts relating to that representation. Our close reading of Ellen Forney's *Marbles* in the next section explores what happens when that body is not in full command of itself due to disease and disability. We also explain how style in graphic memoir can be used as a focalization marker that signals the what it's like of not being in full command.

Body and Style:
Ellen Forney's *Marbles*

Embodiment is a phenomenological concept that directs attention away from an everyday sense of the body and toward the more fundamental question of what it means to be a body. In his study *The Absent Body* (1990), Drew Leder examines the basic notion that although the body is ever-present in daily tasks and routines, it is absent phenomenologically from awareness of these tasks. Leder, who is both a phenomenologist and a medical doctor, draws on the German distinction between *Leib* (lived body) and *Körper* (physical body) to foreground the lived body, which is often absent from consideration. The physical body is seen from a third-person perspective, the body as it appears to the doctor. The lived body, on the other hand, is experienced from a first-person perspective, the body as it feels to oneself. However, there is an important problem with this self-perception: My body usually contributes anonymously to my experience while being itself absent from conscious attention. In performing the everyday activities of seeing, walking, and talking, my body is phenomenologically absent from view. In an important way, embodiment is thus concerned with an absent body, a body that is in flight away from itself in its engagement with the world. Only when this routine interaction with the world breaks down in some way, due to disease or disability for example, does the lived body come to awareness. From a phenomenological point of view, disease therefore opens up the unique possibility to truly see and experience the lived body.

At the same time as it opens up a perspective on the lived body, however, disease also complicates processes of self-recognition and self-identification. *Marbles* (2012), Ellen Forney's graphic memoir of her struggle with bipolar disorder, lays bare the difficult process of creating an image of the body that overlaps with, reflects on, and is intently linked to the mind. That process is set in motion through the crucial initial scene in which the memoirist gets her back tattooed with a cartoon image created by her friend, the cartoonist Kaz. In this expository passage, the memoirist introduces herself through a scenario of displaced authorship, as that authorship is being played out on and through her body. The idea for the back tattoo has sprung to Ellen's mind on one of her brisk walks, fired by the manic phase that opens the memoir. But the actual blueprint for the tattoo was produced by Kaz according to Ellen's specifications, and the tattooing itself was performed on Ellen by the tattoo artist Owen. When readers are finally shown the finished tattoo, what they actually see is a highly mediated image, consisting of Ellen's rendering of a photo that Owen took of her back (10; figure 3.3). Several layers of focalization are at play in this panel, as what readers see is framed by the information they have been given about how the tattoo image was designed and produced. From the start, *Marbles* radically—if playfully—disrupts the idea of the memoirist as the sole author, artist, and creator of her life story.

Similarly disrupted is the idea of the artist as a creator of her own style. A close connection between the subjectivity of an artist and the style of their art often forms the background to stylistic analysis in comics, especially concerning graphic narratives that draw on the tradition of artists' sketchbooks. That tradition is explicitly evoked through graphic memoir's frequent self-portraiture of graphic artists with their sketchpad. In *Marbles*, Forney includes a black-and-white photograph of her sketchpad (93) and several facsimile reproductions of the sketches in it (figure 3.4). She draws a close connection between the materiality of the sketchbook with its specific paper quality (highlighted through the high-resolution images) and the body of the artist who uses the sketchpad to draw a series of suggestive, surreal self-portraits that speak to how she processes her world and her experience as a person with bipolar disorder.

Stylistically, these sketches are distinct from the cartoon drawings that make up the bulk of Forney's memoir. In *Marbles*, Forney's cartooning style relies on thick, bold black linework and simplified characters and is generally characterized by a lack of detail, especially background detail. Panels often intersperse visual images and text in unusual patterns, suggestive of mind-mapping techniques or collage posters. They present an appearance of surface that has been edited to carry a message, spelled out in text boxes or interspersed comments. The sketchbook images, by contrast, are sometimes drawn with a thin ink pen, sometimes with charcoal, and occasionally with a soft lead pencil. They often present as scraps of paper with torn edges haphazardly

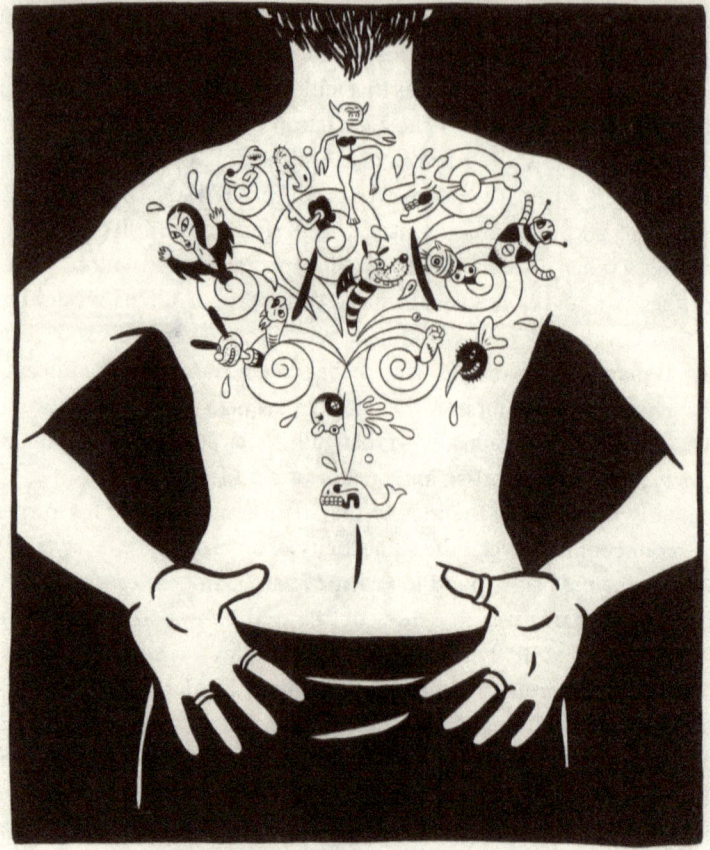

FIGURE 3.3. Forney, Ellen. 2012. *Marbles: Mania, Depression, Michelangelo, and Me*. Gotham. p. 10.

and loosely placed on the page. Layers of crisscrossing lines on some of the sketchbook images indicate a drawn-out creation process through which the images gradually emerged in line with the tentativeness generally associated with the sketchpad.

These different ways of drawing express different ways of seeing the world. They mark different kinds of focalization through which readers can access

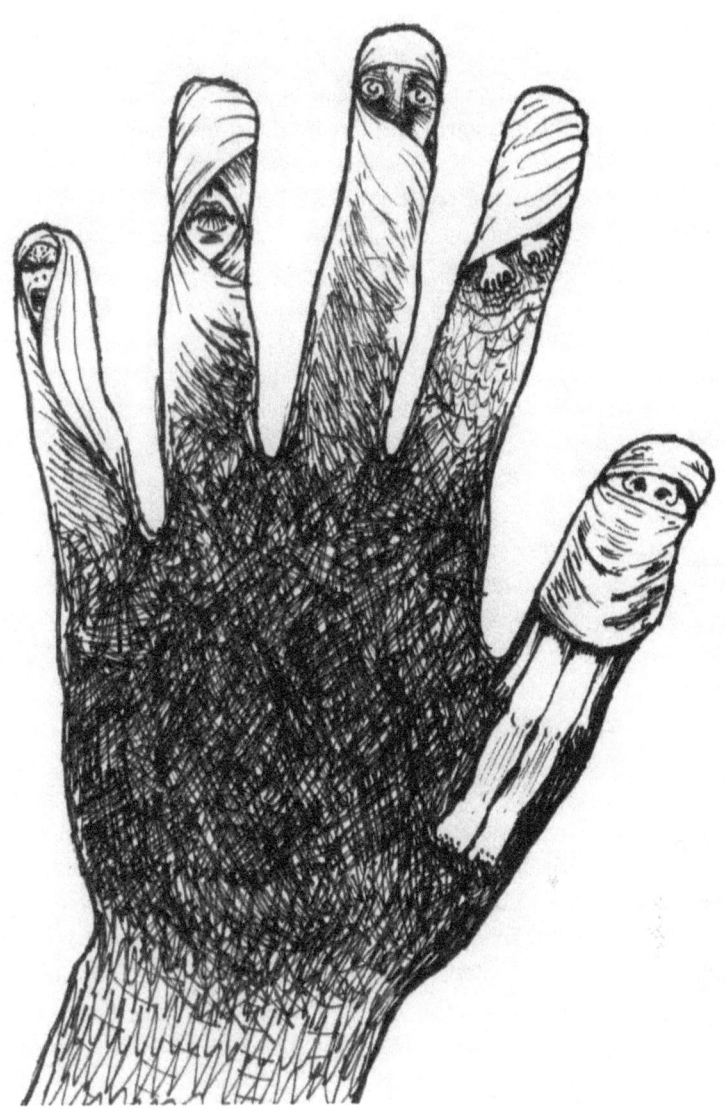

FIGURE 3.4. Forney, Ellen. 2012. *Marbles: Mania, Depression, Michelangelo, and Me*. Gotham. p. 102.

multiple versions of the memoirist's self and the process through which these come into being. Read in conjunction, the multiplicity of styles within the sketchbook and the stylistic distinctions between sketchbook and cartoon memoir images point to a multiplicity of selves—to Forney being torn between distinct kinds of what it's like in her manic and depressive states. They also point to the ways in which distinct types of images can process these states. However, the use of distinct styles and the association of stylistic elements with the authorship of others (Kaz and Owen) introduces serious complications into any attempt to connect the memoir's visual style solely to the subjectivity of the memoirist and thus to interpret focalization, while the recurring depiction of Forney's body in a variety of styles invites reflection on the relation between interior and exterior aspects of selfhood. We will return to the important point that the multiplicity of styles in *Marbles* makes about the inherent sense of self. First, however, we explain what we mean by style in this context.

When speaking about style in connection with shifts in register, and thus in connection with focalization, it is important to draw a sharp distinction between the style of an artist and the form of their work. Because this distinction is often not clearly made in comics studies, and style is readily confused with form, we turn to the art historical tradition of style attribution for an explicit discussion of such a style concept. According to Heinrich Wölfflin's *Principles of Art History* (1915, 1932), style is not something that is objectively given in a work of art, but a way of seeing the world that is inseparably bound up with the artist's subjectivity. In narratological terms, this style concept can be connected to a very broad understanding of focalization, as the style of a painting or of a painter's oeuvre is understood to give access to that painter's subjective perspective. For Wölfflin, style is expressive of the artist's perception of his world and also serves to open up that perception to the viewer.

Although an art historical style concept that links style to authentic expression may prove problematic—one only has to look at the tradition of icon painting to understand that not all paintings express a subjective view of the world—it can prove useful when considering the role of style in graphic memoir. Many graphic memoirs connect style to authenticity of expression; however, they do so in a tentative manner, through repetition, variation, transformation, and juxtaposition. The sequential presentation of different styles in graphic memoir places particular demands on readers, and calls for an understanding of style that takes the role of the recipient into account.

For art historian Whitney Davis, style as a way of seeing does not lie so much in the artist's eye as in the viewer perceiving something as style in the work of art. Viewers learn to see style when they perceive the painter's identity in a painting, in and through the way the painter paints. In a way, style is the opposite of representation: It makes us think about the cause of an artifact—its maker—rather than about the artifact's reference to the objects it depicts. "To see style in an artifact," Davis writes, "is to sense its attributability to a maker who existed before and outside of us, even though *we* see the affiliation. And to see representationality in an artifact, or to see its pictorial aspects, is to sense its resemblance to things . . . outside us, in a virtual world beyond us, even though *we* see the correspondence" (49). Davis' reception-oriented style concept helps us address questions of focalization along explicitly visual terms. When we see style in a graphic narrative, we perceive presentational aspects such as line work and composition as expressions of subjectivity. This perception proceeds from cues in the text. However, because these cues need to be interpreted, readers have to weigh whose subjectivity is being expressed.

The assumption that style points to its maker's personal take on the world is an important one for Ellen Forney, as it is for many other comic artists, and nowhere more so than in the genre of graphic memoir, with its emphasis on the authenticity and sincerity of personal expression. But the referentiality of Forney's style is not a simple one. Forney introduces this important point in *Marbles* when she locates the origin of her narrative in a scene of displaced authorship. In the back tattoo panel discussed above, the cartoon image comes from Ellen (who figures as author in her graphic memoir), but the style comes from Kaz, or, more precisely, it constitutes the outcome of an intersubjective and intericonic dialogue with Kaz's art. This dialogic production challenges received ideas about stylistic origin, as well as about the individuality of the autobiographic subject. However, this does not mean that Ellen is not in command of the narrative. Rather, it signals her playful approach to the self and its creative authority, at least in the first part of her memoir. Forney shows how subjectivity develops in a close exchange with other subjects and with objects in the world, as that exchange is played out across the body.

This process is important not only for the inherent understanding of style in *Marbles* but also for the sense of embodiment developed in it. In the memoir's first section, following upon the tattoo parlor scene, the memoirist's body and the memoir in which it is depicted begin to blend into each other. Through a process of metonymic displacement, individual elements of the tattoo image, which shows a number of cartoon characters splashing through water being spouted by a whale figure at the small of Ellen's back, recur in panels indicating the memoirist's mood and, sometimes, (her view of) herself. Just as she did in her dialogue with Kaz leading to the blueprint for the back tattoo, Ellen adapts symbols and other iconic elements that have come from another person to express her subjective sense of herself.

Opposite the back tattoo, a panel stretching the width of the page shows Ellen walking home at night as she reflects on the warmth on her back creating "a yin and yang balance with the air"—"everything was magical & intense, & bursting with universal truth" (11). As the small Ellen character walks through the bright light of a street lamp, the dark sky above her is a crisscross pattern of broken white lines that intersect with the shapes of a fat Buddha, a pointing

FIGURE 3.5. Forney, Ellen. 2012. *Marbles: Mania, Depression, Michelangelo, and Me*. Gotham. pp. 50–51 (above and facing).

hand, a heart, a diamond, and a flying horse through which the cartoon microcosm on Ellen's back receives an allegorical macrocosmic counterpart. Since many other panels also indicate the memoirist's thoughts, moods, and feelings through text and graphic symbols surrounding her avatar figure, this macrocosm pattern may be taken to express her current sense of being in the world.

A second way in which *Marbles* challenges received notions about the subjectivity of style concerns the visual contrast between manic and depressive states of mind as portrayed in different sections of the memoir. During one of Ellen's manic phases, an unnaturally long-legged Ellen strides wide-eyed across a double-page spread, rubber-tube arms forming loops as ideas for her thirtieth birthday party spring from her body (50–51; figure 3.5). The unnaturally wide and long extensions of Ellen's body parts are here analogous to the excessive exuberance of her mood. The following double page reduces Ellen to a stylized head with no nose, overly large eyes and mouth, and a pattern of five-pronged stars drawn onto her forehead. Rays shoot out of her eyes, while long, stylized flames separate fields that detail her party plans (52–53). In both instances, the representation of Ellen's body portrays neither an outside view nor an inner sensation of the body. Rather, it expresses the memoirist's mood and general sense of being in the world.

By contrast, during Ellen's depressive phases, perception goes inside the body. Ellen's sense of crisis "at the end of a high" (68) as the depression settles over her is depicted as "a cage of frantic rats" (69) in her open skull. The following page shows the first of a number of self-portraits from Ellen's sketchbook. Just like the cartoon images of Ellen in the first part of the memoir, the sketchbook images in the second part do not so much portray an outer appearance as they indicate an inner sense of self. In these images, Ellen's external world goes dim, and the self is isolated, cut off from its surroundings. Stylistically, too, the sketchbook images are distinct from the cartooning style that serves as their backdrop. If the tattooing scene draws attention to the fact that the style through which the memoirist expresses herself does not have to originate in some interior core but can emerge out of a dialogue with other subjects and objects, the hauntingly atmospheric sketchbook drawings make the additional point that the relation between style and self does not have to be one-on-one. A multiform self may very well need multiple styles to record different senses of being in the world.

A third point to take note of concerns the relation between style and the body. Representations of the body in *Marbles*, as in many other graphic memoirs, are often less concerned with physical appearance than with how the body is experienced from the inside. As suggested above, different styles in *Marbles* express different kinds of self-perception and experience. Ellen describes her sketchbook as a place "where I could face my emotional demons in a wholly personal way" (92). The resultant self-portraits are a series of "mental image[s] that I needed to get outside of me" (93), showing not what Ellen looks like to the outside world, but rather "how I was feeling" at the time (99). They include several sketches of her grossly distorted body that she penciled while trying to understand how her symptoms impact her experience of self. From various versions of her head sprouting from her skull (138) or parts of her body poking through each finger of a bandaged hand that presents as a tracing of Ellen's hand (figure 3.4; 102) to a squished, contorted ball of a body lying in a thorny nest (97), Ellen struggles to understand her condition and its impact on herself through images of her body. Although the exact meaning of these sketchbook self-portraits is uncertain, they speak to her effort to imagine her bipolar self across the body. Ellen addresses the intersection of style, body, and mind when she explains: "I soon learned to keep drawing until I really nailed my feelings down. I didn't get nearly the same relief if I only came close" (96).

Throughout *Marbles*, a subjective what it's like is expressed through the juxtaposition of styles and the repetition and variation of tentative images. Both the cartoon drawings and the sketchbook images are expressive of Ellen's qualia. Despite the consistent use of internal focalization through Ellen, however, focalization in *Marbles* is not uniform as Ellen's sense of self, body image, and experience of the world shift radically between her manic and depressive phases. These shifts are marked stylistically, with the filtering through distinct styles also implicating readers in distinct what it's likes. Besides making the specific point that mentally ill people may have several radically distinct senses of the self and modes of access to the world, the graphic memoir also shows how in a more general sense a sense of self is not clearly separable from other subjects in a shared world, and neither is the visual art through which that sense finds its representation. Thus, the subjective experience to which *Marbles* gives its readers access emerges out of a tight mesh of retrospective evaluations of individual thoughts and feelings, of interactions with others, and of the visual means through which these are expressed. Narratologically speaking, such a complex experientiality does not always allow for a clear distinction between internal and external focalization. In the next section, we delve deeper into this "tangling" of the subject—a metaphor we borrow from Sarah Leavitt's graphic memoir, *Tangles*—and we inquire into the consequences that such a tangling has for entangling readers.

Tangling the Subject: Sarah Leavitt, *Tangles* and David Small, *Stitches*

Subjects do not have experiences in isolation. Where the idea of subjectivity performed in autobiographical writing may at times suggest an absolute subject-object distinction, the phenomenological concept of experience emphasizes the mutual dependency of subjects and objects in a shared phenomenal world. In experience, the subject does not meet up with something that is already given; rather, subject and object establish each other. Consequently, experience cannot be the immediate effect of an external stimulus because it resides in an in-between, in which apprehensions of qualities are tied to an entire perceptual context. As Maurice Merleau-Ponty stresses, "the phenomenological world is . . . inseparable from subjectivity and intersubjectivity, which establish their unity through the taking up [*la reprise*] of my past experiences into my present experiences, or of the other person's experience into my own" (2012: 8). Graphic memoir foregrounds this tangling of subjective experience with the material world of objects, with an intersubjective context, and within the physical, perceptual, and cognitive conditions set by the human body.

Many graphic memoirs explicitly emphasize the intersubjectivity of experience by focusing not on the story of the memoirist's self, but on the story of another—at least partly. Alison Bechdel's *Fun Home* tells of Alison's coming out as a lesbian by exploring the biography of her father, a closeted gay man. Sarah Leavitt's *Tangles,* one of our sample texts in this section, engages the biography of Sarah's mother, who suffers from Alzheimer's disease. David Small's *Stitches,* our second sample text, repeatedly combines one half of a self-portrait with half portraits of other family members to reflect on the memoirist's identity. Lastly, David B's *Epileptic,* which we analyze in the final section of this chapter, is concerned with David's development across time, but also with his brother, who has epilepsy. By telling the story of the self through and across the story of another (or others), these and similar graphic memoirs (such as *Maus, Mom's Cancer, Can't We Talk about Something More Pleasant,* or *Flying Couch*) highlight the affiliative dimension of identity. With their emphasis on the way lives and selves are always entangled in the lives and selves of others, they show that subjectivity is relational and intersubjective, thereby opposing a view of the self as autonomous and independent.

Often, textile metaphors in titles such as *Stitches, Blankets,* or *Embroideries* evoke a communal perspective of self. Marjane Satrapi's *Embroideries* (2005), for instance, is set in her grandmother's sitting room, where a group of eight Iranian women share tea while exchanging personal stories. Each story intersects with the stories of the other women who are listening to but also interjecting the telling with requests for clarification and elaborations. These women craft stories about marriage, sex, love, bodies, and other intimacies that stitch their lives and identities together. A white page with an entangled thread hanging from a needle announces the first story told to the group by Marji's grandmother (13). That storytelling and stories serve to knit these women together is further suggested when their faces are drawn grouped around and united by their questions and exclamations (47, 53, 70, 94, 106). These confidential stories that are marked by revelation and secrecy, sharing and hiding, weave lives, emotions, and desires into a tight web of interconnectedness. Like several other graphic memoirs, *Embroideries* presents individual experience as being bound up in a web of what may be called, with Alan Palmer, "social minds" (2010). Their focus on the social and communal aspects of subjectivity invites us to rethink focalization in more relational terms. If subjectivity is not quite individual, then neither is the subjective filtering at work in focalization. Bridging the distinction between internal and external focalization, these graphic memoirs employ different forms of intersubjective focalization either by mutually embedding different focalization types or by presenting a spliced focalization that combines internal and external aspects.

Entangled stories and shared subjectivities characterize Sarah Leavitt's *Tangles: A Story about Alzheimer's, My Mother, and Me* (2010), an Alzheimer memoir about Sarah's mother, Midge. Although *Tangles* speaks on behalf of another, the narrative focuses not on Midge as an isolated person, nor on her disease, but rather on "the tangled story of my mother, and me, and Alzheimer's," as the author states in her introduction. On one level, the title word "Tangles" refers to the brain tangles of Alzheimer's disease that result from the disintegration of protein in nerve cells. However, "tangles" also provides a metaphor for the wrapping, weaving, sewing, or binding together of characters, of their minds and perceptions that structures experientiality in Leavitt's memoir. Moreover, "tangling" refers to the formal and stylistic choices the author has made in laying out her book. Alzheimer memoir, by the very nature of that disease, tells the story of someone who is unable to articulate their own story in a coherent manner; it is always a speaking on behalf of another. Leavitt, however, focuses neither on her mother and the progress of her disease nor on herself and the impact the disease has on her. Instead, she explores the relationship between disease, mother, herself, and others—doctors, Sarah's husband Robert, and other relatives—through a shifting, at times communal focalization.

Tangles is comprised of forty-six short chapters drawn in a faux-naïve style of flat outlined figures against a meager backdrop. Its memoirist, Sarah, is also the book's focal character, filtering the book's events and coloring their depiction with her what it's like. However, the visual content of individual panels as well as the overall style of the narrative emphasizes that Sarah's what it's like cannot be disentangled from that of other family members, especially from her mother. Thus, the book's lack of visual detail relates to the nature of Alzheimer's with its attendant loss of detail, memory, and orientation. Its visual sparsity also points toward Sarah's attempt to understand and communicate the disease, which intimately binds her own sense of self with her mother's altered experience, characterized by confusion and anxiety and by gaps in memory, thinking, and behavior. Stylistic choice in *Tangles* is thus not identified with any one character, but with Midge's experience with Alzheimer's as it intersects with Sarah's new reality and Sarah's trying to imagine her mother's reduced take on the world.

FIGURE 3.6. Leavitt, Sarah. 2010. *Tangles: A Story about Alzheimer's, My Mother and Me.* Broadview. p. 37.

In *Tangles*, style foregrounds selfhood as always existing and shaped in relationship with others. When a doctor informs Sarah and Robert of the Alzheimer diagnosis, the lack of background detail serves to focus attention on the grouping together of characters—Sarah, Midge, and Robert sitting across from the doctor; Sarah and Robert leaving the room; and Midge herself. It also accentuates the tension between various perceptions of this scene, in particular between Sarah's anger at the doctor for not addressing Midge directly (in fact, he mostly addresses the only other male even though Robert is neither the patient nor a direct relative) and Midge's remark, at the bottom of the page, "Oh, that doctor was just so nice!" (37; figure 3.6). A blending of subjectivities, minds, and viewpoints is further suggested with the featureless groupings of black figures often used during emotionally charged moments,

FIGURE 3.7. Leavitt, Sarah. 2010. *Tangles: A Story about Alzheimer's, My Mother and Me.* Broadview. Title page.

such as when Midge resigns from teaching (19) or confesses that she is "not really much of a person right now" (98).

The groups of featureless characters focus attention on shared emotions and stances in response to the Alzheimer diagnosis. In this context, the title metaphor may be taken to refer to Midge's failure to think straight, to her confusion and potential misreading of the situation. But "tangles" may also have a more literal meaning: A tangle is something disordered, something that needs to be straightened or combed out. Indeed, curly, disorderly hair is one main external similarity between Sarah and Midge. On the book's front cover, their curly hair provides some of the main detail in a layout dominated by straight and plain lines. This may be taken to suggest that the border between mental wellness and illness is more porous than the doctor may think (as Sarah's hair is curly, too). It also points to an intermingling of subjectivities, a blending of Sarah's sense of selfhood, which was acquired through her relationship with her parents and especially her mother, and Midge's, which is very much in flux because she is progressively becoming dependent on her daughter's help. The panel on the title page where Midge's and Sarah's arms merge with each other strongly indicates such tangling (figure 3.7).

A tangled view of selfhood also sets the basic narrative pattern of *Tangles*. The comic does not consist of individually framed panels separated by gutters, as the grid pattern is here adapted so that each frame separates, but also unites two panels. This type of gutterless panel sequencing provides a more ambivalent kind of border between the building blocks of narrative, a border that thwarts distinct enclosures and thereby implies that the border line separating subjects can more easily be transgressed than we would like to think. Thus, "tangling" also refers to the formal and stylistic choices the author has made in laying out her memoir. This chimes with the rich poetological resonance of all textile metaphors. When we think back to how this formal choice impacts the concept of the self, the elision of the gutter suggests that the new reality introduced by Midge's disease is not something that concerns Midge alone. Rather, it requires a mutual negotiation of this new reality shared by all family members. At the same time, the narrative chronicles what we may call the author's untangling of herself from her mother's story following Midge's death, and it portrays her achieving an individual and highly original means of expression through her drawing. In the final instance, her attitude toward tangles or entangled subjectivities is therefore at best ambivalent.

David Small's *Stitches* (2009) takes a much more negative attitude toward an entangled subjectivity, as its title-giving stitches refer to a decidedly brutal textile work method: the surgical sewing together of a painful, disfiguring, and debilitating wound. *Stitches* recounts how David, the son of emotionally withdrawn parents, suffered from breathing problems as a child. His father, a radiologist, submitted him to a series of 2–400 x-ray treatments, giving him throat cancer as a side effect. After an operation that his parents postponed for no less than three and a half years, David lost his voice while gaining a huge disfiguring surgical scar down the side of his neck. Ultimately, he became a graphic artist whose eerie watercolor drawings evoke his silenced childhood. Given David's enforced silence, it is not surprising that *Stitches* makes extensive use of wordless panels, sequences, and pages. The graphic memoir is low in verbal dialogue but rich in visual interactions as characters gaze at each other and at their surroundings.

From the start, the memoirist depicts himself as a child drawing comics to escape the mental anguish of his family's unrelenting tensions. A series of expository panels moves from Detroit's 1950s cityscape to the Small family home and finally into the living area where David lies on the floor cartooning as his mother washes dishes (11–14). At a later point and immediately following a description of his mother's "silent fury" rolling over six-year-old David "like a black tidal wave" (46), a full-page panel shows him similarly lying on the living room floor drawing cartoon characters. On the next page, a cartoon

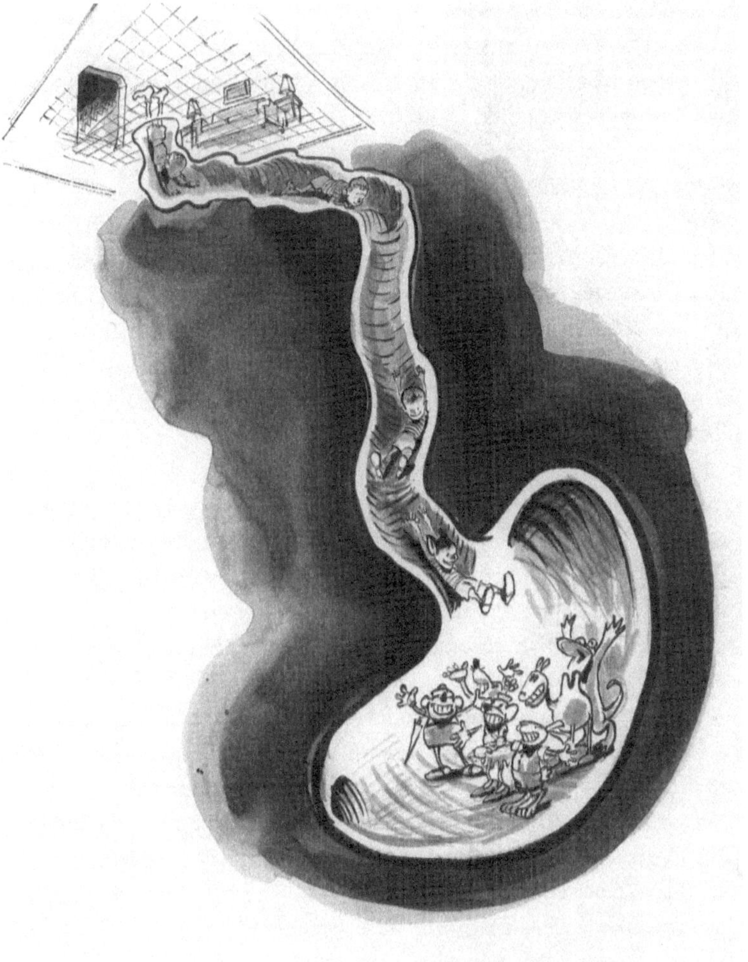

FIGURE 3.8. Small, David. 2009. *Stitches: A Memoir*. McClelland and Stewart. p. 63.

character jumps out of David's drawing sheet dancing, singing, and making merry (49). The cartooning motif climaxes when David flees from a group of bullies, securing safety by diving into his drawing sheet. The interior world of the drawing is represented as the inside of a giant stomach where David is greeted by a cast of jolly cartoon characters (63; figure 3.8). Cartooning, we come to understand, is David's alternative private language. His imaginative engagement with comics is his way of disappearing into an interior fantasy world that provides him with an escape, albeit a temporary one, from the overwhelming torment of his real world. As in the other graphic memoirs we discuss in this chapter, however, subjective interiority is never wholly separated out from the outside world and from other subjects.

Stitches is a rewarding memoir to analyze in relation to focalization not only because it is visually rich but also because it focuses self-reflexively on different languages and forms of expression. Its autobiographical path tracks David's loss of voice and his regaining of expression by means of the visual. In this process, the title-giving stitches holding together David's surgical wound after the excision of the cancerous growth from his throat play a charged role. A full-page panel that shows David looking at his stitched-up neck for the first time in the mirror is accompanied, on the opposite page, by three separate images of the scar (190–91; figure 3.9). This repeated portrayal of the wound sets up an ambivalence of inside and outside that questions where physical integrity begins and ends and where the boundaries of the self are. It thus places David's subjectivity in question. Is a person who is portrayed through a surgical scar—rather than through his face—a self in the full sense? "Surely this is not me," David says, and the wound seems to answer: "No, friend, it surely is." To readers, this mini-dialogue offers two possible options for interpreting focalization: one in which David, as a whole person, considers his wound and one in which David himself becomes refocalized through the image of the speaking wound—a disturbing reversal of experience and of subjectivity.

Stitches further explores borders of the self through a series of panel composites where characters are spliced together, often transgressing the borders between the body and its environment, between subjectivities, and between the human and the nonhuman. In a key scene set during one of David's visits to the hospital where his father works, the six-year-old boy discovers the gruesome hallway display of a fetus in formaldehyde (39). David is both fascinated and repulsed by the fetus in the jar, which hovers uneasily between life and death, preserved at a moment when it had not acquired autonomous selfhood, yet might have done so had it been let to live. In this scene, David provides what the fetus never had: He imagines it coming to life and returning his gaze by staring out at him through the jar. The pacing of the sequence representing this encounter strongly suggests that this imaginative act also reflects David's own self-perception as panels switch quickly and repeatedly back and forth between images of David's eye and images of the fetus's eye as it is imagined by David. When his fear intensifies, David enters into a visual dialogue with the fetus, with images of the fetus developing from closed eye through open eye and

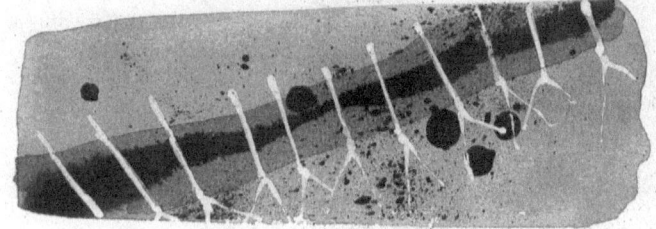

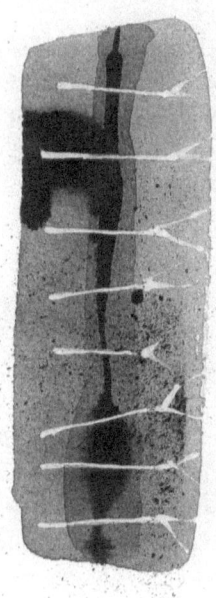
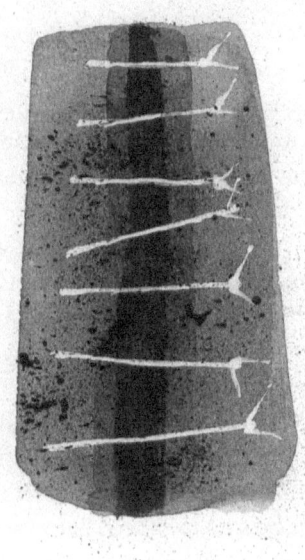

FIGURE 3.9. Small, David. 2009. *Stitches: A Memoir.* McClelland and Stewart. p. 191.

onto staring eye. Finally, David's eye and that of the fetus almost unite in the face of one imaginary chimera character when half-images of both combine in one composite portrait (figure 3.10). The two identities merge in the combination of the two eyes—one David's and the other belonging to the fetus—and in the way the fetus's pupils are mirrored in the boy's, a two-part visual cue used throughout *Stitches* to comment on psychologically intense moments.

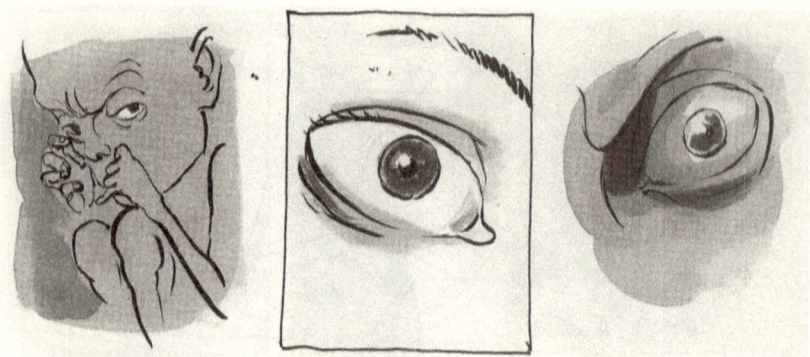

FIGURE 3.10. Small, David. 2009. Stitches: A Memoir. McClelland and Stewart. p. 39.

Scenes of juxtaposition where two panels showing halves of different faces indicate an imagined hybrid identity abound in *Stitches*. Always involving half-portraits of David, they address David's questioning of his identity in relation to others, and express feelings of anxiety and unspoken reproach between himself and his parents. However, the juxtapositions do not stop at these feelings. Their repetition and their variation—from fetus to mother to father—are part of a dynamic process at the end of which David transcends real and imagined bonds and gains subjective freedom through his artistic creativity. The repeated act of portraiture serves less to ground the self in an embodied narration than to overcome the limitations of the body and the familial entanglement producing it.

The fantasmatic suturing of panels can be read in light of the memoir's title: On the level of formal composition, the juxtaposition of half-faces constitutes another stitching method. The point of this suturing, however, is not to depict David's tie to others, but to establish his difference, especially from his family. Like Sarah Leavitt's *Tangles*, *Stitches* follows autobiographical genre conventions by distinguishing between a narrating and a narrated self. However, both also complicate that binary by repeatedly reflecting on the way the self is always entangled with others. Both books show how the self's looking is bound to a familial inheritance. Moreover, *Stitches* repeatedly makes the point that the sense of self derives from what others have said and by how others have looked at the self. In these graphic memoirs, subjectivity is always intersubjectivity.

Since the tangling and untangling of subjectivity is a dynamic process, readers, too, become bound up in intersubjectivity. In the hospital sequence in *Stitches*, readers witness the fetus transforming under David's scrutiny. The repeated switching from visual perception to imagination, from what David

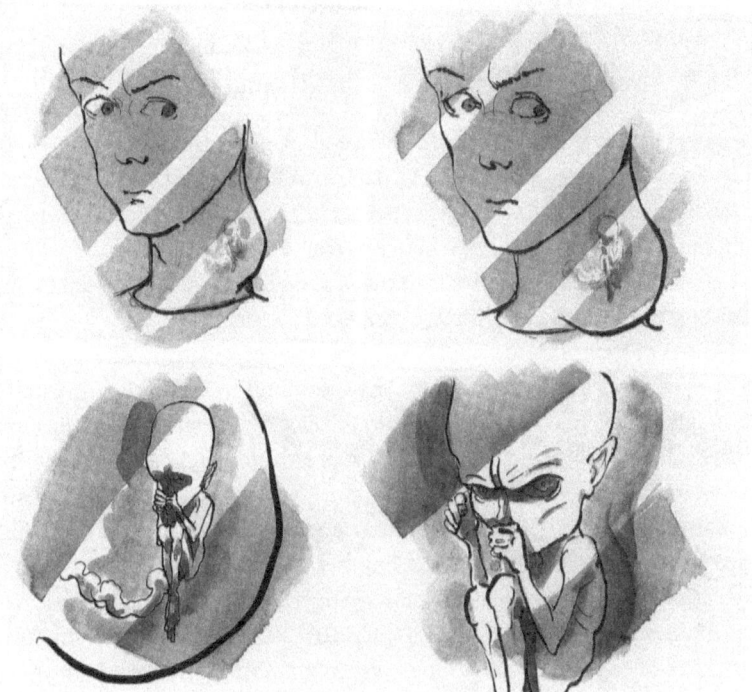

FIGURE 3.11. Small, David. 2009. *Stitches: A Memoir*. McClelland and Stewart. p. 147.

sees to how David understands what he sees, is designed to pull readers into David's six-year-old world. This is a world where fear makes inanimate objects come to life. The use of frameless panels, which digress from the intratextual norm of panel frames, indicates that what unfolds here is the result of David's subjective perception and imagination as he processes what he sees and feels. In narratological terms, the frameless panels mark a character-bound focalization. When the fetus, at the end of the sequence, jumps out of the jar and chases David down the long, empty hospital corridor, readers are firmly inside David's experience of this vivid fantasy, and are asked to sympathize with its emotional charge. David's fear is so tangible that the imagined monstrosity— half man, half alien—even troubles his dreams that evening (45).

The character-bound focalization of this sequence, however, is offset by two later scenes in which the fetus resurfaces as a symbol of David's maturing aspectuality and developing understanding of what his disease means for his sense of self. In the second fetus scene, an eleven-year-old David examines the freshly diagnosed tumor on his neck (146–47; figure 3.11). Switches back and forth between David's subjective perception and a more objective way of seeing the world indicate the maturation of his perception and cognitive processing. Moreover, David's perception has become more psychologically complex, another indicator of a maturing mind. From an external menace that David can outrun, the fetus has turned into an internalized alter ego by the adolescent David. As in the first fetus scene, David's visual interaction with the world develops over a sequence of panels. When the fetus slowly comes into focus, growing in size, so too does the scene's complex layering of focalization come into focus as it develops between David's character-bound focalization, the memoirist's retrospective external focalization, and the reader's understanding of the scene and what it means for David.

The repeated representation of the fetus suggests a focal filtering designed to draw readers into David's experience and into his emotional investment in the memoir's events. However, in *Stitches*, such a character-bound focalization is embedded within the aesthetically sophisticated style and composition of the memoir, expressive of the more mature aspectuality of David-the-grown-up-comic-artist. Through this layering, readers are asked to see and experience *with* David the six-year-old boy but also to see *through* him. Readers are exposed to a multiform subjectivity that develops over time and through repeated, often tentative portraits that mirror the self in others. The implied processes of cognitive evaluation and emotional response, too, are not as individual as they first may appear to be. *Stitches*' opening chapter positions David within a network of subjectivities by describing his childhood predilection for getting sick as a contribution to the family's shared practice of expressing themselves wordlessly (12–19). His subjectivity and its representation are never untangled from the emotional and mental complexity of other characters.

The need to adopt a more mature perspective regarding David's encounter with the fetus is made blatantly obvious when at the age of thirty David returns to the hospital and sees the fetus for what it is: just a fetus in a jar (309). This last visit to the fetus, prompted by his mother's hospitalization, signals the fulfillment of David's psychological needs, which he has been trying to meet all his life but which could only be fulfilled once his mother died. This final scene with the fetus openly dramatizes David's increased mental awareness and his coming to terms with himself as a subject free from his mother. Readers become aware of David's perception of his own role in understanding his story (and in representing it).

In her study of autobiographical comics, Elisabeth El Refaie devotes an entire chapter to "Drawing in the Reader," arguing that graphic memoirs actively strive to involve readers in their telling (2012: 179–220). Rocco Versaci makes a similar point, noting several devices used by graphic memoirists to draw readers into the narrative world, including word balloons, text boxes, ellipses, the use of alter egos, and artistic style. A close reading of David Small's *Stitches*, however, shows that how graphic memoirs entangle their readers in the memoirist's experience depends not so much on individual narrative devices, but rather on the way style, content, choice of symbols, image composition, the juxtaposition of panels, and the braiding of passages across the length of a comic book come together to create an atmosphere that evokes the memoirist's qualia as they appear to the memoirist in retrospect and in light of the experience of others. Focalization cues are thus dispersed across multiple resources that together articulate and bring readers to experience the what it's like of David's experiences that are, in turn, embedded in the perception and judgments of other characters as well as in the evaluation of these by the mature comic artist.

The memoirist establishes a relationship of trust with readers by showing a maturing mind that remembers what was in order to ascertain and make clear to readers what is. David's recognition that what he believed was real to him and did impact his experience, coupled with the recognition that his mind has matured, that he sees and understands things differently now, establishes truthfulness as an internal standard. It bestows authority on the telling—an authority that lies with how the memoirist frames his reality and that is established because David guides his readers to see how reality has been interpreted for them through him. That truthfulness exists only as a framed truth, a point rendered particularly evident in the comics medium that foregrounds its handmade quality and therefore exposes the very act of textual framing.

Our analyses of *Tangles* and *Stitches* illuminate some ways in which lives and a sense of self are bound up in the lives of others and in the emotional ties of families. They also emphasize the active processes through which such ties can be creatively crafted or through which they can be violently imposed, painfully severed, or reconfigured. The staging of intersubjectivity indicates how a character-bound focalization in graphic memoir does not necessarily translate into a singular subjectivity. Whereas the embedded focalization structure of *Tangles* addresses how characters imagine the experiences of other characters and how those imaginings of what it's like to be another impact their own sense of self, focalization in *Stitches* stages a similar entanglement of subjectivities but does so to put into play a pronounced dismantling of distinctions between inner self and physical body as well as self and other. That character-bound focalization is not essentially internal to the diegesis is strongly suggested through *Stitches*' engagement in a retrospective vantage point on the experiencing self and on its environment.

Searching for Symbolism:
David B., *Epileptic*

Titles such as *Tangles, Stitches,* and *Embroideries* hint at the role of figurative language in highlighting the intersubjective dimension of autobiographical narratives. In these and other graphic memoirs, metaphors provide an important tool for the self-conscious exploration of subjectivity. In the final section of this chapter, we consider a visual take on figurative expression by analyzing the search for symbolism in David B.'s *Epileptic* (2005). We ask how the repetition and modification of visual metaphors can serve as focalization cues that reveal a maturing mind. *Epileptic* was originally published in six volumes between 1996 and 2001 that narrate graphic artist David B's (born Pierre François Beauchard) growing up with an older brother (Jean-Christophe) who developed a particularly severe form of epilepsy. Readers learn about the family's struggle with the disease and their attempt to understand what the disease means for Jean-Christophe's identity and also for their relationships with him and with each other. The memoir's original French title, *L'Ascension du haut mal* (literally, *The Rise of High Evil*), captures the sense of the temporal unfolding of this process.

Two recurring visual metaphors signal the semantic fields that the family, especially David, draw on in their struggle to understand the disease: the machine metaphor, which addresses the family's experience with the medical system that treats Jean-Christophe, and the dragon metaphor, used first to express the family's view of Jean-Christophe's disease, then David's relation to Jean-Christophe himself, and finally a past understanding of the disease. When we call these images metaphors, we draw on Paul Ricoeur's theory of live metaphor as an aesthetically innovative form of expression, rather than on the linguistic concept of everyday "metaphors we live by" (Lakoff and Johnson). The machine and dragon metaphors in *Epileptic* provide no shortcuts to established patterns of meaning. Instead, their "semantic pertinence," to borrow from Ricoeur, transgresses established usage. The machines in *Epileptic* are not representations of actual machines and the dragons do not refer only to mythological animals. Communicating one thing but simultaneously seeming to communicate not that thing but something else entirely, they perform a doubling of discourse that Ricoeur calls the "paradox of the copula." This paradox places particular demands on readers, who at once juggle both meanings. It also grants readers the freedom to find their own (plausible) interpretation for the relationship between the two levels of meaning. Live metaphors are creative metaphors, and their creativity implicates both their author and readers.

FIGURE 3.12. B., David. 2005. *Epileptic*. Pantheon. p. 41.

In *Epileptic*, however, readers are implicated not so much through creative innovation—dragon metaphors are not highly rarefied—but through recurring metaphors, variations on those metaphors, and commentary on them in the verbal track. Because of the tentative use of these metaphors, through repetition and variation, and because of their shifting status in relation to the narrative reality they are meant to capture, we also speak of a "search for symbolism," even though single recurrences of these images are, strictly speaking, figurative tropes and not symbols. Their figurative character is clearly discernible in their lack of realism that clashes with the dominantly realistic style of their context, their incongruence with the biographical narrative, and the accompanying shift in semantics—from disease to mythological animal, from medical care to science fiction, and from patient intervention to warfare. Their meaning depends less on the figurative images themselves than on how these are used in context, how they communicate the family's understanding of the disease, and finally on how they address readers. In short, the images gain in meaning through the active work they accomplish as markers of focalization.

The dragon image is first used as a metaphor for the sense of menace associated with Jean-Christophe's disease and thus transports a medical view of diseases as enemy creatures that have to be vanquished. The machine metaphor, first introduced when Jean-Christophe undergoes a series of invasive gaseous encephalograms that violate his personal integrity, expresses the associated medical view of the human body as a machine that needs fixing (through the use of technologically advanced machines and doctors who know how to use them; figure 3.12).

Imagining Professor T., one of many doctors eager to experiment on Jean-Christophe, performing the procedure, David comments: "I visualize my brother in the clutches of mad scientists" (41). The horizontally elongated panel illustrating David's visualization breaks the three-by-three page layout to present a frontal view of the top part of Jean-Christophe's shaven head encircled by robotic machines with long, winding hoses attached to them. Two miniature versions of the stark-looking Professor T. straddling two of the many hoses frame Jean-Christophe's head. Together with David's verbal comment, the image communicates David's sense of Jean-Christophe's debilitation at the hands both of the disease and of the doctors who are eager to treat it. It tells readers that David sees Jean-Christophe reduced to an object at the mercy of an ethically flawed medical system that leaves him no space for self-determination.

Focalization in *Epileptic* is bound to David, whose narrating self overlaps with his experiencing self in a simultaneous present. David's perceptual and emotional experience and his evaluative judgments color what is said on the verbal track as well as what is shown in the visual panels. The coincidence of the knowledge, perceptions, and diegetic centering of the narrating and experiencing self, coupled with the spatiotemporal narrative synchronization of the two tracks, produces a sense of immediate reporting that intensifies the reader's entanglement in the memoir's events, but also in the mind of its focal character. This close entanglement breaks down when the machine imagery recurs, and the dragon metaphor is introduced, some thirty pages later, not in the context of David's but of his mother's experience (72; figure 3.13). This time, the machine image occupies over half the page and shows Jean-Christophe from the shoulders up. It follows immediately upon one of Jean-Christophe's seizures that leaves his mother devastated. "In her mind," David tells us, "this sends us all the way back to square one. She has a vision of her son back in the hospital, his head shaved" (72).

David's statement sets up a doubly embedded focalization structure in which the image shows what David believes his mother experiences in this particular moment by drawing on his own earlier imagination of Jean-Christophe's medical treatment. In this panel, a miniature version of the distressed mother, stricken with fear and sadness, sits limply atop her son's head while Professor T. stands casually atop a dragon's head, both hands in his pockets as he looks attentively at the side of Jean-Christophe's head. Three miniature assistants straddle the dragon's tail while looking on from the other side of Jean-Christophe's head. Compared with the human characters, the dragon, with its paw stretched over Jean-Christophe's shoulder and its tongue flickering across his face, is an overwhelmingly large and active

FIGURE 3.13. B., David. 2005. *Epileptic*. Pantheon. p. 72.

force that the panel's frame cannot contain. Whereas its head, tail, and paws encircle Jean-Christophe and carry the doctors in their pursuit for fame, its body, which presumably runs across Jean-Christophe's torso, is not shown. The modified emphasis on small, passive human agents and the dragon illness follows a series of critiques David aims at the various methods adopted and efforts made by his family to destroy "the family ghost" of Jean-Christophe's illness (65). Disillusioned, David fears that the illness is winning the battle. The juxtaposition of inactive "stupid" (76) adults and active shrewd dragon communicates David's growing rage at how epilepsy effaces everyone except Jean-Christophe and leaves "every man for himself" (34).

A third variation of the panel occurs over a hundred pages later, following an embedded story that transcribes a 1997 dialogue between David and his mother. Through this dialogue, an adult David learns that his mother tried different treatments herself, because she hoped that if she "could use the doctors' technology [she] could discover the origin of Jean-Christophe's seizures" (202). The narrative caption of his mother's voice is paired with the familiar image, but here Jean-Christophe's large head is depicted horizontally with eyes

FIGURE 3.14. B., David. 2005. *Epileptic*. Pantheon. p. 202.

closed, while his mother has replaced the mad scientist and now operates the machines connected to Jean-Christophe. In this instance, the meaning of the image is somewhat enigmatic. Does David mean to criticize his mother's efforts, just as he criticized others who treated Jean-Christophe's epilepsy to no effect? Or does he imply that, like them, she was only doing her best to help Jean-Christophe? The repetitions and variations between the three recurrences and the different focalization types they cue force these and similar unresolved questions into consideration.

The imposition of his mother's narrative voice onto the familiar image indicates that David's story and the way he understands it is entangled in her story and her understanding of their shared experiences with Jean-Christophe's epilepsy. The link between David's subjectivity and his mother's is further suggested in the following panel where the image is reproduced yet again, this time with David operating the robotic machines that have hoses linked not only to Jean-Christophe's now-exposed brain but also to the body of his grandfather's ghost (202; figure 3.14). Reclaiming his narrative voice, David reflects how "it's odd how [his] mother and [he] have the same dreams" of saving his brother (202). This verbal admission and the visual substitution of his mother with himself in the familiar image strongly suggest that his mother's narrative voice is representative not only of what she felt but also of what David feels (note that the narrative returns to the use of the present tense when the voice is David's). Just as the two narrative voices and perspectives are distinct and yet meld into one, so too are the images both unique and combined visions.

The repetition *and* variation that characterize the recurrence of this visual metaphor ensure that one rendition does not substitute or override the narrative significance of another. Instead, they come together to instate a semantic overdetermination, a densification of detail and meaning, but also a perspectival layering and enmeshing that can only be discerned and appreciated through a multidirectional, nonlinear reading pattern of returns and semantic adjustments on the part of readers. Every repetition poses a challenge for readers wishing to determine what in the panel is a significant repetition and a significant variation, but also why these repetitions and variations are meaningful within the overall narrative. They do so by cuing subtle, but significant adjustments to focalization.

•

Individual minds and perceptions necessarily intersect with the body in graphic memoir, where a narrating-I and an experiencing-I interact across two narrative tracks. Graphic memoir differs from the fictional graphic narratives that we discussed in chapter 2. Although graphic memoir focuses on one subject and its embodied experience and couches that experience in a language of authenticity, it also thwarts expectations of authenticity and truthfulness that "stand at the center of autobiography" (García 159). It does so not only through its complex narrative structure but also through its visual engagement with self-portrayal, its concern with style, and its presentation of an embodied sense of self, all of which can serve as focalization markers in the communication of subjectivity.

The tendency toward self-reflexivity and even metanarrative ruptures that make the perceptive, emotive, and cognitive processing of the memoirist accessible to readers is strong in many graphic memoirs (I. Williams 356). Resisting the myth of solitary perception, graphic memoir creates patterns of intersubjectively tangled perception. A subject and its experience, we learn from a critical reading of graphic memoir, are not two separate things, since a sense of subjectivity only emerges out of the experiences that we have.

Graphic memoir manifests as a meta-phenomenological genre that reflects on the very nature of experience, on the self having experiences, and on the relation between subject, object, and other subjects in experience. Often portraying the self as tentative, developing, and embedded in a web of social relations, graphic memoir seems as interested in exploring, on a fundamental level, what it means to be an individual, to have an identity, and to communicate that identity to self and others as it is in telling the story of an individual. In these common instances, graphic memoir foregrounds the intricate relations between a subjective perception of self and world, the refraction of that perception through the experience of other people, and the representation of different perspectives through drawing and self-portraiture. It is thus a particularly rewarding genre for the study of focalization.

With its frequent highlighting of a split self, often imagined through distorted body images, graphic memoir makes it impossible to separate a thinking and judging mind from physical, material, corporeal experience and, consequently, the subjective representation of experience from the representation of subjectivity. The difficulty of describing in narratological terms what exactly happens especially in silent passages, such as those found in *Stitches*, suggests that narrative theory may still be tied too much to a thinking in essences, to mind against body inside the diegesis, and to narration against focalization on the level of representation.

When focalization is understood as a relational concept regulating levels of experience and their transmission to readers, however, it can be a helpful concept for studying subjectivity as a shared and embodied performance of graphic memoir. The following chapter will develop this inquiry into the relation between narration and focalization in comics, which we only touched upon in this chapter, in the context of graphic historiography, while chapter 5 will delve deeper into the role of visual metaphors for entangling the reader of comics.

CHAPTER 4

Graphic Historiography

Graphic memoir closely overlaps with a second group of comics that has been steadily gaining in popularity: documentary comics that do not tell autobiographical stories, but similarly promise an authenticity of expression and a truthful depiction of reality from a subjective perspective. Frequently, their narratives are internally focalized, presenting readers with the subjective what it's like of a focal character who is also the narrator and graphiator. However, unlike graphic memoir, that subjective perspective is not concerned with subjectivity itself, but with matters external to the self—historical events, politics and society, or travel to foreign countries. The focus on external subject matters has consequences for the type of focalization in these comics, which is internal in relation to the character-narrator (hence, corporeal, affective, often producing closeness), but external in relation to the depicted events (hence, distanced, evaluative), leading to a multilayered, often ambiguous take on the represented events.

Generically, comics in this group have been subsumed under a number of headings, including "documentary graphic novels" (Adams), "graphic journalism" (Schack; Schlichting; Worden), "historio-metagraphics" (Polak 4), and "nonfiction comics" or "graphic nonfiction" (Acheson; Gorman; Irwin). As these designations suggest, documentary comics do not belong to a single, fixed genre in the sense of a taxonomy, but perform and are shaped by a number of related genres (see Frow 27). Indeed, some of the texts in this group have also been productively analyzed as graphic memoirs. This particularly concerns Art Spiegelman's *Maus* (1986, 1991). Nonetheless, documentary comics share several formal and thematic features that make it productive to group these texts together under a "family resemblance" model of genre that focuses on similarities between texts (see Swales 49).

Documentary comics draw on forms of reportage, often foregrounding a character narrator who occupies an outsider role in relation to the narrated events. This creates a situated perspective geared toward readers who are also outsiders, seeking to capture the experience of others at the same time as the narrative distances itself from these others (Chute 2016: 252). A main thematic concern of documentary comics is with the reconstruction and presentation of evidence. Thus, these comics exploit the comics form to draw attention to the work of framing that happens in all media, but that becomes particularly manifest in comics due to the sequential grammar of panels and gutters (Chute 2016: 16). Questions of reliability and accuracy move to the foreground, both regarding the multimodal presentation of evidence and its interpretation by focal characters. When the filtering of focalization is self-consciously highlighted, readers too are invited into the difficult work of assessing the facticity of events and the plausibility of their representation.

In this chapter, we focus on a subgroup of documentary comics that engage historical events of global significance: the Holocaust, the Israeli-Palestinian conflict, the Rwandan genocide, and the history of the People's Republic of China. We describe the comics that we analyze—Art Spiegelman's *Maus* (1986, 1991), J. P. Stassen's *Deogratias* (2006), Li Kunwu and Philippe Ôtié's *A Chinese Life* (2012), and Joe Sacco's *Palestine* (2003), *Footnotes in Gaza* (2009), and *Safe Area Goražde* (2002)—through the genre term "graphic historiography" because these texts challenge our thinking about the writing of history, particularly of atrocity history, in similar ways to the challenge that graphic memoirs pose to ideas about the self. Depicting history from the point of view of a variety of people, from active perpetrators of genocide to its victims and to uninvolved bystanders or belated witnesses, graphic historiographies show that the telling of history always carries a perspectival index, and they reflect on how artistic styles of representation express such a perspectival ownership.

Like graphic memoir, graphic historiography often uses meta-phenomenological narrative strategies, employing a variety of focalization markers to make the felt quality of a world and its characters available to readers while simultaneously drawing attention to its representational choices. Many graphic historiographies highlight the specificity of a particular vantage point on historical events by grounding their mode of documentary in the person of the comic artist, who serves as a witness and scribe of history. The sensual quality of comics drawing and the affordances of the comic form are self-consciously exploited to structure history differently (Chute 2016; Polak). The narrative strategies used in graphic historiographies to emphasize a personal and subjective grounding include metanarrative reflections on the writing of history by a narrator who guides readers through the story, the assertion of doubt and not-knowing on the part of narrating and focal characters, and an explicit engagement with the role that interpretation and imagination play in the creation of historical narratives.

Graphic historiographies grant unique insights into what it is like to live through extreme experiences of genocidal atrocity, civil war, famine, and the revolutionary rebuilding of societies, while simultaneously offering meditative explorations of how these experiences can be represented, and how that narrative representation relates to reality. Through combinations of panel size, framing, layout and ordering, shading, line work, and the use of visual metaphors that mark focalization, they direct attention toward the angle through which historical events become focalized and through which readers access the felt quality that characterizes historical experience, as well as its later processing. Indeed, the graphic historiographies that we analyze in this chapter take pains to emphasize the secondary and belated processing of historical events that is associated with the figure of the narrator, over against the experience of characters who lived through these events. Focalization in graphic historiography therefore typically involves a cognitive focus that builds well-known problems of historical understanding into the fabric of the narrative.

As in several of the graphic memoirs that we analyzed in chapter 3, focalization in graphic historiography often also has intersubjective aspects. The focalization of character narrators can embed the aspectuality of others, and the same scenes and events may therefore be refocalized explicitly or implicitly. In *Maus,* subsequent panels focalize the same scene through different characters. *Deogratias* deliberately obscures the focal origin of enigmatic dream passages, which can be read both in terms of the protagonist's self-understanding and in terms of the way others perceive him. In *A Chinese Life,* focalization through the character narrator is explicitly designed to stand in for the experience of an entire nation, while the graphic journalism of Joe Sacco embeds a plurality of characters' voices within the reportage of the graphic journalist. Our analyses in this chapter therefore focus on how the mediation of historical events in comics format allows for a multilayered take on historical experience that is simultaneously inside and outside, providing intimacy as well as critical distance.

Against a positivistic understanding of historiography as the representation of historical events, graphic historiography highlights the doubt and ambivalence as well as the interpretative work involved in the telling of history. In addition, the self-conscious crafting of a relational, multiple, or collective subject position invites readers to reflect on the dialectics between personal and communal experiences of history. In the following section of this chapter, we explain what consequences the complex narrative structure of graphic historiography and the often ambiguous or multiple focalization of these texts have for narrative ethics before turning to the analysis of our sample texts.

History, Postmemory, and Narrative Ethics

Graphic historiography's self-conscious reflection picks up on debates about the narrative and literary dimension of history that have been ongoing in historical scholarship since the late 1970s. In his seminal collection *Tropics of Discourse* (1978), historian Hayden White argued that the telling of history is not so much representative of a set of underlying facts as it is structured by literary tropes, plot structures, and rhetorical devices. This emphasis on the inherently narrative dimension of history writing became especially salient in debates about literary contributions to representing the Holocaust. Thus, Geoffrey Hartman argued that literary Holocaust representations preserve history in a unique way because they are "more personal and focused than public memory yet less monologic than the memorializing fables common to ethnic or nationalist affirmation" (107). White himself proposed that "modernist" or experimental modes of representation that are more readily available to imaginative literature than to historical writing "may offer possibilities of representing the reality of both the Holocaust and the experience of it that no other version of realism could do" (1992: 52). He thereby suggested that imaginative literature is uniquely able to communicate a phenomenologically inspired take on history, an idea that we extend toward comics in this chapter.

It is in this academic climate that Art Spiegelman's *Maus*, serialized from 1980 to 1991, quickly rose to prominence as a key text in relation to which many core ideas about history and representation were first formulated. *Maus* tells the story of Vladek Spiegelman's Holocaust survival from the perspective of Vladek's son, Artie, across a historical distance of three decades. Through the combination of two distinct narrative voices with a character-bound focalization that consistently interrogates the comic artist's representational choices, articulates doubt, and repeatedly offers competing versions of the same image, *Maus* creates many opportunities for a multifaceted engagement with history that allows for the adoption of different perspectives on the same characters and events (see S. Horstkotte and Pedri 2011).

Faced with the widening gap between the individual recollection of Holocaust survivors and the collective memory of subsequent generations, *Maus* uses the bimodal comics format to bridge the chasm between authentic personal witnessing and indirect fictional engagement. Its multilayered narrative shows that Artie's take on the Holocaust, although he was born in 1948 and thus has no individual recollection of it, does not exist independently of his father's experiences—even if many of Vladek Spiegelman's memories did not become explicitly formulated until his son interviewed him. Many self-reflexive scenes that stop on the act of drawing the comic book we are reading, as well as the use of animal metaphors to denote ethnic identities throughout the two volumes, invite readers to ponder Artie's aesthetic choices and ethical positioning regarding his father's story and thus to participate in the affiliative transmission of memory.

When it became widely studied, *Maus*'s narrative structure and approach to representing history changed how scholars think about the Holocaust and its aftermath and about memory more generally (see Hirsch 1993, 1997, 2001, 2008; 2012; Liss 1991, 1998). Marianne Hirsch, who is herself the child of Holocaust survivors and one of the first academics to study *Maus,* coined the term "postmemory" for the intersubjective transmission of memory in *Maus* and in other intergenerational Holocaust accounts (1997). Whereas memory relates to individual recollection, Hirsch argues, postmemory describes "the experience of those who grow up dominated by narratives that preceded their birth, whose own belated stories are evacuated by the stories of the previous generation shaped by traumatic events that can be neither understood nor recreated" and is "distinguished from memory by generational distance and from history by deep personal connection" (1997: 22). In *Maus,* Art Spiegelman's memory is "delayed, indirect, secondary—it is a postmemory of the Holocaust, mediated by the father-survivor but determinative for the son" (Hirsch 1997: 13). Confronting his father's memories and his own postmemory, Hirsch explains, "Spiegelman's challenge is to be able to inscribe in the story his ambivalence—both his passionate interest and desire and his inevitable distance and lack of understanding" (13).

Through our analyses in this chapter, we argue that focalization plays a crucial role for implicating readers in the affiliative process of postmemory, and thus for the narrative ethics of the comics we study. Following Vera Nünning's work on narrative ethics, we show how graphic historiographies alter the beliefs of readers by "spreading values, emotional dispositions, and cognitive practices" (38). Narratives in all media, Nünning explains, have the potential to engage their recipients in an "imagining-other perspective" that entails "imagining how the other feels in a given situation" (42). Narrative strategies and stylistic features that foster the adoption of an "imagining-other perspective" include the perceived realism of a story, access to a character's thoughts and feelings by means of internal focalization or narratorial comments, and the creation of suspense (44). However, Nünning emphasizes that these strategies can be used to create distance as well as closeness (45), a conclusion that we also reach through our readings in graphic historiography in this chapter. Indeed, Nünning suggests that distancing devices are ethically significant because they "contribute to an awareness of the differences between readers and characters" (47). Such an awareness is germane to a present characterized by multiplicity, heterogeneity, and alterity, in which narrative perspective-taking may help readers "to accept otherness, to refrain from stereotyping and categorizing others, and to abandon the insistence on closure" (47). When narratives highlight shifts in focalization, they "ask the reader to practice a cognitively complex process of 'confronting' perspectives and forming his or her own opinions as well as positioning oneself in the face of such contradictions" (49).

In the past two decades, many graphic historiographies have adapted the narrative model established by *Maus* to their own purposes, granting a diverse reading audience insight into better- and lesser-known atrocities including the Rwandan genocide (*Deogratias*), the catastrophic famine of the Chinese Great Leap Forward (*A Chinese Life*), the plight of the Palestinians (*Palestine*; *Footnotes in Gaza*), and the Lebanese civil war (*A Game for Swallows*). Representing history from a variety of perspectives, often noncanonical ones, graphic historiographies lend themselves to questions concerning reader engagement and the accessibility of experiences within the diegesis. These comics not only transmit historical memories to their readers through a process of postmemory but also invite reflection on that process of transmission and on the different ways in which readers can position themselves in relation to the memory of others.

As Kate Polak explains, the comics form, with its segmented and bimodal narration, is apt at expressing complex ethical questions, "particularly those surrounding how we narrate and receive history and how we affectively engage with historical atrocity" (1). Graphic narratives "engage the reader's emotions and ethical norms in complex ways in the representation of historical atrocity, and fictionalized treatments seek to comment on representational ethics, the ethics of spectatorship, and how point of view creates pathways for identification" (2). Atrocity comics have an affective impact on readers because "their staging of the gaze and their staging of questions surrounding both how and what we remember prompts readers to consider their emotional and ethical relationships to the text" (2).

Creating a situated perspective on the embodiment of others, comics are uniquely able to capture experiences of pain and suffering and to recover forgotten trauma (Chute 2016: 201, 252). In the following sections of this chapter, we investigate the impact that different focalization types have on making those experiences available to readers. Through a close reading of *Maus*, we show how its double-layered narrative structure functions as a form of dialogic communication that accentuates shifting personal understandings of historical detail, and we discuss how such dialogism affects readers and implicates them in an affiliative postmemory. Our second sample text, *Deogratias*, adopts a more distanced attitude toward its historical subject matter, presenting a fictional story about the traumatic aftermath of the 1994 Rwandan genocide. The narrative follows the boy Deogratias, who participated in the bloody massacre, repeatedly showing flashback memories of butchered corpses being gnawed by dogs as well as a haunting series of hallucinations in which Deogratias himself turns into a dog. But Deogratias is not the artist of the images, and their source is not explicitly indicated. We consider what implications this combination of an impersonal narration with an uncertain focalization has for the graphic narrative's overall attitude toward its protagonist and toward his crimes, and thus for the book's narrative ethics.

For our third analysis, we turn to *A Chinese Life*, a seven-hundred-page history of the People's Republic of China, collaboratively authored by Chinese graphic artist Li Kunwu and French writer Philippe Ôtié. Although the narrative focuses on the singular experience of its protagonist, Li, the foreword by Philippe Ôtié explains that this protagonist is neither identical with the artist Li Kunwu, nor a true individual. Instead, Li is described as a compound character that "contains all the Lis, Zhangs and Chens of China." Li's expression, too, is a compound, since the words of *A Chinese Life* were penned by a foreigner, a Frenchman whom the foreword identifies as "Dupont, Durand, Schmidt, Popov, Martin and Smith, all at once." We examine this evocation of collectivity through the lens of theories of "we" narration to assess if it expresses a truly collective experience, and we question how focalization functions in the context of such communal expression. Finally, we conclude with a consideration of three comics by Joe Sacco: *Palestine*, *Safe Area Goražde*, and *Footnotes in Gaza*. In these, Sacco depicts himself as a news correspondent, employing the narrative stance of the uninvolved witness to mediate the traumas of the Palestinian conflict and of the war in Bosnia. As in *Maus*, attention is directed at what is being told, but also at the mediating role of the narrator and cartoon artist and at his thematic, structural, and stylistic choices.

Framing Historical Knowledge:
Art Spiegelman, *Maus*

In comics studies, *Maus* is often regarded as the text that "granted 'legitimacy'" to the comics medium (Hathaway 249) and that "changed everything" in the comics world (Beaty and Woo 17). It is quite likely the best-known work of graphic historiography worldwide. As we indicated in chapter 3, *Maus* shares many genre features with graphic memoirs. Like *Tangles* and *Fun Home*, *Maus* centers on a parent-child relationship and consists of a dialogic interrogation in which the memoirist tells his own story through the life narrative of another. Other features, however, set *Maus* apart from the graphic memoir genre and suggest that the book is more productively discussed in the context of graphic historiography. The story of Artie's father Vladek is not only the individual story of a parent, but a survival narrative of the twentieth century's most widely known atrocity. Vladek's act of witnessing and the insistent questioning of historical detail in the dialogues between father and son make him a representative of all Holocaust survivors. The focus of his narrative is therefore less on a subjective what it's like than on collective questions about history, witnessing, and ethics.

Another important distinction that sets *Maus* apart from the bulk of graphic memoir concerns its narrative structure, which combines two character narrators, each with their own focalization. Throughout the two volumes of the book edition, Holocaust history is related on two temporal levels. The main (extradiegetic) narrative is set in 1970s New York, and is narrated as well as illustrated by Artie. It relates how Artie interviews his father about his Holocaust survival, compares his father's memories with historical knowledge about the Holocaust, and struggles to find an appropriate visual vocabulary for representing his parents' experience. The second (intradiegetic) narrative is set in 1940s occupied Poland and tells Vladek's survival story in his own, heavily accented voice, but visualized through the cartoon images produced by Artie. It thus combines two narrators, one verbal, one visual, each of whom also serves as an internal focalizer, creating many opportunities for intersubjective intersections of feeling, perception, and cognitive processing.

Maus often draws self-conscious attention to the comics form and its bimodal narration. This particularly concerns the representation of all characters with stereotypical animal heads: mice for Jews, cats for non-Jewish Germans, pigs for Poles, and dogs for Americans. Several cultural meanings are at work in animal metaphors (Marcus 128) and in the cat-and-mouse binary that runs through *Maus*. Associations with anti-Semitic vermin stereotypes go hand in hand with allusions to Aesop's fables and Mickey Mouse cartoons (Frahm). Through this representational vocabulary, *Maus* reflects on the unusual choice of the comics form for representing the Holocaust, creating jarring inconsistencies between a prevalent view of comics as a lowbrow, mass-cultural form of entertainment and the atrocities of the Holocaust—between story and discourse (Huyssen 2003: 125; see Huyssen 2000). At the same time, the animal metaphor also provides many opportunities in *Maus* to dwell on the genocidal stereotyping of humans as ethnic species in the Nazi period and on how such stereotyping lives on in the present (Hirsch 1997: 27).

These reflections are particularly rich and complex because *Maus*'s extradiegetic narrative consistently exposes the conversational origin of the narrative, highlighting moments of uncertainty, ambivalence, and doubt when Vladek's memory fails or deviates from historical source material such as photographs or maps or when Artie contemplates how to illustrate his father's story. In *Maus*'s first volume, the animal metaphor seems to amplify the subjective quality of Art Spiegelman's drawings, putting the book's imaginative stance toward its historical subject matter on the surface. In the second volume, *And Here My Troubles Began*, however, several episodes, such as when Artie contemplates how to draw his wife Françoise (11) or representations of mouse-cat children to indicate the offspring of a Jewish man and his non-Jewish German wife (131), deconstruct this visual conceit by highlighting the tentative quality of its historical interpretation.

A number of sequences in both volumes of *Maus* indicate that Artie's understanding of events and characters is tentative, always open to revision and reinterpretation. In our article "Focalization in Graphic Narrative," we drew attention to a striking sequence in which Vladek tells Artie about an episode that occurred when he was an Auschwitz prisoner (S. Horstkotte and Pedri 2011: 340–43). The sequence relates how during one of the endless role calls at Auschwitz, an old prisoner suddenly protested to the camp guards that he was unjustly imprisoned, claiming, "I'm a **German** like you!" (1991: 50). We considered how the episode is focalized first through Vladek, the story's verbal narrator, and then through Artie, who draws the images that render Vladek's experience visible. We focused on the visual shifts that occur when Artie portrays the old prisoner, first as a mouse, then as a heavily shaded cat, and finally again as a mouse to show how a meshing of voices can make it difficult to distinguish between character-bound and narratorial focalization in graphic narrative.

Here, we return to the sequence to delve deeper into how its complex layering of narration and focalization exposes the uncertainty but also the creativity inherent in the work of interpretation that underlies Artie's visual rendering of Vladek's story (figure 4.1). We show how the repeated represen-

FIGURE 4.1. Spiegelman, Art. 1991. *Maus: A Survivor's Tale. Part II: And Here My Troubles Began.* Pantheon. p. 50.

tation of the same scene is used to explore different interpretations of history by marking different types of focalization. The sequence opens with two long panels depicting rows of prisoners at the top of the comics page, with the old prisoner protesting in the second of these panels. Two symmetrical panels that zero in on the old prisoner make up the next row. The first panel individuates the protesting prisoner and sets him apart from others through a large close-up portrait of his mouse head and upper body. The second panel reproduces the prisoner's portrait, equally large and identically framed, speaking the same words. However, it introduces significant changes: The prisoner's mouse head is substituted with a cat head, the portrait is heavily shaded, and a 1980s scene of Artie and Vladek in conversation is superimposed into the foreground of the panel.

Both the heavy shading and the superimposition of the conversation scene indicate that this second panel makes a different kind of claim than the first.

Whereas the first close-up portrait is congruent with Vladek's verbal story, the second, cat portrait does not translate Vladek's verbal account into a visual idiom, but halts the narrative, stepping outside the process of translation to reflect back on what is being told. The contrasting of two incompatible visual renditions of the prisoner's identity, one in the style used throughout *Maus*, the other in a shading technique that stands out from the rest of *Maus*, suggests a weighing of different options on Artie's part. In this sequence, the shading indicates Artie's processing of Vladek's story and thus functions as a focalization marker.

That readers are here confronted with alternative interpretations of Vladek's story is also discernible through the speech balloons in each of the panels. While the speech balloon in the first panel emanates from the old prisoner, who states, "I have medals from the Kaiser. My son is a German soldier!," the second panel overlays the intradiegetic speech balloon that is as heavily shaded as the cat's head from which it emanates with an extradiegetic one in which Artie asks Vladek, "Was he *really* a German?" Together with the accentuated "really," the shading indicates the second panel's tentative status. It presents a trying-out of a possible representation that sidesteps the referential status that the other similarly stylized panels in *Maus* possess, despite the surrealism of the animal metaphors. Finally, the closing panel of the page visually supports Vladek's verdict that "for the Germans, this guy was Jewish" by showing him as a mouse being clubbed to death by a cat camp guard.

The shift from mouse to cat and back again sets in motion a complex dynamic of focalization in which Vladek's aspectuality contrasts with but also sits alongside Artie's tentative alternative interpretation of Vladek's firsthand witnessing and of the guard's motivation behind killing the prisoner. The juxtaposition of tentative portraits, a technique we have already encountered in *Black Hole* (chapter 2) and *Stitches* (chapter 3), invites readers to compare different dimensions of the narrative world and to weigh not only different options for interpreting events but also different versions of those events as these are understood by individual characters. Individually, the cat and mouse panels constitute two distinct instances of internal focalization, one bound to Vladek, one to Artie, but both drawn by the visual narrator, Artie. Taken together, the panels highlight an intersubjective dimension that often pertains to focalization in graphic narrative. Focalization in the cat-and-mouse sequence emerges out of a dense situation in which the thoughts, perceptions, interpretations, and judgments of at least four characters interact: the prisoner's, Vladek's, the guard's, and finally Artie's. This dense situation involves Vladek's storytelling, Artie's processing of Vladek's story, Artie's hesitation on how to draw the old prisoner, Artie's visual embedding of Vladek's assertions, and the ensuing juxtaposition of versions, but also the guard's concrete actions.

This intersubjectivity also encompasses readers of *Maus*, who have to assess the plausibility of one way of representing the prisoner over against an alternative way. When the juxtaposition of panels makes readers consider whether Artie's tentative cat panel might be a more suitable representation of the old prisoner, a highly immersive reading experience can emerge in which readers, too, wonder how to understand the old prisoner and in which they share Artie's doubt. If this effect is reached, it constitutes a higher-level immersion quite unlike the feeling of getting lost in a narrative world that many theories of immersive reading focus on (see Ryan 2001). In the cat-and-mouse sequence, readers do not get lost in the events or characters of the story, but in Artie's interpretation of them. Thus, focalization in a higher-order sense makes not only the world, characters, and events of *Maus* available to readers, but more than that the representational choices out of which that world is built.

The refusal to fix focalization in one spot also has important consequences for our understanding of the animal metaphors used throughout *Maus*. That the old prisoner can be represented in two incompatible ways shows that the comic's animal imagery does not account for the complexities informing identity, such as that of an assimilated German Jew. Refracting the event through differing, but equally plausible understandings, the switching back and forth between mouse and cat emphasizes that *Maus*'s animal metaphors should be approached not as a statement about essential ethnic character traits, but rather as a representational choice bound to the perspectives of different characters that can be read in different ways. Through the interplay of different focalization types on two temporal levels, readers are persistently reminded that the subject matter of *Maus* is not a concluded history in the past. Rather, it is the unfinished work of postmemory that continues in the present and that implicates Artie, born after the Holocaust, just as much as Vladek, its survivor. The dual focalization in *Maus* also implicates readers in this unfinished process.

Over the course of her work on postmemory, Marianne Hirsch has become increasingly convinced that the transmission of survivor memories reaches beyond the familial memory of children and grandchildren to encompass the affiliative memory of all those born after the Holocaust (2012). Readers of *Maus* are included in the narrative's postmemorial structure when they are invited into a complex network of attitudes, postures, and perspectives that bear on each other. In this context, focalization does not mark a fixed position into which we can step. Rather, focalization functions as a generator of perspective-taking in readers, who can adopt different or multiple perspectives on events and characters, as well as on the rendition of those events, on the two character narrators who mediate them, and on possible alternative representations suggested within the text or outside of it. This is often the case with focalization in all media. Renate Brosch, for one, argues that readers do not automatically identify with focal characters, but make use of their ability to project different mindsets and imagine several points of view simultaneously; hence, mental representation is never uniformly attached to a specific fictional character (2008: 65). But *Maus*'s insistent use of counter-focalization foregrounds the possibility of shifts in empathy to an unusual degree—so much so that it becomes difficult to think about empathy toward any one character at all. Indeed, the narrative structure seems to direct attention much more toward these constant shifts than toward the identification that can occur between them.

This becomes particularly apparent in a sequence in *Maus II: And Here My Troubles Began* in which Artie openly grapples with his role as the narrator and graphiator of the two *Maus* volumes, and thus with the artifice of the entire project. In the chapter "Time Flies," Artie sits hunched over his drawing board, balanced atop a pile of rotting corpses (1991: 41). Insects buzz around him as he smokes a cigarette and draws provocative parallels between his story and that of his parents. Tellingly, Artie is not portrayed as a mouse, but as wearing a mouse mask that does not entirely cover his face, revealing a sliver of stubble on the side of his exposed face (figure 4.2). This change in portrayal suggests Artie's shifting self-perception following the completion of the first volume of *Maus*, its overwhelming success, the birth of his daughter, and Vladek's death. These life-defining events come to light in a series of captions that draw provocative parallels between Artie's history and that of his parents, and in Artie's subsequent discussion with his psychiatrist, Pavel, a Holocaust survivor who is also drawn as a human wearing a mouse mask.

The mask sequence, which Art Spiegelman later described as risking "unbalancing the book" (2011: 165), adds to the overall narrative complexity of *Maus* in several ways. Its singular focus breaks away from the central storyline. It draws attention to Artie (and, as we discuss below, his psychiatrist Pavel) as a fully fledged human being and palpably conveys the complex interplay between past and present that informs postmemory. The sequence portrays a "new layer of time the reader enters into," with Artie in a present that follows the publication of *Maus I* and that unfolds during the writing of *Maus II* (Spiegelman 2011: 147). Moreover, it changes readers' understanding of the preceding narrative by openly questioning the mouse imagery operative throughout *Maus*. Portraying a human Artie in a mask as he struggles with

FIGURE 4.2. Spiegelman, Art. 1991. *Maus: A Survivor's Tale. Part II: And Here My Troubles Began.* Pantheon. p. 41.

how he is implicated in his father's history, the sequence exposes the mouse imagery as too essentialist and reductive to encompass the multiple aspects of Jewish identity, which also includes elements of hybridity, self-identification, and self-fashioning.

By proposing that Artie does not see himself as being quite as mouse-like as those who experienced the Holocaust firsthand, the sequence also establishes a distance between the story told in *Maus* and Artie, who is responsible for its representation and who is intrinsically bound up in it. This distance is also accentuated by the mask-donning psychiatrist who, like Artie, has positioned himself apart from the trauma of the Holocaust. Although Pavel is a Holocaust survivor, the mask suggests he does not have to wear that identity at all times. In this fashion, the mask sequence breaks the animal metaphor, launching readers into a new narrative frame in which Vladek is absent, but in which his lived experience continues to bear on Artie. It performs the work of postmemory by inscribing both a critical distance toward the past and a profound affective relationship with it.

By foregrounding the constructedness of the stereotypes used throughout *Maus*, the mask sequence also highlights the interplay between fiction (as imaginative invention) and documentation (as the recording of fact) at the heart of graphic historiography. Readers are made aware that Artie is questioning his own adherence to stereotypes. The introduction of the mouse mask at this late stage in the telling shows readers that Artie, as narrator, graphiator, and character, is asking himself who can claim such identifying categories, who is entitled to bestow them upon others, and how their meaning can be grasped. Focalization in this metanarrative rupture is internal, but relating not to Artie's present experience but to the representational choices of Artie the narrator and to the later evaluation of those choices.

To its readers, the complex dual structure of *Maus*, with its layering of generational perspectives and its frequent shifts between different options for representing past experience, offers the lesson that it isn't always possible or desirable to hold onto one perspective on historical events. Combining its bimodal narration with a dual temporal structure mediated through two character narrators, *Maus* exposes different aspects under which historical experience can be considered, including intersubjective as well as individual aspectualities. Its acknowledgment of doubt, uncertainty, and the difficulty of understanding historical details may well fuel the reader's transference of self into the experiences—physical and emotional, real and imagined, remembered and learned—of the cartoon other. Accentuating uncertainty and doubt as productive states that impart knowledge about what is told and the telling, about history and historiography, focalization in *Maus* opens up a space for readers to engage not only in the what it's like of characters but also in the overarching process of evaluating and interpreting historical evidence. It thereby allows them to engage in graphic historiography's meaning-making processes. In the next section of this chapter, we will deepen this point through a close reading of J. P. Stassen's *Deogratias*, which uses animal metaphors to mark a much more ambiguous focalization, inviting readers to engage with the ethically compromised experience of a child participant in the Rwandan genocide.

An Oblique History: J. P. Stassen, *Deogratias*

The Rwandan genocide was one of the most horrific atrocities of the twentieth century. Over a period of one hundred days, members of the Hutu ethnic majority participated in the meticulously planned state-organized slaughter of the Tutsi minority group, butchering friends and neighbors with machetes that extremists in the Rwandan government had ordered and distributed specifically for this purpose. Although it has been fictionalized a number of times, details of the Rwandan genocide are not widely known. In this section, we consider how this lack of knowledge impacts readers' ability to engage with historical experiences in J. P. Stassen's *Deogratias*, which narrates the events of the genocide in an oblique fashion and in retrospect, without ever showing the butchery directly.[1]

Stassen draws on several of the narrative innovations introduced by Art Spiegelman in *Maus*, including the layering of past and present storylines and the use of animal stereotypes to denote ethnic categories. *Deogratias* combines a main plotline set some time after the events of the genocide with interspersed flashbacks to a time period leading up to and during the hundred-day slaughter. Its narrative structure differs from all other works of graphic historiography discussed in this chapter by employing an impersonal mode of narration to offer a fictional account of the Rwandan genocide. Apart from two enigmatic stream-of-consciousness passages, it contains no verbal narrative voice. Visual images, too, have no immediately discernible origin, which may point toward an external focalization. However, some panels also appear to express the internal focalization of the protagonist, while simultaneously integrating the perception of other characters.

Like its narrative structure, the use of animal metaphors in *Deogratias* differs from that in *Maus*. With one exception, all characters are represented as humans. Only the protagonist Deogratias is shown turning into a dog in a number of surreal sequences whose incongruency with their context suggests that the transformation is to be read metaphorically. As we explained in chapter 3, visual metaphors often serve as focalization markers in graphic narrative. However, the focalization marked in these sequences is ambiguous, as the animal imagery is bound up in the protagonist's self-perception, but also in the perception and judgment that other characters form of him.

The question whose aspectuality is expressed by means of comics style and the choice of symbolism gains new salience in this heterodiegetic context. Identifying focalization becomes particularly difficult in *Deogratias* since the narrative withholds crucial information concerning both the events of the genocide, which are represented only briefly and late in the book, and the crime plot unfolding in the narrative present in which Deogratias murders three men and attempts to kill a fourth. Since readers do not learn until the

---

1. While the English-language translation of *Deogratias* includes a preface that details the historical background to the Rwandan genocide and its political consequences, the French original edition does not provide such information (see Ciment and Groensteen).

end of the book how each of these characters was culpable in the genocide, they struggle to determine the meaning of allusions to Deogratias's state of mind and to find reasons for his way of seeing the world. At the same time, identifying focalization is critical for understanding *Deogratias*. In our following analysis, we address each of these points in turn. We begin by examining the comic's narrative structure and its use of animal imagery, and we then consider how both implicate the reader in the what it's like of unspeakable events and the characters who experienced them firsthand.

A silent panel portraying the protagonist in a tattered T-shirt opens *Deogratias* (1; figure 4.3). This gesture of confrontation, where readers join the anonymous narrating/graphiating instance through the artifice of the comic artist to look at Deogratias as he looks back at us, sets the tone for the ensuing narrative, and puts in motion an ethically complex narrative structure. *Deogratias* narrativizes the Rwandan genocide across two temporally distinct, yet closely related narrative layers, unfolding without narrative interjections across a sequence of rectangular panels, some framed by a black line to indicate the present and others unframed to signal events in the past. The pairing of framed and unframed panels to mark distinct, but related periods of time leads to a doubling over of space: the same locations and characters are shown before and after the genocide, inviting readers to comparison. Sometimes, this doubling, where near-identical past and present scenes are placed next to each other in adjacent panels, is based in Deogratias's flashbacks, which trigger narrative transgressions across time. But present occurrences in Deogratias's life—familiar people or places as well as feelings of loneliness, desire, guilt, and disgust—also push the narrative present into the time leading up to the genocide. Often, jumps in time produce uncertainty over where the focal center of scenes and sequences lies, leading to several possible interpretations, as the external focalization of the book's impersonal narrator gives way to an internal focalization through Deogratias. This creates a multilayered, often unreliable view of the relation between past and present that readers have to decode. In the past, Deogratias is a teenage schoolboy intent on winning the hearts and sexual favors of Tutsi sisters Benina and Apollinaria. In the present, by contrast, Deogratias is traumatized by his past involvement in the genocide. His violence against the sisters and their mother Venetia haunts him despite his desperate attempts to keep memories at bay with Urwagwa, a locally brewed banana beer. This haunting is made apparent through Deogratias's flashback memory of butchered corpses being gnawed by dogs that culminates in a series of hallucinatory scenes in which Deogratias transforms into a dog. As he becomes increasingly inebriated over the course of the narrative, these episodes gain in length and intensity until past and present blur and coalesce in

FIGURE 4.3. Stassen, Jean-Philippe.
2006. *Deogratias: A Tale of Rwanda*.
First Second Books. p. 1.

the final part of the book. On both temporal layers, *Deogratias* functions like a detective novel, with the reader trying to discover what Deogratias did in the past to make him the way he is today, while also following the crime plot around the poisoned Urwagwa that Deogratias administers first to a French sergeant who served as a military advisor to the Hutu majority government; then to two Interahamwe militiamen, Bosco and Julius; and finally to Brother

Philipp, the American missionary who fled the mission school and abandoned his pupils when the genocide started.

From the start, the narrative's focus on Deogratias—his participation in and reaction to the genocide but also his blankness toward the reader, his lack of knowledge about himself, and his hiding from others—is accentuated through the introduction of animal stereotypes that expose the book's narrative process of showing and hiding. These stereotypes refer to two distinct classes of animals, real and metaphoric ones. However, that distinction is deliberately veiled in *Deogratias*, with appearances of real animals creating metaphoric associations, while metaphoric animals are made real through the characters' actions, through Deogratias's self-perception, and through the sequences in which Deogratias transforms into a dog. In the realistic frame of reference, dogs gnaw the corpses of slaughtered Tutsis and cockroaches infest the village where Deogratias lives. But both kinds of animals also have a pronounced metaphoric side. In the present, Deogratias is as mad as a dog; in the past, Deogratias, the French sergeant, and Bosco were as brutal and unthinking as dogs, and acting in a pack like dogs, while radio broadcasts called for the extermination of Tutsi cockroaches. These levels of reference associated with the two animal stereotypes are linked together throughout the book, creating interplay between real and imagined animals.

The first encounter with animals occurs in an introductory sequence that begins in the present, but quickly switches between past and present, as well as between real and metaphorical animals. Deogratias is in a bar drinking beer with the French sergeant, who has returned to Rwanda as a tourist. It is his return visit that sets the novel's events in motion. Just as the sergeant reminisces nostalgically about the "soft little thighs" of the Tutsi women he killed, a cockroach skitters across the bar table (5). The sergeant's declaration triggers a flashback of Deogratias stealing money from the missionary station and offering it to Venetia, a prostitute and the mother of his friends Benina and Apollinaria. When the narrative returns to the present, the conversation has turned to Venetia; at the same time, the sergeant discovers the cockroach on the table and crushes it. With one stroke, the crushing of the *real* bug sends Deogratias into memories of his friends being killed *like* bugs. In shifting from present to past experience, Deogratias also switches from cockroach to dog associations, exclaiming: "The dogs . . . They're eating the corpses . . ." (5). This is the first of many mentions of dogs eating corpses, all coming from Deogratias. Although readers may surmise a connection with the genocide, the precise content of his memories is not revealed at this point, and the specific parallels between past and present thus remain uncertain. Apart from Deogratias's verbal exclamation, the sequence contains no internal focalization markers, presenting readers with an external focalization that provides no insight into the protagonist's what it's like.

In a later passage, Deogratias walks through the streets of the village as a group of youths shouts at him "Arf! Arf! Hey Deogratias, doggie! How's it going? Still see too many stars?" (14), metaphorically likening Deogratias to a dog. However, it is not until Bosco says to Deogratias, "You're not thinking you're a dog today, are you?," that the narrative reveals to its readers what the characters have known all along: Deogratias not only witnessed the gnawing of corpses; he also thinks himself a dog (17). This self-perception becomes visually manifest over a series of sequences in which the protagonist transforms into a dog. The first of these transformation sequences, which offer unique insight into Deogratias's what it's like, occurs when Deogratias returns from a visit to Bosco's house. A series of intensely blue panels show Deogratias walking deeply bent along a country road under a starlit sky when the sound of barking dogs sends him off into a monologue that extends his earlier exclamation about corpse-eating dogs into a surreal fantasy: "They devour the bellies, and the bellies spill open." / "The insides of bellies rise up to the stars and dissolve them." / "From up there, they are watching them fight. You are watching me." / "The dogs, and my head that's evaporating, spilling out into the night. I'm afraid of the night. The stars are dissolved by the bellies, and my head is filled with cold" (26–27).

Only the first of these utterances is designated as Deogratias's verbal speech by means of a speech balloon. The second utterance is in a text box; no tail connects the words to Deogratias's body as he scrambles into a shack on all fours. The third and fourth, although associated with Deogratias's thoughts and memories, appear as unframed text between and under the three panels on the next page (figure 4.4). While the top left and bottom panels show a hilly landscape under a starlit sky, the top right panel zooms in on Deogratias, whose posture, shortened limbs, and facial expression resemble those of a canine. A parallel passage in which Deogratias is once more on the road to Bosco's house shows the protagonist similarly moving from an upright to a crouching posture while his ears become more pointed and his face more snoutlike with every panel (47–49). After a flashback in which Deogratias observes Benina and Apollinaria, this passage ends with two dark panels, one in which two dogs with pointy teeth are barely visible against a background showing Deogratias drinking Urwagwa and one of the starlit night sky. In this second transformation scene, Deogratias's interior monologue has been shortened to one utterance: "My Urwagwa . . . I am not a dog" (49).

These two scenes lay the groundwork for *Deogratias*'s central transformation sequence, which follows immediately upon the second scene, but occurs

FIGURE 4.4. Stassen, Jean-Philippe. 2006. *Deogratias: A Tale of Rwanda*. First Second Books. p. 27.

during the day. The sequence opens with a small panel of Deogratias in the present, crouched on the ground asking after Bosco, followed by a larger close-up panel of Deogratias's face, which has morphed into a dog's snout (52). After three rows of panels depicting his full-body transformation into a dog, the two-page sequence closes with three panels in which Deogratias has regained his human appearance. As with the two preceding transformations, this sequence switches between the transforming Deogratias and views of the starry sky. These familiar motifs, now pictured in the daylight, are once more accompanied by Deogratias's monologue that unfolds across speech balloons and captions. Unlike the previous sequences, the text is connected to Deogratias by speech balloon tails that, together with the daylight, may indicate a higher degree of self-awareness in the protagonist, as is also suggested by Deogratias's question, "What's happening to me?," and his subsequent monologue in which he tries to control his traumatic memories by ascertaining, "There are no dogs . . . There are no bellies" (52).

The verbal monologue across these three transformation sequences functions like voice-over narration in film, positioning Deogratias as an intradiegetic verbal narrator who provides readers with insight into his thoughts and feelings. But while the verbal text marks a character-bound focalization, the source of the images accompanying it is more difficult to ascertain. Does the transformation into a dog show Deogratias's own self-understanding or does it present an external view of him? Whose aspectuality do these images express—that of Deogratias, other characters, or the external focalization of the narrator?

A fourth, much briefer transformation scene with no accompanying monologue takes up the visual motif of Deogratias crouching doglike in his hut (57). As before, events and characters that trigger this transformation scene are not made explicit; hence, connections between the transformation scenes and the narrative context in which they occur can only be drawn belatedly—possibly during a subsequent reading. The riddles around Deogratias are finally resolved for the reader in the two final transformation scenes that frame two tightly interwoven passages in which the past and present narrative layers culminate (67, 76). In the present, Deogratias confesses to murdering the French sergeant, Bosco, and Julius to Brother Philip, whom he also tries to poison. In the past, Benina and Apollinaria, who have been hiding in the latrines of the mission school, surrender themselves to the Interahamwe militia in which Deogratias serves. Although their murder is not pictured, later panels show piles of rotting corpses and the dogs that gnaw at them, thus providing visual evidence for the traumatic memories that haunt Deogratias. At the end of these revelations, Deogratias transforms into a dog both in the past and in the present and is arrested for the murder of the three men (77). *Deogratias* ends with a shocked Brother Philip remarking, "He was a creature of God," and a large panel of the familiar starlit night (78).

When read in light of the book's ending, the transformation scenes can be seen to contain subtle allusions to Deogratias's role in the slaughter and to his present murder spree. Each occurs immediately before or after Deogratias commits the murders. Moreover, the fourth transformation leads into a past episode in which Deogratias has just had sex with Benina. His question, "Did it hurt?," gains a second level of meaning when a radio in the background broadcasts the government's call to murder: "Rise up, brothers! Rise up and go to work! Sharpen your tools, pick up your clubs! This race of cockroaches must be eradicated!" (57–58). In light of the book's closing revelations, this can be read as a foreshadowing of Deogratias's rape and murder of Benina and Apollinaria. As in other transformation scenes, however, it remains unclear whether this belated knowledge is to be associated with Deogratias's present memories of past events, thereby constituting a character-bound focalization, or whether such revelations about the protagonist are communicated behind his back directly to the reader, thereby constituting a narratorial focalization.

Determining the source of focalization in *Deogratias* is a matter of interpretation, and several options are possible, particularly in panels that do not include Deogratias. For instance, the landscape images in the transformation scenes are connected through an intricate pattern of similarities, repetitions, and variations, but contain no clues as to who experiences these views. In the central daytime sequence, two landscape panels share striking details (foliage, shades of green and blue, and angle of vision) with views of pre-genocide Rwanda found throughout the book, and the landscape in the large panel closing the sequence resembles that of an equally large panel that interrupts a dialogue between two mission priests in the past. Depicting a luscious forest and partial views of local laborers, men, women, and children, it includes a speech balloon in its center coming from a red van that reads, "Did you know, Brother Philip, that when the first white missionary came here, he brought the first pig to Rwanda . . ." (9). The next panel shows Deogratias behind the van's steering wheel, finishing the point, ". . . And he found its meat so delicious that he came into the country with the animal's tail in his mouth" (9). Although it is suggestive that remarks about Rwanda's colonial past draw on animal stereotypes also used to visualize the genocide and its traumatic aftermath, such connections are not explicitly addressed. It therefore remains uncertain whether Deogratias, who appears to be the source of flashbacks, is aware of them.

For Suzanne Keen, the transformation episodes serve to "dramatiz[e] the psychic effects of trauma and guilt" on Deogratias (2011: 140). This may explain why Deogratias's dog characteristics, also visualized through the state of his T-shirt that distinguishes Deogratias in the present from Deogratias in the past, become more pronounced over the course of the book. However, it does not account for the striking visual resemblance between Deogratias's doglike characteristics and those of other characters in the present. Julius and the boys who taunt Deogratias wear spotted T-shirts and have reels of dribbling saliva (53, 55). Cynical, attentive eyes and a wide, growling mouth suggest that

Deogratias's lack of insight when drunk mirrors the state of other characters who, despite their spotted clothes and savage behavior, are unaware of their doglike status. These shared characteristics may indicate the state of being tainted by guilt, but can also be read as a metaphoric reference to a character's animal nature. In contrast to *Maus*, the animals in *Deogratias* thus resist simple schematizing by type and accrue multiple layers of meaning (Keen 2011: 140). Determining the relationship that binds characters to stereotypes is difficult, and readers are left asking which characters are and are not bound up in the stereotypes, and how far the meaning of the stereotypes extends.

In narratological terms, Deogratias can be read as the character-focalizer of some of the images, but in the final instance, focalization cannot be fixed in one spot. The emotional angle through which readers access the what it's like of post-genocide Rwanda emerges out of the interplay between Deogratias's awareness, the lack of awareness of other characters, and visual hints that do not come from Deogratias—between that which is and that which is not shown and between the points where different ways of dealing with the past intersect. When Deogratias fully transforms into a dog, he weeps for lack of hope, wishing only to die (67). Paradoxically, the acknowledgment that he not only acted like a dog, but truly is a dog serves as an indicator of Deogratias's human sensibility but also of his need to soften his pain with alcohol.

In the preface to the English translation, Alexis Siegel describes *Deogratias* as a "compassionate narration" that enables readers to "imagine the unimaginable" and makes them "come through the fire of that experience a better person." Michelle Bumatay and Hannah Warman, too, propose that the central goal of *Deogratias* is "that readers identify with the main character, asking themselves what they would have done in his situation" (334). Conversely, our analysis suggests that *Deogratias*'s impersonal mode of narration and its ambiguous use of focalization together with the presentation of the protagonist as both victim and perpetrator in both temporal frames deliberately thwart such an easy identification and frustrate the desire of readers (and some critics) to empathize with the protagonist. In fact, it is precisely *Deogratias*'s narrative obliqueness that powerfully communicates the what it's like of being a child soldier in the Rwandan genocide, and remembering what you have done.

The combination of internal and external focalization grants readers access to the subjective experience of someone who is not in full possession of himself, providing a noncanonical perspective on a little-known atrocity. By withholding information about how what is shown in some of its key sequences is to be interpreted, moreover, the comic "gestures at the silence surrounding the genocide in the era following it, and deploying memory, anthropomorphism, and point of view to destabilize the reader's allegiance" (Polak 31). As Polak argues, this destabilization in turn subverts anticipated reading strategies: "Rather than creating an environment that encourages understanding, empathetic identification, and political action in the present, *Deogratias* is a warning about the problems posed by these practices" (41).

Deogratias employs variable and indeterminate types of focalization to evoke the ethically uncomfortable what it's like of an atrocity perpetrator. At the same time, the narrative provides very little direct insight into its protagonist's thought processes, thereby putting readers in the position of atrocity bystanders who are complicit in the crimes of the Rwandan genocide that unfolded under the eyes of Western media. Polak describes this as a "noncathartic approach" to representing atrocity. Rather than absolving Deogratias from guilt and providing ethical closure to readers, *Deogratias* introduces readers to shame over the actions of Deogratias as well as over the inaction of the international community, and thus of their own shame (70–71). In the following section of this chapter, we examine another manifestation of an unusual subjective position—that of an individual who is also the representative of a collective—to assess how a shared consciousness expressed through a singular focalization intersects with questions of reliability and the ethics of representation that are central to the genre of graphic historiography.

Collective Subjectivity:
Li Kunwu and Philippe Ôtié, *A Chinese Life*

A Chinese Life, drawn by Chinese artist Li Kunwu and written by French author Philippe Ôtié, creates a highly unique narrative structure. It is a collaborative, dual-authored comic based on personal memories but realized through a hybrid narrative that blends internal and external perspectives into an artificial unity in order to address a largely non-Chinese reading audience. Its chronological narrative relates the history of the People's Republic of China (PRC) from 1958 to 2006, as it was experienced by the protagonist Xiao Li. This Li, however, is not introduced as a realistic depiction of an individual, but as a carefully constructed artificial persona adopted by Li Kunwu, who drew the book and on whose memories the narrative is based. The overall plotting and pacing of the narrative, meanwhile, are not Li Kunwu's. They were contributed by Ôtié, who drafted the storyline and wrote the verbal text for the three books that make up *A Chinese Life*. Ôtié's scenario embeds Li Kunwu's firsthand experience, thus producing a hierarchy of narrative authority rather than a true collaboration. Ôtié's overarching narrative authority also governs

Li Kunwu's artwork. The book's introduction explains how Li Kunwu's drawing style was invented under Ôtié's guidance, morphing from the "smooth, quick, airy, modest" brushstrokes of the first pages into the bold black-and-white ink drawings that make up the bulk of the narrative. Hovering uneasily between claims toward an authenticity of experience expressed through autobiographical rhetoric, on the one hand, and an open acknowledgment of artifice, on the other, the hybridity of *A Chinese Life* is distinct both from the communicative structure of *Maus* with its layering of generational perspectives and from the explicit fictionality of *Deogratias* that enables subtle shifts between narratorial and character-bound focalization.

Although two real individuals, each with their own appearance in the narrative, authored *A Chinese Life*, the verbal introduction by Ôtié emphasizes that both the protagonist Li and the narrator, whose voice is Li's as transcribed and redacted by Ôtié, are fictitious exemplary people. To "dive into [Kunwu's] life. To help him reconstruct it. To negotiate, with the real Lao Li, what inflections to give the dialogue, the story," Ôtié explains, he had to "become Chinese, become Lao Li ['Old Li,' the polite address for Li Kunwu]." To know and communicate Kunwu's history, Ôtié combined the experience of his friend with his own, Western understanding of that experience, thus engendering a hybrid protagonist able to project an inside view of China to outsiders. The introduction further explains that the two authors had planned to treat this made-up protagonist, designed in dialogue between a Chinese artist (who "contains all the Lis, Zhangs and Chens of China") and a French writer (who is "Dupont, Durand, Schmidt, Popov, Martin and Smith, all at once"), as "average," but once the character Li took on a life of his own, Li went "from 'average' all the way to 'representative.'" A tension between the individual and the collective is thus deliberately built into *A Chinese Life*.

In our following analysis, we consider how the emphatically proclaimed dual authorship, realized through a hybrid character whose subjectivity is at once that of an insider and of a foreigner, plays out across the graphic narrative, itself a visual-verbal hybrid. We refer back to our concept of tangled subjectivities, developed in chapter 3, to ask whether it is possible for the hybrid medium of comics to express a truly collective subjectivity of the kind advocated in the propaganda of the Communist Party of China. If such a collective subjectivity even exists, what does its historical, lived experience look like, and how can it be expressed through words and images? To address these questions, we consider *A Chinese Life* through theories of "we" narration and inquire into the access that a communal focalization offers to readers. First, however, we introduce the historical context in which the creation of a collective subjectivity in *A Chinese Life* is set.

The narrative of *A Chinese Life* begins in 1950, eight years before the Great Leap Forward, a state-driven campaign that collectivized every aspect of life in the PRC. Little known outside of China, the Great Leap produced the most catastrophic famine in history, killing between 40 and 45 million people in the three years from 1959 to 1961. Although its devastating consequences were known to Chairman Mao as early as 1959, the Communist Party of China subsequently strove to strip this atrocity from popular memory (Lee and Yang 4). Historians studying Chinese memory culture on a local level, however, have shown that memories of the famine persist into the present, often in the shape of the "monstrous and troubling visions, dreams, and nightmares of famine survivors" (Thaxton 3). Indeed, during China's present-day reform period, famine memories are becoming increasingly contested between different social groups, between town and country, between men and women (whose social situation improved dramatically in the 1950s), and between regions, ethnicities, and generations (Lee and Yang 5). The increasing surfacing of suppressed famine memories witnessed by Thaxton testifies to their renewed salience. Against the PRC's official historical narrative of a nation melded into one single collective unity, memory contests around the Great Leap Forward illustrate that the "typical" Chinese among other "typical" Chinese does not and cannot exist.

A Chinese Life suppresses such ongoing memory contests, all the while inscribing them within its narrative. Its protagonist Li functions as a focal character through whose personal experience and understanding historical events are refracted. Yet despite its heavy reliance on character focalization, *A Chinese Life* takes pains to disassociate itself from conventional Western ideas about the individual's privileged vantage position on history. The book's unique conception and narrative mediation of subjectivity lead to a highly unusual, often contradictory structure of focalization. Readers follow Li through the formation of modern China over the last sixty years as it unfolded in Kunming, the largest city in the country's southwestern Yunnan province. However, the narrative emphasizes that Li's personal experience is representative of "collective euphoria" (29) and "exultation" (267); "mass action" (59); collective famine, hardship, and "destructive consequences" (37); collective "love" and "veneration" (190) as well as grief for Chairman Mao; collective feelings of "the deepest confusion" (228); collective silence (341); and the "deeply rooted feeling[s] many Chinese share" (489). United by "the uniformity of fate" (479), group identities—configured according to cantons, schools, families, professions, and the state—and their collective initiatives, circumstances, and emotions cloak Li's individual experience, rendering it ordinary within the greater Chinese context.

The explicit claims made by the narrative voice make it tempting to consider *A Chinese Life* in the context of "we" narratives. According to Uri Margolin, we narratives are collective narratives that present a group as "the central agent of the actions and events portrayed" (2000: 597). Insisting on a group source, Margolin offers a strict definition of we narratives and acknowledges only a few rare instances. Brian Richardson, by contrast, includes we narratives among other modes of "extreme narration," defining we narration as "a supple technique with a continuous history of over a century that continues to be deployed in a considerable number of texts, particularly those that emphasize the construction and maintenance of a powerful collective identity" (55–56). Especially when combined with more traditional modes of narrating, we narration is "an excellent vehicle for expressing a collective consciousness," often with a clear political agenda (56, 58). With its emphasis on group or collective experience, *A Chinese Life* may be classified within Richardson's spectrum of we narratives. However, although *A Chinese Life* presents a collective subjectivity, it does not rely on a we narrator in the strict sense of "a new first-person *plural* narrator, whose nature it is to possess *collective* epistemological, perspectival, and other qualities" (Bekhta 2017: 166, 170; see also Bekhta 2020). Instead, the use of an individual character narrator whose singular focus is said to give exemplary access to the collective experience of all Chinese is more productively understood as another permutation of intersubjective focalization strategies.

A number of visual and narrative features ensure that Li's experience of a changing China is read as one shared by many, that the impressions Li formulates are approached as collective impressions, and that his understanding of history stands in for a communal understanding. Strategies securing the transference of Li's individual experience to a collective one include the representation of party propaganda; the switching back and forth between a first-person singular voice and a first-person plural one, even within the same sentence; and the reiteration of deeply rooted cultural narratives. These three strategies come together in the book's two-column chapter title pages, which combine popular patriotic songs, photographs of Li Kunwu and his family, and cartoon sketches of Chinese crowds or rural landscapes (figure 4.5). Only the title page of chapter 6 ("Old Li"), devoted to Li's personal life—meeting his future wife and his father's return to his native village and eventual death—breaks this pattern, reproducing a handwritten manuscript of an article published in the *Yunnan Ribao* newspaper, instead of a song and a photograph of Li Kunwu. These collages of personal and communal memorabilia address the conflation of Li's beliefs, attitudes, values, and experiences and those of his fellow citizens. Throughout *A Chinese Life*, collective experi-

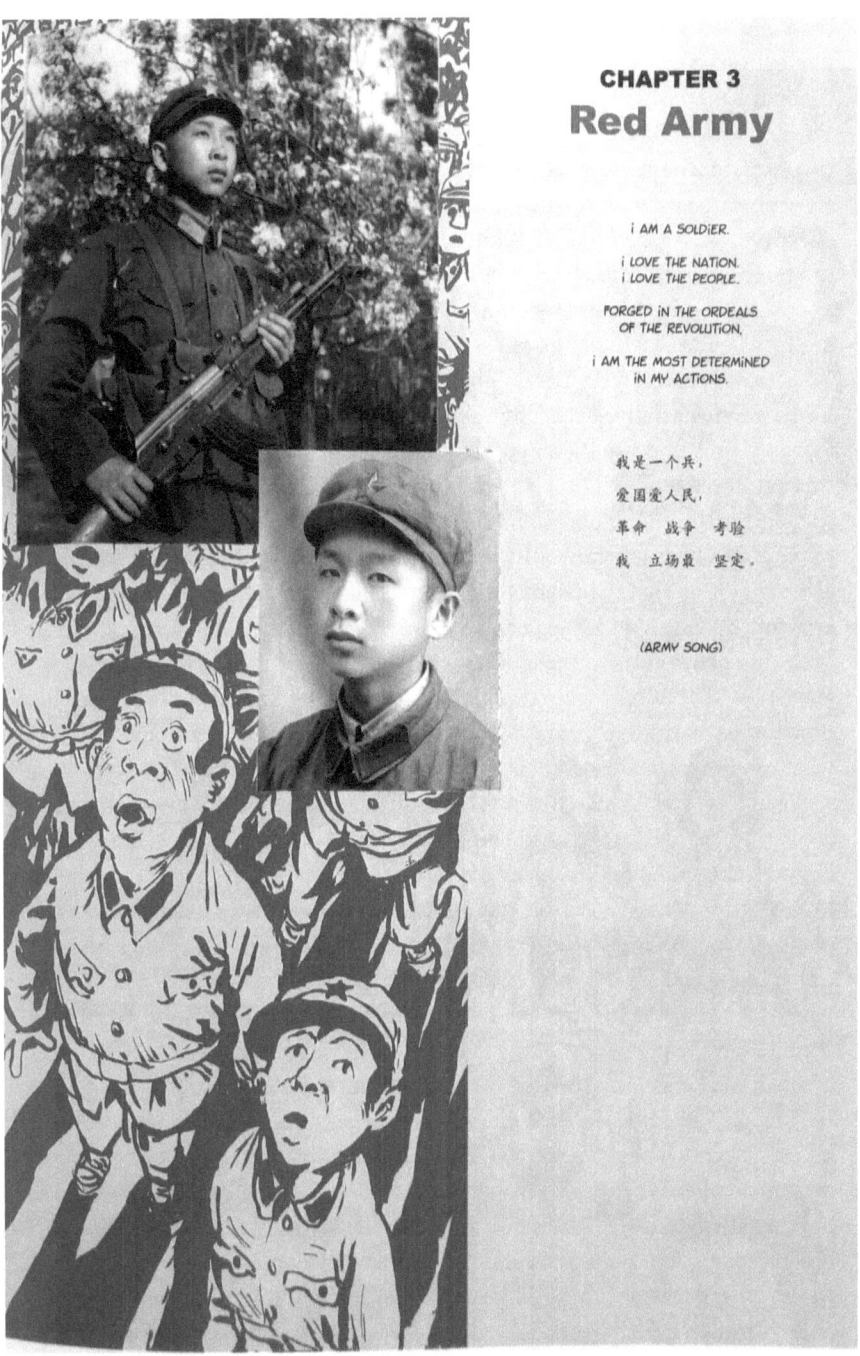

FIGURE 4.5. Kunwu, Li, and Philippe Ôtié. [2009; 2011] 2012. *A Chinese Life*. Translated by Edward Gauvin. Harry N. Abrams. Chapter 3 title page.

ence and sensibility foster a communal consciousness but also incite collective action. Numerous representations of crowds and the use of speech or thought balloons with several tails indicate a group sentiment and a collective sensibility (103; figure 4.6). Li is careful to situate his story within this collective consciousness: He speaks of "the China we all love" (410), insists that "it's a deeply rooted feeling many Chinese share" (489), and warns readers that "whatever we learned then [as children] leaves a lasting imprint" (95). Finally, the book ends with a grand statement about a Chinese life built "from our brows and our children, to whom we bequeath lives that will also be made of hard work and sacrifice" (690).

Despite repeated declarations to represent a truly collective experience, however, the narrative also contains several factors that complicate such ideological claims. Indeed, the singular and the plural stand in an uneasy relationship on every level of *A Chinese Life*'s production and enunciation, artwork, and authorship. Complications begin with the book's introduction, which never states precisely how Ôtié and Kunwu collaborated on the book, while also suggesting that the character Li was designed to conform to Ôtié's Western understanding of his experiences. In terms of the book's narrative structure, this generates a complex enunciative situation in which the narrator's voice says "I," but that voice is authored not only by Li Kunwu, on whom the protagonist-narrator is based. Meanwhile, visual images supposedly represent what Li saw or knows, but their content and style were designed to show not a real, but a typical Chinese collective vision as understood by the two authors.

A Chinese Life further problematizes claims of collectivity when a tension between the individual focus on Li, on the one hand, and the explicit claims toward group experience, on the other, raise questions of reliability. In the book's introduction, Ôtié admits that he and Li Kunwu didn't anticipate that "for foreign readers—or young Chinese people—who knew little about contemporary Chinese history, whatever happens to Xiao Li ('Young Li') would seem to have happened to all his fellow citizens in exactly the same way. Ditto with what he says. And thinks." Li's exemplariness here constitutes an effect of reading: Li appears as an exemplary character because Western readers do not know very much about Chinese history. If that is true, however, the choice to present a collective history through an individual focal character may appear problematic because it leaves no room for alternative experiences.

In fact, *A Chinese Life* contains a number of contradictions that should warn readers against too readily trusting its claims toward a collective experience. Through its choice of Li, the child of a party functionary living in the provincial capital, as a protagonist, it presents the vantage point of a privileged, educated, politically engaged man from which China's political development is

FIGURE 4.6. Kunwu, Li, and Philippe Ôtié. [2009; 2011] 2012. *A Chinese Life*. Translated by Edward Gauvin. Harry N. Abrams. p. 103.

experienced and understood. Persistent claims toward an exemplary viewpoint notwithstanding, Li's experience is thus not typical, but the specific experience of an individual. This becomes particularly obvious when his account of the Great Leap, which highlights well-known events such as the Four Pests Campaign and largely coincides with the official history of the famine, is disrupted by the memories of Li's rural relatives, who were starving under horrific circumstances. Such contradictions invite readers to draw their own conclusions about how representative Li's experience is of China as a whole.

Another episode in *A Chinese Life* that explicitly cautions against a straightforward conflation of the personal and the collective concerns the representation of the Tiananmen massacre. In the book's only metanarrative scene in which Li and Philippe appear in their role as authors, Philippe seems to willfully misconstrue the link between subjectivity, shared consciousness, and reliability when discussing the inclusion of the occupation of Tiananmen Square. Li is hesitant to include it in his visual narrative because, in fact, he was not present at the event. Upon Philippe's insistence, however, he agrees to represent the massacre, but only if he can say "what [he] think[s] . . . instead of what [he] saw" (485). Now it is Philippe's turn to hesitate: He sees Li's condition as one that encroaches on questions of authenticity and trustworthiness. For Philippe, an overt representation of what Li thinks about the massacre, from a future perspective, "means an end to the neutrality [they've] maintained since the beginning" of *A Chinese Life* (485). Although Philippe addresses a neutrality couched in the rhetoric of witnessing, he also equates neutrality with a telling that is free from the teller's own prejudice, from the teller's subjective take on things. Such a neutrality presupposes an emotionally distant focalization that is incompatible with Li's role as a focal character. Both the Great Leap and the Tiananmen episode thus suggest that *A Chinese Life* produces a fallible focalization that distorts events and presents only partial insights.

Li's short two-page sequence about the Tiananmen massacre visually confirms an understanding of authority and reliability as bound up in focalization. He begins by stating that he knows about the "very dark view of 6/4"—the date of the massacre—that has been impressed upon the world through the "terrible images associated with it" (488). He immediately leaves this train of thought to assert, "But the truth is, like almost all [his] countrymen, [his] mind is occupied with so many other things [he] finds even more interesting" (488). Instead of showing the iconic images of army tanks entering the student-occupied square, the page's five panels portray Chinese of all ages enjoying leisure-time activities at the beach on the Yangtze River in Hankou that Li visits after his discussion with Philippe. The incongruency

FIGURE 4.7. Kunwu, Li, and Philippe Ôtié. [2009; 2011] 2012. *A Chinese Life*. Translated by Edward Gauvin. Harry N. Abrams. p. 489.

between the verbal and visual tracks suggests that the "order and stability" (489) of the present, and not the past, is what Li considers to be the "official line" that many Chinese share. The lengthy caption explaining this reasoning "that might seem shocking, especially to Westerners" (489), is included at the top of a large panel depicting Li sitting alone on a tree stump, looking out toward a cityscape (489; figure 4.7). The same panel was first introduced three hundred pages earlier when Li confirms, "Like many others, I try not to look back too often, to let memory tug me down the slope of remorse" (131). Both times, the panel comes when Li feels that looking forward is what he and the Chinese people want to do. This rare instance of braiding, where Li pauses to contemplate and relate what he thinks, highlights how his subjectivity, what he thinks *as well as* what he sees, colors the story we are reading. It thus draws notice to his focalization.

A Chinese Life contains few overt clues of its account's potential unreliability. As a work of graphic historiography, however, the validity of its account may be assessed through a comparison with other sources, for instance the testimony of villagers' traumatic memories collected by Ralph Thaxton and the conclusions about distinct memory communities drawn by Ching Kwan Lee and Guobin Yang. Read in this light, *A Chinese Life* is ethically problematic in its uncritical stance toward the history it tells: Its account criticizes some effects of collectivization, but ultimately sees Chinese collectivity as an inevitable outcome of the PRC's history, thus reflecting an official political climate where only some things can be voiced and overt criticism is suppressed. To a Western reading audience, the ethical dilemma of an overdetermined ideological positioning may become visible in the contradictions born from the book's portrayal of a single life and its claims that it is exemplary of the nation as a whole. The same problem underlies *A Chinese Life*'s presentation of authorship, which embeds Li Kunwu's art within the narrative authority of Philippe Ôtié so that although the book accentuates a collective subjectivity, it articulates an individual outsider's understanding of Chinese collectivity.

Careful consideration of these incongruencies between individual and group experience as expressed through Li, a hybrid character-focalizer whose subjectivity is simultaneously unique and exemplary, Chinese and Western, leads us to conclude that *A Chinese Life* is not a we narrative in the strict sense. The book may propose a communal focalization, but because it does so hesitantly and somewhat ineffectively through Li's contradictory positioning, it ultimately engages readers in an assessment of the ethics and politics of historiography—even if this goes against the book's explicitly stated goals. The double authorship of *A Chinese Life* and the contradictions and tensions its negotiation produces within the diegesis may thus lead to a distanced reading, an effect more usually associated with a non-character-bound narratorial focalization. Our following analysis of Joe Sacco's three graphic historiographies, *Palestine*, *Safe Area Goražde*, and *Footnotes in Gaza*, extends this argument by considering how these books combine a plural focalization with character narration by an outsider and asking what challenges the layering of multiple personal takes on historical events poses for readers' ethical engagement with contested histories.

Focalization in the Plural: Joe Sacco, *Palestine*, *Safe Area Goražde,* and *Footnotes in Gaza*

Maltese-born Joe Sacco is one of the main proponents of graphic journalism, a form of graphic historiography that presents a mix of reportage and investigative journalism and grants a central role to the cartoonist-journalist and to the act of reporting. He is renowned for bringing to light forgotten or underrepresented atrocities to which he himself has no immediate connection (Chute 2016: 201). Sacco's graphic journalism focuses on the experience of others but presents that experience from an explicitly subjective perspective. His drawings reflect this double focus by casting the comics journalist simultaneously inside and outside the frame, creating a record of experience that seeks to capture the pain and suffering of others while including his own situated perspective in the narrative. As Hilary Chute explains, Sacco shares with Art Spiegelman the preoccupation with inhabiting someone's experience through drawing: "Drawing someone carefully is a form of dwelling (to invoke *inhabit*'s Latin root) in the space of that person's body, taking on their range of postures that themselves reflect experience" (2016: 249). Graphic journalism as practiced by Sacco thus joins other forms of graphic historiography in that it does not hide its subjective viewpoint.[2]

Palestine, the first graphic narrative by Sacco that we consider in this section, is related by a narrator who is also the book's main focal character. Modeled on Sacco's real-life appearance and biography, the character narrator Joe provides readers with a gateway into unfamiliar experiences. Readers are invited to identify with this avatar character and to participate in his story of discovery. Each chapter title page of *Palestine* includes an easily recognizable portrait of Joe, often wearing an inquisitive expression or one of bewilderment or surprise. These point-of-view images mark an internal focalization and highlight the narrator's task of understanding. Throughout *Palestine*, countless images show Joe, camera in hand, photographing what presumably serves as material for the book we are reading. *Palestine* also includes many other visual markers of a character-bound focalization. These include numerous self-portraits, often drawn with exaggerated facial expressions that sum up an event's emotional weight and Joe's reaction to it; Joe gripping a comics panel that introduces the incident he is observing (33; figure 4.8); backdrops where Joe is pictured multiple times looking around frantically as he struggles to include all that he is being told and shown (38, 258); and arrow-tailed

---

2. See Versaci (114) and K. Williams (52, 55), who refer to Sacco's comics when examining graphic journalism's inherent subjectivity.

FIGURE 4.8. Sacco, Joe. 2003. *Palestine*. Jonathan Cape. p. 33.

narrative captions that direct readers through Joe's process of perception and evaluation (59, 73, 173). Many of these markers, as well as the book's enunciative situation as a whole, echo the genre conventions of graphic memoir. However, the book's content is not primarily autobiographical in nature.

In relation to the history recounted in *Palestine*, Joe does not claim to present an objective account, instead openly relying on his own experiences and observations that serve as a critical lens for dissecting what he learns as he wanders through streets and talks with the locals. He concedes that he is not a knowledgeable narrator, often addressing his difficulties in collecting and understanding historical evidence and in processing what he sees, experiences, and learns from others. Throughout *Palestine*, Joe's stance remains that of an outsider whose principal aim it is to create a comic book about Palestinian history. Visually and verbally highlighting his own processes of reporting, Joe repeatedly draws attention to the presentation of evidence. From his ever-present camera or notebook and pencil to his looking, reading, and other explorative acts, Joe makes readers aware that his is a mission to gather information, and that it is fraught with the conceits and predicaments of his outsider perspective. Through Joe, experiencing and reporting, feeling and informing overlap so seamlessly that readers are immersed in the unpredictable unfolding of events and discoveries. His openly subjective take on what he discovers encourages readers to walk alongside him as he tries to untangle the complexities informing Palestinian history. Ultimately, this creates an overwhelming sense of being present, in an intimate way, in what Joe experiences and narrates with words and images. Readers of *Palestine* thus experience Joe's growing knowledge and sensitivity, which coalesce to present an intimate picture of people, place, and historical reality.

An abundance of scenes indicate Joe's active participation in the telling of Palestinian history and the processing of lived experiences. However, the graphic narrative also contains an equal number of instances when Joe steps "outside the frame" (Dong 43) to let others tell their own stories. Throughout *Palestine*, individuals are often made to speak for themselves, grounding history in the firsthand accounts of Palestinians (67; figure 4.9). The book is full of portraits of speaking subjects, some named and others nameless, their intradiegetic stories spilling out into speech balloons that float over Joe's speech balloons and, at times, overtake his narrative text boxes. This overlaying suggests that the different vantage points of these others are as legitimate as Joe's. Their urgency to have someone listen to their often silenced experience mirrors Joe's persistent efforts to collect their stories. Although the accounts of Palestinians are rendered through Joe's narrating voice and presented through his drawings, markers of the speakers' subjectivities abound. For instance, the inclusion of what may or may not be disclaimers—"he says," "she says," "he told me"—with which Joe qualifies their intradiegetic narratives draws attention to his goal of collecting a "different slant" on what he is reporting across these accounts (132).

FIGURE 4.9. Sacco, Joe. 2003. *Palestine*. Jonathan Cape. p. 67.

The testimonies of Palestinians are left intact alongside Joe's reporting, creating a proliferation of focal characters. By including a variety of voices, Sacco enriches his story with the feeling, emotion, engagement, and understanding of Palestinians. However, just as Joe's process of understanding colors his narrative, so too does each speaker imbue their telling with their own personal

FIGURE 4.10. Sacco, Joe. 2003. *Palestine*. Jonathan Cape. p. 2.

contexts and interests, their own what it's like. Visually complex crowd scenes, for instance, unite Palestinian voices and perspectives with Joe's interior monologue (2; figure 4.10). Joe is always present when Palestinians speak of their experience—as the interviewer who asks about the type of things he wants to learn about, such as what something felt or looked like; as the journalist who collects stories and photographs; or as a critical listener. But he never takes up an authoritative position in relation to their personal take. Their views may clash with Joe's or the views of others, but they are legitimized nonetheless. Personal stories mix with Joe's reporting, his attempts at understanding, and his critical reflection to account for multiple agencies, multiple perspectives and positionalities vis-à-vis the events being represented.

The drawings that portray both those Joe is listening to (often while sipping tea) and the events being told further suggest that multiple perspectives are meant to be equally valid in *Palestine*. Not only does "Sacco routinely illustrate the stories he hears from his informants, investing them with the same visual presence he gives to events he witnesses firsthand" (Singer 73); he also renders them in the same cartoon style used throughout the book. The consistency in drawing style suggests that Joe's focalization does not carry more weight than that of other focal characters; all stand on an equal footing. However, by embedding Palestinians' perspectives within Joe's journalistic mission, Sacco maintains authority as the graphic journalist who compiles and presents *Palestine*'s narrative. At times, this creates an uneasy tension between the explicit dedication to pluralism and Joe's privileged position, through whose drawing style, narrative voice, and choice of narrative situation and genre the experience of Palestinians becomes accessible to readers. As in *A Chinese Life*, the adoption of a drawing style associated with an outside position in relation to that which is being shown makes all claims to represent the experience of others somewhat problematic. At the same time, the embedding of different character-bound aspectualities in *Palestine* grants readers a much larger choice of perspectives to take on the represented history.

In *Safe Area Goražde: The War in Eastern Bosnia 1992–1995*, Sacco adopts a different narrative strategy to give access to a plurality of experiences. Nine firsthand accounts of the Serb siege against the Bosniak enclave Goražde are presented across several pages. A thick black border separates these from Joe's extradiegetic account, and narrative captions containing direct quotes of the person speaking suppress Joe's narrative voice so that the telling of past experiences is left to the character narrators who experienced them (109; figure 4.11). There are, however, some indications that Joe hasn't fully stepped outside of the frame. These include a voice-over caption that provides contextual information, first-name labels that identify characters or speakers, an unaccompanied speech balloon in which questions are posed from a source outside the frame, and a shift in style. Notwithstanding, the personal narratives are presented intact, free of Joe's commentary. Not subject to his critical, sarcastic, compassionate, or self-reflexive stance, the black-bordered narratives transpose readers into the experiences and minds of firsthand witnesses.

FIGURE 4.11. Sacco, Joe. 2002. *Safe Area Goražde: The War in Eastern Bosnia 1992–1995*. Fantagraphics. p. 109.

Each story thus marks a shift in focalization, and together they multiply the perspectives presented in *Safe Area Goražde*.

Although *Footnotes in Gaza* does not make use of dark borders or other stark visual signs to mark a shift in focalization, the history it relates also unfolds across a plural focalization. The book sets out to "record the stories of Palestinian eyewitnesses to the events in Khan Younis and Rafah" (x), when in November 1956, Israeli forces bulldozed Palestinian homes in two neighboring towns and killed almost four hundred people. The narrative follows Joe as he collects eyewitness testimony to these atrocities. *Footnotes in Gaza* presents these oral stories as personal accounts of a collective experience told either across several first-person voices (at times, collected on the same page) or across the adoption of a second-person plural narrative. As the telling of firsthand experiences transfers from one speaker to the next, a multilayered focalization strategy adds narrative texture to the historical account. In this later work, a stage direction—in the form of a full name followed by a colon or a portrait panel with a caption indicating the person's name—often announces a change in speaker but also in character-bound focalization. Single events come into focus as each eyewitness accentuates details, actions, emotions, and cognitive processes that they remember having lived through. Although grounded in the personal context of the speaker—"To be honest, from my point of view, they were shooting just to terrify the people, but afterwards people told me that the killing had sometimes been on purpose," explains Mohammed Zidan as he sketches out the lay of the land (216)—the eyewitness testimonies stack together to produce an overpowering impression of how things unfolded.

In the chapter "The Day of the School," for example, no fewer than fifteen men provide testimonies across seven pages (262–68). Portrait panels complete with name captions are scattered across backdrops that zoom in on and out from a crowded scene of wounded men huddled together with their hands folded over their heads (265; figure 4.12). The testimonies of these men wind together into a rich, emotionally charged tapestry. Through them, readers discover that on that day, "there were many people—nations" (263) retained "in one barbed wire area" (263) as Israeli soldiers shouted orders—"put your faces on the ground!" (263), "'tata rosh!,'" or "tatu rosh," or "tatahosh!" (264)—and shot at them (264). The men were forced to sit "with each other like watermelons" (265), feeling "very pressured, very crowded" (265). "Some of the people inside the school were injured, and their blood was flowing" (266), "the smell came from the blood of the people around me" (266), who were also "pissing on themselves" (266). "No one [was] allowed to stand up. Nothing offered to them. Nothing at all. No water. No food" (267). One man emphasizes how there was nothing to do but give "ourselves up to God" (264). Through the memories of the fifteen men, details and sensations, facts and emotions accumulate into a vivid, complexly layered picture of the events, but also of what it felt like to be there.

While these personal stories seem to be left intact, Joe mediates the remembered experiences, embedding the what it's like of historical experience within his own story in which he sets out to discover facts, assess and edit evidence, and expose discrepancies between competing versions of events. For

FIGURE 4.12. Sacco, Joe. 2009. *Footnotes in Gaza*. Jonathan Cape. p. 265.

instance, Dr. Abdullah El-Horani, a witness to the Khan Younis attack, fails to recall how many people were hiding in the room with him. In answer to Joe's inquiry, he responds, "I'm trying . . . the memory . . . I remember only one of them, a teacher with me called Atta El-Ostaz" (104). But when he describes how they were put against a wall, Dr. El-Horani states, "We were around 10, 11, 13, I don't know" (105).

Throughout *Footnotes in Gaza,* Joe often interrupts the narrative to highlight the difficulties for the understanding and writing of history such gaps create and the problems involved in ascertaining the reliability of the information he collects through interviews. After collecting the Khan Younis stories, Joe interjects: "Now allow me to kick the pillars upon which our story stands. I don't need to tell you, memories change with the years, and the memories we have excavated here are decades old. Memory blurs edges; it adds and subtracts" (112). He thereby indicates his narratorial processing of the information he gathers, assessing the degree of exaggeration and the accuracy of details, but also summing up what needs to be taken away from the oral accounts he gathers. In another instance, one man remembers running from a firing squad after his three brothers had been shot; by contrast, his sister-in-law and nephew are certain that he was not there (113–15). Faced with this major discrepancy, Joe urges readers not to "forget the essential truth" of the story despite "the problems that go along with relying on eyewitness testimony" (116). Throughout *Footnotes in Gaza,* Joe repeatedly adds his understanding of things to that of his eyewitnesses as he highlights the relation between memory, truth, historical fact, and consciousness. Ultimately, this embedding of focalization produces a disorienting effect that invites readers into Joe's shoes and asks them to reach their own assessment of historical facts.

In the three works of graphic historiography that we have analyzed in this section, Joe and the eyewitnesses he interviews each describe and interpret historical events from individually specific vantage points. Readers of these books are given the choice to engage with the focalization of eyewitnesses or with Joe's narratorial focalization as he assesses and processes their remembered firsthand experience, or with both. By layering diverse subject positions, Sacco's graphic narratives draw readers into the narrative universe, urging them to sift through the complex details and reach their own conclusions about the history, events, and people they are reading about.

●

Whereas theories of historiography often focus on how history is narrativized, this chapter examined noteworthy ways in which history is focalized, granting particular attention to noncanonical forms of focalization that can enable alternative takes on significant historical events. The examples of graphic historiography examined in this chapter are explicitly concerned with understanding historical facts, events, and people, all the while openly recognizing the difficulty, if not the outright impossibility, of reaching a full understanding. They do so by visualizing historical events and people in nonrealistic ways through the use of visual metaphor but also through the juxtaposition of versions and interpretations of history by exploiting the co-presence of panels and the interaction of text and image on the comics page. The difficulties of historical understanding are built into their narratives through narrators who serve as uninvolved bystanders, members of a second generation, or foreigners. This situated perspective is often explicitly aimed at readers who are also outsiders in relation to the represented events. By exposing the problems and obstacles involved in grasping and representing the what it's like of traumatic historical experience, each book endeavors to make readers aware of the processes of, and the relationship between, looking and seeing, observing and knowing. In doing so, these graphic historiographies emphasize the belated and secondary processing of history over against the experiencing of events firsthand, thereby providing a position in relation to history into which the reader may step.

Focalization in graphic historiography carries a cognitive focus that may involve corporeal reactions, but to a lesser extent than is the case in graphic memoir. While the internal focalization of character narrators may foster the adoption of an "imagining-other perspective" (Nünning), leading to affective closeness and empathy, the external focalization in relation to the depicted events offers a more distanced, evaluative position to readers, who are invited to reflect back on processes of affiliative transmission and on the different ways in which we can position ourselves regarding the memory of others. The presentation of alternative versions of a historical event, exchanges between and the negotiation of different sources and types of historical knowledge, and the assertion that historical facts are always, at the very least, tinged with a drop of doubt invites corresponding acts of counter-focalization from readers. Thus, graphic historiographies set in motion a dynamic process of transmission in which understanding, achieved by accessing historical experience through acts of focalization and counter-focalization, becomes a task for readers.

CHAPTER 5

Wordlessness

Comics can express astonishingly complex processes of a character's or noncharacter narrator's perceptual, cognitive, and emotive engagement with the narrative world. A variety of storytelling strategies introduce readers into the aspectuality of focal characters. As we have highlighted in chapters 2 and 3, the most common of these expressive means include point-of-view images, self-portraiture, shading and line work, panel size and framing, layout, the repetition of identical or similar panels, and the use of visual metaphors, as well as the style and genre of a comic book. When these features operate in conjunction, they often mark a multilayered focalization in which the subjective what it's like of individual characters becomes part of a social web of experiences, perceptions, memories, and retrospective appraisals, which are in turn embedded in the mood, tone, and atmosphere of a narrative world. Graphic narratives offer a rich and detailed reflection on what it's like to have experiences, as well as on the aesthetic means by which experiences can be expressed and on the ethical positioning this expression offers to readers. For this reason, we consider comics as a meta-phenomenological medium that offers new insights into the experientiality of narrative and into the processes of focalization through which that experientiality becomes available to readers.

In this chapter, we extend our inquiry into focalization in comics by considering a semiotically distinct corpus: *sans paroles*, wordless, or silent comics (see Beronä 2001, 2008). Composed entirely of images, except for the occasional intradiegetic sign, poster, or chapter title, wordless comics sidestep the word-and-image dynamic that plays such an important role in the storytelling practices of bimodal comics. While bimodal comics have the potential to employ nondiegetic narrative text to ascertain the identity and aspectual orientation of narrators and focal characters or to pinpoint temporal, ontological, and epistemological relations between pictorial elements, wordless comics rely on exclusively visual means to evoke the what it's like of a world and its experiential processing by one or several characters. As we have pointed out in our discussion of wordless sequences, for instance in *Jessica Farm* (chapter 2), such an exclusively visual access presents a particular challenge for interpreting focalization.

Wordless comics, which are more obviously united by their semiotic structure than by a common theme, share a situation of address and a rhetorical function. For this reason, we include them in the genre-based organization of our study. Moreover, their semiotic structure also has thematic implications, as the formal features of wordless comics lend themselves to certain types of narratives more than to others. The narrative interest of wordless comics often lies in accentuating a particular mood or atmosphere, rather than plot and character; where subjective experiences are evoked, these often center on basic emotions such as love, desire, fear, or anger. As Barbara Postema notes, "wordless narratives are more likely to be associative, stream-of-consciousness, or surreal" (2018: 71; see Postema 2017: 206).

The dissolution of inside-outside boundaries and a focus on experiences of disorientation and estrangement are frequent in wordless comics. The deliberate withholding of a certain type of information—verbal narrative in captions, which typically contains basic information about time, location, and the identity of characters that is crucial for orienting readers—makes wordless comics particularly apt at creating ambiguity, indeterminacy, and confusion. This pertains both within the diegesis, where a character's lack of orientation in an unfamiliar environment is frequently addressed, and outside of it, as the disorientation of readers often mirrors that of the character. Thus, although wordless comics can, in principle, deal with a wide range of topics, their semiotic structure makes them prone to an indeterminacy that is at the heart of a specific poetics—a poetics of the fantastic, of gothic and horror stories—and this too lends wordless comics a genre profile.

When speaking about the fantastic in comics, we work with a broader, more recent understanding of the term than that offered by Tzvetan Todorov's classical definition of the fantastic as a border genre between the uncanny (in which strange events are rationally explained) and the marvelous (in which events remain rationally inexplicable). Broader definitions of the fantastic focus on the ontology of fantastic world building (M. Horstkotte; Schmeink and Böger) and describe how fantastic narratives transgress the boundaries between a fictional reality, which is accepted by characters inside the diegesis, toward a second, alternate reality system (Durst; Simonis). For Clemens Ruthner, the fantastic is in many ways a genre of border crossing and liminality: Its supernatural incidents question epistemological standards; its protagonists fall into a liminal mental state; and its texts are themselves aesthetically liminal, often excluded from the canon of high culture. The fantastic thus confronts readers with the blind spots of their knowledge system and its anxieties (59).

The three wordless comics that we analyze in this chapter—Josh Simmons's *House* (2007), Eric Drooker's *Flood!* (2007a), and Shaun Tan's *The Arrival* (2006)—are productively read in terms of the fantastic because their narratives revolve around blurred inside/outside boundaries between characters and their surroundings and between different worlds. Their tendency toward dissolution, their sophisticated use of metaphors and symbols, and their often ambiguous deixis, where the origin of symbols remains unclear, make them rewarding texts for a theory of focalization. This is because focalization, too, becomes fraught with ambiguity in a narrative environment that withholds important information, blurs boundaries, and obscures the deictic center of a narrative's experientiality. However, at the same time as wordless comics challenge and complicate our understanding of focalization, they also take pains to direct attention toward processes of focalization. Across different intensities, their visual narratives guide readers through the expectations of a narrative universe by placing a sustained focus on a particular psychological state that overrides all other narrative considerations, such as those of setting, time, and even plot development.

The duration of such narrative instances can vary considerably. A three-page, 144-panel spread in Eric Drooker's *Flood!* narrates the protagonist's emotional anguish, which culminates in his fading away into a blue smear. In George Walker's *Book of Hours: A Wordless Novel Told in 99 Wood Engravings*, a single-panel page shows a heavily shaded person from an unusually low angle, arresting the narrative's temporal flow to capture the fear and disorientation felt by many New Yorkers shortly after the first plane crashed into the Twin Towers on September 11, 2001 (2010: 187). In both of these instances, an intensification of focalization positions readers within the emotional lives of characters and within the world that is experienced through this emotional life. Images communicate an expansion of emotion, an intensified emotional engagement with the storyworld that overrides all other narrative concerns to accentuate the narrative world's psychological map.

Although wordless comics communicate through visual images alone, they appeal not only to the sense of sight, but to all the senses, evoking emotional charge and mental complexity and creating affective impact. Analyzing wordless comics therefore requires a high degree of visual literacy. The discussion about the narrativity of still images that has developed in the subfield of visual narratology since the 1990s offers important tools and concepts for such an analysis. In the following section, we outline the most important contributions to this discussion and explain how the work of visual narratologists such as Mieke Bal and Emma Kafalenos can enrich the study of wordless comics (and of comics generally). The subsequent analyses of *House, Flood!*, and *The Arrival* focus on visual focalization markers that are frequently used in wordless comics, including the use of light and darkness, the blurring of inside/outside boundaries, and visual metaphors. We also explain how wordless comics often evoke ambiguity around the source and type of focalization by drawing on a fantastic poetics, and discuss the consequences that such a deliberate evocation of ambiguity has for drawing a distinction between internal and external focalization.

Sans Paroles and Visual Narratology

The history of wordless comics has been traced back to the mid-nineteenth century when silent strips made their first appearance in Germany and France (Groensteen 1997: 60–62). In the 1920s, Belgian artist Frans Masereel began publishing novels without words in the style of expressionist book illustrations, dealing with what critics considered serious topics and thus raising the profile of visual storytelling. While Masereel was mainly known as a book illustrator in the mid-twentieth century, he has recently been rediscovered as the inventor of wordless comics and "the father of the modern graphic novel" (Walker 2007: 19). His woodcut stories influenced German artist Otto Nückel and American artists Lynd Ward, Milt Gross, and William Gropper, "who developed Masereel's novels in pictures in the 1930s" (Beronä 2001: 19). Although the popularity of wordless novels was short-lived, the impact of these early works on comics should not be underestimated (Eisner 2008b: 140). Indeed, recent work in *sans paroles* by cartoonists Rebecca Dart, Eric Drooker, Peter Kuper, Shaun Tan, Masashi Tanalca, Lewis Trondheim, George Walker, Jim Woodring, and others continues to explore the possibilities of purely visual narratives (Nières-Chevrel 129).

Despite the long history of *sans paroles*, contemporary comics theory has so far underestimated their critical importance. For instance, Benoît Peeters devotes a short section of his *Lire la bande dessinée* to wordless graphic narratives, describing their discourse as simplistic and arguing that a purely visual narrative must avoid insurmountable ambiguity (129). For Marie-Laure Ryan, sophisticated comics narration needs to exploit the contrast between two semiotic channels in order to achieve a high standard of narrative versatility (Ryan and Thon 142–43). Meanwhile, classical narratology has generally associated the representation of interiority with verbal activity. Techniques for indirect, nonliteral representation of mental activity such as Dorrit Cohn's "psycho-narration," on the other hand, are usually considered to convey non-complex or nonconscious mental activity.

As Barbara Postema shows, such a logocentric attitude glosses over the narrative potential of images and, by extension, the intricate narrative structure and complex creation of narrative worlds in *sans paroles* (2014, 2015, 2017, 2018). The general undervaluing of wordless comics is particularly disconcerting given that narratologists studying visual narrative practices have long highlighted the narrativity of visual images, drawing a close parallel between verbal and visual narration. Mieke Bal, in particular, argues that "the principle of meaning-production is the same for verbal and visual art" (1997: 164; 2009: 167). In several of her books, Bal introduces images (including Baroque paintings but also contemporary abstract paintings, collages, and multimedia art) as narratives that can be analyzed with the tools and concepts of narratology (1991, 1999), concluding that "the analysis of visual images as narrative in and of themselves can do justice to an aspect of images and their effect that neither iconography nor other art historical practices can quite articulate" (2009: 166). For Bal, that missing aspect is the time of an image's reception, which she analyzes as a narrative that unfolds between the image and its spectator. In that unfolding narrative, spectators distinguish between images presented through an "external focalizor," where "the event represented [in a visual image] has the status of the focalized object produced by focalizors," and those that embed an "internal focalizor," where "the 'reality'-status of the different objects represented is variable and contingent upon their relation to the focalizor" in the painting, who presents events as they are seen by him or her (2009: 166). Thus, while narrativity has to be imported into the painting through the process of reception, focalization is inherent to the image itself, even if—as Bal admits—the distinction between external and internal focalization "is not always easy to point out" (166).

Emma Kafalenos, too, has examined the narrativity of visual images, particularly paintings. She proposes that narrative paintings can compress the *syuzhet* into a single scene, leaving the spectator to unfold this into a plot (1996). For Kafalenos, the narrativity of paintings rests on the condition that narratives create worlds with the aid of the cognitive and imaginative faculties of their viewers. Thus, "a viewer of a visually represented isolated moment interprets the depicted scene in relation to prior and subsequent events," just like "a reader, beginning to read a narrative, interprets the events that are initially recounted in relation to prior and subsequent events that . . . she too selects from extratextual information, or supplies from her imagination" (2001: 138).

Within comics theory, the conviction that the meaning of comics is made in the gutter mirrors Bal's and Kafalenos's point that the narrative compression of visual images becomes untangled in the viewing and interpreting process of spectators. By "dividing the picture into several distinct frames," graphic narrative "uses the eye of the spectator moving from panel to panel to keep narrative time running. The reader (for the eye movement amounts to an act of reading) constructs a story" (Ryan 2004: 141; see Ewert). The theoretical work by comic artists Will Eisner and Scott McCloud also emphasizes the structuring of comics narrative by means of grids and gutters: Comics break the narrative flow down into discreet panels and thereby open up a space between the panels that offers a way in for readerly engagement and imagination (Eisner 2008a; McCloud). For Eisner and McCloud, the reader's psychological closure or filling in of the gaps created in the gutter is at the core of how comics narrate. Our analyses in preceding chapters have indicated, however, that readerly engagement with the narrative world is bound to focus not primarily on the space between panels, but rather on what panels show as well as on how panels speak to each other.

As film semiotician Christian Metz has demonstrated, the images in a visual narrative do not function as signs in a manner comparable to words in a sentence. Each image in a visual narrative may be understood more productively as a full statement whose relation to preceding and following statements is much "less embedded in paradigmatic networks of meaning" than that of words in a sentence (26). Since narrative directionality in comics is not dictated by technology, as it is in film, graphic artists may, and increasingly do, choose other ways to organize narrative information or present a course of action than that of grids and linear sequences, either exclusively or intermittently. The versatility of comics narrative grants a high degree of freedom to the readers of comics, regarding both the path and order in which a comic is read and the work of interpretation that integrates the distinct aspects of a comic's visual presentation. This creativity becomes particularly noticeable when considering focalization, which is itself at least partly an interpretative category, especially in wordless comics.

Narrating exclusively across images, *sans paroles* draw from a range of intericonic and intertextual references. They make extensive use of symbols, stereotypes, and metaphors, and evoke painterly and comics styles and genres much more blatantly and consistently than most bimodal graphic narratives. The three wordless comics analyzed in this chapter unsettle assumptions about the integrity of world, the identity of characters, and the mechanics of comics storytelling through the construction of fantastic—split or double—worlds. Contrary to the standard belief that thought is (quasi-)verbal in nature, these *sans paroles* expose visual, pictorial, and metaphorical thought as crucial for narrative meaning. Moreover, their sophisticated symbolism invites a renewed investigation into the narrative complexity of still images and into the reading practices engendered by that complexity. In our following analyses, we build on our discussion of visual metaphors in chapter 3 to explain how metaphors in wordless comics evoke the complex experiential, perceptive, and thought processes of protagonists and narrators as they engage with the narrative world. Visual metaphors, we argue, often function as focalization markers in wordless comics by introducing mental and emotional nuance into the story-world and by establishing an atmosphere that disorients readers, pulling them into the confusion experienced by characters as they enter a fantastic world.

The Graphic Fantastic: Josh Simmons, *House*

In Josh Simmons's deceptively simple wordless comic *House*, the extraordinary details of a spooky house at once foster and reflect the deteriorating mental states of its three young protagonists. The central action takes place outside and inside an abandoned house that has properties that are incompatible with everyday reality. Larger inside than it is outside, the house contains a huge crater lake in which several dilapidated houses are chained to its walls and floor, and beyond the house's rooms lies a maze of dark corridors, passages, and crawl spaces from which there is no escape. *House* thus operates with a number of tropes that are familiar from fantastic literature and film, especially from postmodern variants of the gothic (M. Horstkotte): the trope of the haunted house in the woods in which the youthful protagonists meet a gruesome but mysterious fate, the "fantasy trope of structures that are larger on the inside than on the outside" (Purcell), and finally the house as a metaphor for the protagonist's body or mind familiar from many texts in the gothic tradition. Thematic allusions to these tropes, as well as a number of visual cues in *House*, bind the unnatural properties of the house to the minds of the novel's protagonists, which is why the novel is of interest to us in the context of focalization theory.

Of the three texts examined in this chapter, *House* is the one that most closely and deliberately aligns itself with the fantastic theme of world transgression and with a fantastic mode of storytelling in which the rhetoric of a text produces a "sense of wonder" in readers (Mendlesohn). To account more closely for the persuasive power of the fantastic, which enables an immersive reading in which readers obtain imaginative entry to the narrative world, Farah Mendlesohn distinguishes between four categories of the fantastic: portal/quest fantasy, immersive fantasy, intrusive fantasy, and liminal fantasy. Since Mendlesohn's four categories offer a helpful taxonomy of fantastic subgenres, we will explain them in some more detail before turning to our analysis of *House*.

Portal/quest fantasies invite the reader into the fantasy world through some kind of entryway (Mendlesohn 1–58). The reader's role is that of a companion-audience, bound to the protagonist, who functions as a point-of-view character. Common in children's literature, portal fantasies focus on the protagonist's access to the alternate world, and they often include lengthy explanations of its peculiarities by a wise inhabitant of that world. By contrast, immersive fantasies introduce a complete alternative secondary world without external influences (portals, breaches, or invasions) (59–113). That world is taken for granted by characters and readers alike because the narrative does not draw attention to its deviation from the real world. The narrative rhetoric employed in immersive fantasies binds readers to the perspective of a protagonist, but readers do not have to accept the protagonist's version of events, as immersive fantasies open up the possibility of subversive readings. In narratological terms, portal/quest fantasies typically involve a narratorial focalizer, while immersive fantasies follow a character focalizer to whose perception and judgment readers are bound.

Intrusion fantasies, Mendlesohn's third category, are frequent in ghost stories and gothic novels in which the fantastic enters the narrative world from outside through a rhythm of latency and escalation, as places become spooky (114–81). Although the revelations of intrusive fantasy are not based in evidence, as in portal fantasy, but rather in the unreal and subconscious (fear, intuition, etc.), the rhetorical function of the intruder can lie in making the narrative world appear more real in comparison to the alternative world. Finally, in liminal fantasy, there is no firm proof of the fantastic, and the fantastic is always just out of sight, remaining continually uncertain (182–245). The liminal fantasy results in possible and not in necessary readings. Both intrusion and liminal fantasies are also often associated with character focalizers. As Mendlesohn repeatedly points out, these four categories are fuzzy, and single texts can fall into two or several of them.

House combines thematic and structural characteristics of portal, immersive, and intrusive fantasies. The narrative begins when a teenage boy hiking through the forest comes upon an abandoned house. Together with two girls—one light-haired, the other dark-haired—he pries open the house's door and begins to explore its interior. The theme of portals and border transgressions is an important one in the first half of the graphic novel, concerning not only the protagonists' first entry into the house but also a number of thresholds inside the house. When they delve deeper into the house's vast interior, the three teenagers come upon a crater lake into which they dive, discovering a number of floating houses anchored in place with large chains. This episode marks one of several key moments in the story where the protagonists enter an interior space through some kind of portal. Despite the obvious allusions to the fantastic portal trope, however, the bizarre peculiarities of the underwater world inside the house are never noted or explained, but rather are simply taken for granted, as in immersive fantasy.

House's progressively accentuated focus on the experiences of the three characters, without recourse to an external vantage point from which their experiences could be assessed, is also suggestive of an immersive rhetoric. As in *Jessica Farm* (which we discussed in chapter 2), comic artist Josh Simmons combines an impersonal narration with an extreme form of interior focalization in *House*. While the graphic narrative initially appears to be externally focalized, the second half increasingly focuses on the frightening experience of the three protagonists, marking an internal focalization through the stark use of light and darkness and through the size of its characters. Yet, as the protagonists' experience gains in detail, the house, too, turns into a more active agent, setting in motion a narrative rhythm of latency and escalation that characterizes intrusive fantasy. Many cues toward an identification of the house with the desires and fears of the three teenagers also suggest an intrusive rhetoric, complicating the ascription of focalization.

A number of key scenes in *House* indicate that the house externalizes the interior mental states of characters, and that readers can therefore become immersed in the characters' what it's like by way of exploring the house. For example, the discovery of the water-filled enclave not only shifts readers' understanding of the house from a spooky to a surreal or metaphoric habitat; it also marks a turning point in the three characters' emotions. The boy and the blond girl kiss, revealing their attraction to each other and provoking the dark-haired girl's jealousy. After a brief return to the house's roof, the teenagers enter a room dominated by a striking portrait of a uniformed, bearded man, who appears to stare down at them. Reproduced on both covers of *House*, the portrait is given a special status in the narrative. It also stands out from its surroundings because it is the only object in the house that is not marked by decay. The portrait's clearly marked special status invites speculation about its meaning and the identity of the bearded man, who might be the house's owner or even a personification of the house (or vice versa). The portrait's stern glance has a strong effect on the three teenagers, who appear completely captivated and follow its invitation into yet another interior space by crawling into a secret passage beside the fireplace over which the portrait hangs.

Once in the house's underbelly, things begin to go very wrong for the protagonists. The blond girl falls through rotten stair boards and lies badly hurt in the darkness for the rest of the comic. After walking away from the dark-haired girl, the boy sees a phantom at the end of a hallway and chases after it into a dark passage out of which he never emerges. And the dark-haired girl has visions of light pouring into the dark space toward which she runs, crashing full force into the stone wall and eventually expiring wounded on the floor. Graphically as well as thematically, the tone shifts in the second half of *House*, from light, playful, and adventurous to gloomy, dark, and fearful. As we detail below, throughout *House*, black panels mark transitions between storylines and shifts between light and darkness mark focalization.

In *House*, black panels are repeatedly used to cut from one strand of the narrative to another and to separate out scenes and sequences pertaining to a specific character. This ensures that the three storylines develop in a parallel fashion, giving readers equal insight into the experiences of all three protagonists. Abruptly terminating a given sequence, black panels signal to readers that the thread of that storyline is complete, and thus facilitate their transition from one storyline to another, from one character's experience to that of another. This use of black panels to mark switching points between the focalization of different characters can be productively described through Rick Altman's concept of following-units. In *A Theory of Narrative*, Altman proposes the term "following" to describe the reader's sense of moving with a character from scene to scene (15; see chapter 1). It is this sense of following that, for Altman, turns a mere account into a full-fledged narrative. Since a narrative is made up of a series of "following-units" focusing on one or several characters, an important goal of narrative analysis lies in determining the "following-pattern" of a narrative, as for instance a dual-focus pattern that alternately follows two characters or a multiple-focus following-pattern with more than two protagonists (55, 241).

In *House*, the use of black panels becomes more nuanced and its effect on the reading process more complex as the narrative progresses. The positioning of black panels comes to express the feelings developing between the three characters, as well as their understanding of their own and of each other's feelings, thus marking internal focalization. For instance, a dark panel that shows the dark-haired girl from the waist up, eyes wide open and arm partly extended, closes a six-panel page portraying her initial walk through

FIGURE 5.1. 2007. Simmons, Josh. *House*. Fantagraphics. n.p.

the house's underground corridors (figure 5.1). Her two companions are not pictured as the narrative narrows in on her. On the left-hand side of the page, two of the three panels picture the girl from the waist down, with particular attention on her walking feet. By contrast, the column of three panels on the right-hand side of the page shows her from the chest up. In the first two panels, she looks up at some cracks in the wall, aided by her flashlight. In the third, she looks down, stricken with fear, into what appears to be a dark abyss. The carefully orchestrated interplay between upward and downward perspectives suggests that the girl is the character focalizer of this scene. While the first two panels express her lack of awareness that she is in danger, the final panel clearly indicates that she is now becoming aware of the danger she is in.

WORDLESSNESS • 157

FIGURE 5.2. Simmons, Josh. 2007. *House.* Fantagraphics. n.p.

Just as the dark-haired girl is about to fall into the abyss, the boy saves her by pulling her back. Now it is the blond girl who feels threatened and abandoned. The following page opens with a dark panel that directly echoes the one that closes the sequence we have just discussed (figure 5.2). It shows the blond girl by herself, eyes glancing downward, mouth drooping, just as she was portrayed on the previous page when she witnessed the tenderness between her two companions. However, in the dark panel, her face and torso are shaded. Her darkened face reinforces her sadness and alienation, and thus contains a hint of her understanding of the other characters' feelings. The introduction of a black backdrop where the stairs and the two other teenagers all but drop away may similarly indicate a darkening mood. The slight visual suggestion of the brunette's presence in the panel's foreground, with only the top of her head barely visible in its bottom portion, further highlights the blond's awareness of the threat posed by the blossoming love between her companions. The use of light and darkness in these panels draws connections between the subjective experiences of both girls, and indicates the mood with which they experience their surroundings. The panels that follow confirm the blond's understanding of the situation. She plummets through the stairs and, despite the boy's efforts to aid her, is left wounded and alone in a dark space below the partially collapsed staircase.

As the teenagers' understanding of their situation intensifies, so too does the use of black panels. At the beginning of *House*, a continuous, predominantly white succession of panels relates how the teenagers play together lightheartedly. By contrast, three dark panels on a double-page spread signal the point in the narrative where each teenager realizes that she or he is alone. The absence of black panels when the mood is light and their increased use as events weigh on the teenagers associate their use with a heightened emotional awareness. In this manner, *House* gives visual expression to the emotional experience of being under duress often described as "losing one's mind." From this point on, the three teenagers begin exhibiting behaviors associated with fear, rage, or despair. After falling through the staircase, the blond girl wails, screams, and drags herself across the floor, but eventually calms, seemingly resigning herself to impending death. The dark-haired girl, who has been abandoned in a dark corridor by the boy, bangs her head against a white stone wall and repeatedly punches it and the floor until she lies bleeding and crying, her eyes slowly closing as she too presumably dies. The boy wanders through the house's passageways, where he sees a ghost that he tries to capture without success. When he understands that death is inevitable, he becomes monstrous, moving on all fours, clawing away at the earth, vomiting, screaming, and crying in a curled-up position as he fades away into the darkness.

The three death scenes move in striking unison. Plummeting further and further into despair, the features of each teenager darken as the black line shading mixes with blood and tears. As their anguish and exhaustion increase, the characters fade away, first shrinking in size, then reduced to a speck, and eventually erased altogether, as indicated by the use of black panels and pages. In *House*, the three characters who had been individuated when they competed for each other's affections turn into a collective consciousness, sharing a set of experiences but also thoughts and emotions. In the final instance, they become just another part of the all-engulfing consciousness of the house.

The change in layout and color scheme establishes a tight link between the mental space of the teenage protagonists and that of the house, translating their emotional states in spatial terms. As the characters' anguish increases proportionately to the duress inflicted by the house on each of them, the comic panels darken. The three teenagers experience the haunted house in a crescendo of horrific surprises, and their growing fear is graphically reflected by an increased use of black. The rapidity with which the panels telling of the teenagers' descent grow dark translates pictorially the mental disintegration of each of the characters. The dark panels are tightly linked together until, eventually, they invade the whole space of the page as the teenagers get smaller and smaller until only tiny fragments of what they were peek out from a predominantly black page.

House's panel crafting and use regulates pacing and time but also serves to create atmosphere, set the tone, and expose the inner worlds of characters. Panels communicate the characters' what it's like through black-and-white contrasts and thus mark character focalization. But they also narrate how the house takes over as a main story agent while the human characters' mental, emotional, and physical presence diminishes, which suggests a more narratorial focalization. At the end of the book, when the characters' mental state fully deteriorates under the menacing pressure of the house, only darkness remains. Is *House*, then, a psychological narrative or a horror story? In the final instance, it remains unclear whether the house physically consumes the teenagers, especially given that nothing explicitly referenced in the diegesis menaces them. An alternative reading could explain the end in terms of metaphorical expression: The characters' anguish and despair wear on their psyche so that, ultimately, they feel so little and so claustrophobic that they experience themselves as fading into nothingness. As Josh Simmons acknowledges, "horror is usually a version of melodrama, of heightened reality. In that framework, you can work toward an emotional truth" (2012). For the most part, *House* explores not the characters' adventures, which are predictable and not expanded upon with each repetition, but rather their psychological engagement with events and their eventual disintegration. As in many wordless comics, intense emotion steals the show away from action.

Thierry Groensteen comments that it is not by chance that wordless comics privilege fantastic storyworlds where supernatural or uncanny events are perceived against the backdrop of a natural world, since the fantastic often evokes dream worlds, which are essentially visual (1998: 98). However, the fantastic appeals to wordless comics not only because of their dependence on the visual but also because fantastic narratives evoke psychologically and emotionally intriguing worlds characterized by instability and uncertainty. Especially in immersive and intrusive rhetorics of fantasy, details and events are evoked rather than told in a straightforward fashion. This is also true of wordless comics that adopt a fantastic poetics, making it unclear whether panels depict exterior aspects of the narrative world (narratorial focalization) or an intensely subjective experience of that world (character focalization).

For Todorov, the main characteristic of the fantastic is the uncertainty it evokes in readers, who follow the ambivalent response of characters to inexplicable events. Because they lack orienting verbal detail, wordless comics are particularly apt at producing such uncertainty. Frequently, there is no way to distinguish between visual details depicting an exterior world and those pertaining to a character's interior world of dreams, visions, and imagination. In terms of focalization, this means that panels and sequences can be simultaneously read as narratorially focalized statements, where the authority of expression and the represented content are congruent with each other, and as the internally focalized expression of a focal character's mental and emotional experience.

In *House*, connections between the psychological state of characters and the narrative world's mood are communicated across visual strategies that mark shifts in focalization. However, the comic adopts several characteristics of fantastic narratives that leave readers in doubt as to whether focalization invites them to consider the instability of the storyworld, its characters' (individual or collective) emotional states, or both as reflective one of the other. The following sections of this chapter will further explore this inherent ambiguity of focalization in wordless comics by focusing on two other ways in which wordless comics blur boundaries: narrative metalepsis in *Flood!* and the use of visual metaphor in *The Arrival*.

Border Crossings: Eric Drooker, *Flood!*

Flood! builds up a veritable crescendo of ambiguity, stretching from an expository first chapter set in a realistic city, through a second chapter delving into its protagonist's unconscious mind and creativity, and up to the third and final chapter, which breaches the ontological boundary between life and fiction when the protagonist, a comic artist, breaks into his art by entering the cartoon pages he has created. In this process of intensifying ambiguity, focalization moves step by step toward the protagonist, from an external take of him in chapter 1, to a representation of his dream life in chapter 2, and finally into his comic art in chapter 3, where he is both the character focalizer and the intradiegetic graphiator of the narrative. *Flood!* employs a number of narrative devices that are familiar from our reading of *House* to evoke a storyworld whose terrain constantly shifts between inside and outside, objects and ideas, world and art. These include contrasts between lightness and darkness to evoke mood, a marked change in the size of panels indicating a constriction or expansion of experience, and the gradual introduction of surreal visual details that are incongruent with the realistic world expectations raised by their surroundings and that can thus be read metaphorically.

The meaning of individual symbols in *Flood!*, which include the protagonist's beating heart and skeleton visible from the outside, scattered bones, and fish skeletons, often remains enigmatic, but their use clearly connects different narrative levels as well as inside and outside worlds. The identification of character and world, which increases throughout *Flood!*'s three chapters, parallels the mirroring of the house and characters in *House*. To these familiar patterns of a fantastic poetics, *Flood!* adds a metafictional dimension by introducing a strongly marked narrative metalepsis, and making use of many other visual strategies to self-consciously reflect on the different ways in which an alternate world can be accessed, for instance through the psyche, as well as through myth and fiction.

Flood! presents a disorienting image of the protagonist's life in a city that indiscriminately engulfs its inhabitants in its dark entrails. Identified by the author Eric Drooker as New York City at the end of the twentieth century (2007b), the city is overwhelmingly vast, crowded with an amalgam of faceless people who flood its streets. Its buildings and trains are defaced with graffiti, poster art, and advertisements; apartments are run down and sparsely furnished; and economic prospects for its inhabitants are poor. The protagonist is a factory worker who one day finds his workplace shut down without prior warning. Disappointed in love when the woman he met at a bar turns out to be a prostitute demanding payment, and increasingly uncomfortable because of the constant torrential rain that adds to the city's apocalyptic atmosphere, the protagonist is weary but alive. His heart visibly pulses at times as he searches for a raison d'être or a way to pass the time. While the graphic style of *Flood!* is directly indebted to Frans Masereel's city depictions and to the German expressionist woodcut tradition, the close identification of city and hero also points to the heritage of the fantastic.

As is frequently the case in fantastic narratives, *Flood!* offers no clear distinction between a subjective perceiver and his objective and inanimate surroundings. Instead, everything around the subject becomes infused with feelings and with ideas of movement, force, and intensity. Read through the lens of focalization theory, *Flood!* can therefore be productively considered as a noteworthy example of a wordless comic devoted entirely to the question of character-bound focalization and its relation to narrative structure, theme, and mood. At first, it appears as though the narrative is composed of two more or less separate ontological domains: a real world filtered through the protagonist's experiences and impressions of it and an unconscious interior world that is also tinged with the protagonist's mental processes. As the story unfolds, it becomes more and more apparent that the two worlds are so tightly identified with each other that there are no clear boundaries between them.

Several panels explicitly highlight this mutual infection of separate ontological domains. The clearest instance of this occurs in a panel in the graphic novel's third chapter, when the rain has flooded New York so badly that the artist is drowning inside his apartment as the blue ink that had previously colored the cartoon pages he creates empties out into the extradiegetic storyline.

But even panels that seem to be more grounded in real-world expectations, such as those depicting the protagonist as he walks through a recognizable New York, are always to some extent colored with his aspectuality. For example, the unceasing rain that falls on the city could initially be seen as a bad weather strain of catastrophic proportions. However, the rain's crucial role in enabling the narrative metalepsis in chapter 3 suggests that the weather serves as an external expression of the protagonist's interior state. So, too, with the debris of shit, bones, and skeletons that litters New York, but that may similarly express the protagonist's disillusioned perception of his world and life. This impression is strengthened when the visual vocabulary in the cartoons he draws mirrors the style of the first two chapters with its perspectival distortions—bending houses, surreally long streets—indebted to German Expressionism, a movement that also focused on representing mental responses to modernity.

Although the images that comprise the book's first chapter, "Home," communicate, for the most part, concrete details and events pertaining to the protagonist's everyday life, its closing pages transpose readers into his emotional reality. The more the protagonist wanders through the streets of New York, the more he loses his sense of self and his grounding in the real world. Slowly but steadily fading away, the protagonist becomes first a shadow, then a stick figure, until eventually not even a trace of him exists. Other visual indicators, too, mark his complete physical and mental absorption in the city. Among its alienating crowds, the protagonist repeatedly figures as a translucent person with his skeleton exposed "to suggest a feeling of vulnerability . . . and impermanence" (Drooker 2007b; figure 5.3). Visual distortion and exaggeration also express the city's menacing influence on the protagonist and the inner turmoil that results from it. From being reduced to a stick figure walking through the city, the protagonist resurfaces as a supersized man seated on the roof of a building, hunched over in the dark utterly discouraged as he looks down at a street lamp (figure 5.4). On the final page-sized panel of "Home," the city buildings shrink under his massive body.

This is one of a number of striking instances in which *Flood!* uses formal features such as panel size and distorted images to express the protagonist's intense emotions. "Home" opens with full-page panels followed by two-panel pages, then four-panel pages, sixteen-panel pages, sixty-four-panel pages, and then comes to a close with a shockingly dense comic page composed of 256 small panels followed by a splash page of the superhuman-sized protagonist. The shrinking and spatial intensification of panels and their darkening reflect the protagonist's growing despair as he is crushed by the city. By the end of *Flood!,* the city too is buried under torrential rains, its immersion in water

FIGURE 5.3. Drooker, Eric. 2007. *Flood! A Novel in Pictures.* Dark Horse. n.p.

FIGURE 5.4. Drooker, Eric. 2007. *Flood! A Novel in Pictures.* Dark Horse. n.p.

further suggesting its intersection with the protagonist's state of mind. Boldly violating realistic codes of representation as they were used in the story up to that point, the unusual closing two-page spread may indicate that we are now in a fantasy world. Throughout *Flood!*, character focalization renders ontological borders uncertain; it persistently encourages readers to waver between possible interpretations as they realize that all story levels may be about the same emotionally charged experience.

Flood!'s second chapter, "L," engages in a complex use of character focalization to accentuate the story's fantastic structure. The chapter opens with the protagonist descending stairs, framed by graffitied walls, empty except for a bone and a snail, that lead to the subway trains. After securing a seat on the subway, he begins to doze off, first accidentally leaning against a woman who startles him awake with a shove and then a second time without disruption until the end of the chapter when a police officer and his dog wake him up. The sixth page of this relatively short chapter opens with a long panel of the protagonist as he begins to fall asleep for the second time. In this panel, his face is drawn seven times, progressing from a clear silhouette with wide open eyes to a more blurred silhouette to the final image of him sleeping, eyes closed. An equally long panel follows this one; it depicts a group of people in a dark hole around a fire from which protrudes a monstrous figure facing the group with raised arms. Whereas the first panel appears to be narratorially focalized, the second panel shows the protagonist's dream world, and thus his character-bound focalization. From the protagonist's real world, readers have now transitioned into his dream world.

The following pages depict the protagonist walking away from an abandoned subway station down into tunnels and through them to a surreal setting in which he wanders through the bowels of a great water snake to join the group of people and monsterlike figure around the fire. They warmly greet him, and he takes up his place as a drummer, leading the group into a bacchanalian dance. As the sequence unfolds, the growing size of panels, the introduction of jagged-edged panel borders, and the increasingly idyllic character of the images suggest that the dreamer is being drawn deeper and deeper into his dream world. No fewer than four splash panels complete the sequence, the last depicting the protagonist and a lover embracing in a paradisiacal setting. However, the dream sequence comes to an abrupt end with the introduction of a panel showing the stark barking of a police dog when the protagonist is found asleep on an empty subway train. The chapter concludes with the protagonist exiting the subway car and ascending the stairs into the city street.

Several details indicate that the rupture between external world and dream world in this sequence is not an absolute one, as both are connected through the protagonist. Visual cues marking a character-bound focalization include the recurring use of bone, snail, and fish skeleton symbols across both the exterior and interior world. Instances of foreshadowing, too, indicate that the protagonist's what it's like tinges both worlds. For instance, before plunging into the bowels of the water snake, the dreaming protagonist is startled by a howling, menacing dog whose silhouette and stance foreshadow those of the police dog at the end of the chapter. The repetition of details of events, spaces, people, and objects throughout *Flood!* adds coherence to its psychologically charged narrative, linking narrative levels and making them resonate across panels, pages, and chapters.

In the final chapter, the protagonist sits at his drawing board, pencil in hand, as he produces a series of tri-toned cartoon pages that are reproduced full scale on subsequent pages. From a focal character whose relation to a narratorial mediation remains somewhat underdetermined, he turns into an intradiegetic graphiator and narratorial focalizer who draws an autodiegetic graphic narrative about his dreams and visions. This embedded story begins with him holding an umbrella floating up into the rainy sky over Manhattan buildings that were drawn in a similar manner in the previous chapters of *Flood!* This gives way to the protagonist being blown off the page, eventually bursting through a cloud into an amusement park. As he walks back to the city center, the protagonist takes in both peaceful demonstrations, which unfold in dry streets, and violent ones that are overabundantly flooded to the point that people are swooped away and buildings burn under bolts of lightning as people are being arrested and brutally beaten, with tanks and biplanes firing artillery. This apocalyptic narrative is interrupted by images of the protagonist once again sitting at his drawing board, drawing the graphic narrative we are reading, but this time holding an umbrella and immersed past his waist in rain. At one point, he floats out of his flooded apartment with his cat in tow as the blue ink he uses to draw the story mingles with the water inside his apartment. The protagonist drowns in the flood, while his cat survives by sitting on his lifeless head and is eventually saved, in a surreal twist, by the biblical character Noah, who hauls the cat up into his ark as it cruises between the visible tips of New York's skyscrapers. Holding an umbrella, Noah is clearly recognizable as the bearded man from whom the protagonist bought an umbrella as he was making his way home in the rain early in the chapter.

In this surreal sequence, the extradiegetic world of the artist sitting in his apartment and the intradiegetic world of the graphic narrative that he draws mix to the point of becoming one and the same. Visually, this identification becomes possible because both worlds were only demarcated through the use of blue color in the intradiegetic story, while drawing style and panel frames

FIGURE 5.5. Drooker, Eric. 2007. *Flood! A Novel in Pictures*. Dark Horse. n.p.

are the same in both the extradiegetic and intradiegetic story. However, the metaleptic break is not the first time that the blue ink has been used. Toward the end of "Home," a smear of blue indicates the protagonist's disappearance (or, perhaps, disintegration; figure 5.5). In the context in which it first appears, the blue smear seems relatively innocuous. Considered in relation to the use of blue ink in the final chapter, however, it might similarly indicate a jump across narrative levels and cue the protagonist's transference in and out of his own drawings. Once we have experienced the final chapter's blue-dominated universe, a universe created by the cartoon-drawing protagonist, the first chapter with its blue smear begins to appear ambiguous and fantastic. Does the protagonist, for instance, get evicted from his apartment in the real world, or is that a fantasy of his, maybe even a story that he draws? Especially the violation of realistic codes of representation in the page-sized panel of the superhuman-sized protagonist, which follows upon the page on which the blue smear appears (figure 5.5), may indicate a crossing into a fantasy world when it is read in light of the book's third chapter. Thus, the blue smear points once more to the conclusion that *Flood!*'s narrative universe results almost entirely from the protagonist's processing of perceptual and emotional experience.

Delving further into the inherent ambiguity of wordless comics and its relation to focalization, our examination of *Flood!* demonstrates that a number of visual cues marking character focalization break ontological boundaries that separate the protagonist's external and internal worlds. The melding of narrative and ontological levels through a sustained character focalization transposes readers into the physical and emotional ambivalence of a fantasy world. In the following section, we discuss a different type of ambivalence that often pertains in wordless comics, examining how visual metaphors function to create an ambiguous focalization in Shaun Tan's *The Arrival*.

Visual Metaphor and the Problem of Deixis: Shaun Tan, *The Arrival*

In chapter 1, we introduced Manfred Jahn's seminal article "Windows of Focalization," in which Jahn describes the different activities of narrators and focalizers in terms of distinct optical perspectives on story events. Narrators are "'watchers' standing at the windows of the 'house of fiction,'" whose primary activity is "the contemplation of the 'spreading field, the human scene'—the story world, or diegesis" (1996: 251). A number of factors determine what these watchers see: the "shape of the window," the "view afforded by it," the "'instrument' used," but above all the watchers' own consciousness and its construction of reality (251). It is against this backdrop that the perspective of the focalizer comes into play. Jahn describes the focalizer as "a special story-internal character," who sees the story events "not, like a narrator, from a window 'perched aloft,' but from within the 'human scene' itself" (251–52). This character "metaphorically functions as a window" that "*mirrors the world for* these higher-level agents," for the narrator and narratee (252). Where Genette distinguished between zero, internal, and external focalization based on the degree of knowledge separating a narrator from the characters in the narrative world (1980; see chapter 1), and where Bal introduced a clear separation between the narrator, or "(linguistic, visual, cinematic) subject . . . which expresses itself in the language that constitutes the text," and the "focalizor," which is "an aspect of the story this narrator tells" (1997: 15, 18), Jahn revisits focalization by conceptualizing narrator and focal character as two distinct types of "window" through which the reader may imaginatively enter the textual world in two distinctive ways.

According to Jahn's model, a narratorial window is constituted through descriptive language providing a kind of disembodied, panoramic view onto the narrative world and events. By contrast, the window of focalization is anchored in a deictic center with a more embodied spatiotemporal origin (1996: 256, 257). In cognitive literary studies, the term "deictic center" describes a locus in the narrative world that readers use to orient and locate themselves in the process of meaning-making (Zubin and Hewitt). When readers immerse themselves in a story, they undertake a "deictic shift" that allows them to "see things virtually from the perspective of the character or narrator inside the text-world" (Stockwell 2002: 47). Jahn's distinction between a narratorial and a focalization window associates this immersive potential primarily with focalization, locating it inside the "human scene" of the narrative world, rather than "perched above" it. However, as we have seen in our analysis of *Berlin: City of Stones,* a deictic center may also be located outside of any character, affording an Olympic viewpoint that can be associated with the representational choices of narration as well as with the angle of focalization through which the narrative world comes to be experienced (see chapter 1).

In the final section of this chapter, we draw on Jahn's window model to analyze Shaun Tan's wordless comic *The Arrival* (2006). We argue that Jahn's distinction between narratorial windows and windows of focalization is both helpful and challenging. In the analysis of graphic narrative, focalization has to be associated with a deictic center that can, in principle, be situated either inside or outside of the diegesis and associated with a character or with a noncharacter narrator. However, as we indicated in chapter 1, comics often make it very difficult or even impossible for readers to ascertain where the deictic center of a story's experientiality lies. Indeed, our analyses suggest that deixis is often not optically marked, as in the *Berlin* love scene between Marthe and Kurt, with panels depicting an outside view of the two protagonists that is expressive of what the two feel like inside, but also of the scene's overall mood and atmosphere (see chapter 2). Focalization and deixis are here marked by an interplay between panels, and they reside between the two lovers. In *Deogratias*, the impersonal mode of narration and the deliberate withholding of crucial information impede readers from fully accessing the protagonist's first-person insight (see chapter 4). Deixis is also veiled through repeated switches between past and present, reality and metaphor that make it open to interpretation whether the central transformation scenes show Deogratias's self-understanding, indicate an external view of Deogratias (how other characters see him), or are expressive of an extradiegetic narrator's take on Deogratias. Determining whose aspectuality these sequences express and where their deixis originates is crucial to the process of interpretation, but it nonetheless remains out of reach.

Difficulties in determining deixis are exacerbated in wordless comics because they lack the semiotic resources for nondiegetic communication to ascertain the identity and moral orientation of a narrator or to pinpoint temporal, ontological, and epistemological relations between pictorial elements. In chapter 3, we considered the extensive use of wordless panels and sequences in David Small's *Stitches*, concluding that these often obscure deixis or locate it not within, but between characters and narrative agents. Whereas the repeated fetus scene switches between two possible deixes, with David focalizing the fetus but the fetus also refocalizing David, panel composites that splice together different characters transgress the borders between the body and its environment, between subjectivities, and between the human and the nonhuman. The repeated portrayal of David's sutured wound similarly questions the physical integrity of the self as a deictic center. In chapter 4, we showed how the juxtaposition of tentative portraits in *Maus* invites readers to compare different versions of events and to weigh alternative options for interpreting them. Both comics underscore a point we made in chapter 2: Experience in graphic narrative may derive from one or several characters, but it may also be located in between characters and have a social or intersubjective scope. It is thus unproductive to associate focalization too narrowly with the perspective and deixis of individual narrative agents.

The following analysis of Shaun Tan's *The Arrival* builds on these observations by considering how the book's unusual visual metaphors further contribute to and complicate our understanding of focalization and deixis in graphic narrative. In *The Arrival*, detailed pencil drawings systematically exploit a potential for indeterminacy, creating a defamiliarizing effect that relentlessly taxes the reader's understanding. From the start, it is unclear whether the narrative is set in the past, the present, or an imagined dystopian future (Farrell, Arizpe, and McAdam 199). The style of the drawings mimics the tone and detail of early photography, and the characters' clothes and behavior support the impression that the story is set in a late nineteenth- or early twentieth-century world. However, although *The Arrival*'s immigrant narrative is clearly based on iconic patterns of European immigration to the US in that time period (several panels rely heavily on well-known photographs of Ellis Island and its surroundings), the book's many surreal elements bear little or no relation to real-life immigrant experience. In the new world of *The Arrival*, not only the language but also the alphabet, food, modes of transportation, games that people play, pets, and even the earth, sky, and planets look and are initially experienced by our protagonist and by readers as utterly, disconcertingly strange.

From a large serpentlike creature looming behind town buildings to humongous one-eyed masked people populating the homelands of immigrants, *The Arrival* seamlessly couples the familiar and the unfamiliar. This intermingling renders it difficult to know if the extensive defamiliarization of ordinary things is meant to be understood on a metaphorical level that might, in turn, indicate character focalization. Should readers approach unnatural phenomena in an otherwise natural world as indicative of the disorientation that pervades the immigrant experience? Or are we to take them at face value, as is subtly suggested by the protagonist when he sketches his hometown, including the dragon tail, in order to explain his initial fear of a boy's dragonlike pet to a fellow immigrant? Is *The Arrival* set in a nonrealistic world or is it the immigrant's experience of that world that makes everything seem unfamiliar? This uncertainty is heightened by how unfamiliar elements often closely resemble aspects of the real world. The new world's extraordinary animals behave very much like common pets, the bizarre flying ships allow people to travel from one place to another, and the intricate, indecipherable clocks tell time. This creative visual expression for mundane details may be associated with the expressive capacity of the perception and emotional experience of its central character, with unfamiliar elements functioning as visual metaphors that reference experiences of fear, disorientation, and alienation. Wavering between a literal and a figurative reading, readers struggle to understand what they are meant to see, and this struggle mirrors the protagonist's own struggle for understanding.

The book's striking use of visual metaphor plays a crucial role in this process of estrangement. Besides prompting the consideration of multiple meanings, it also introduces an ambiguous deixis, which in turn unsettles readerly expectations regarding focalization. Although the story setting initially suggests an early twentieth-century petty bourgeois milieu, readers are soon confronted with surprising elements that demand an explanation, which is withheld by the comic's silent story. As the protagonist sets out on his journey toward a new land, he walks through the town streets with suitcase in hand alongside his wife and daughter. A large serpentine tail imaged spiraling in and out of the town's densely distributed buildings casts large shadows on the

FIGURE 5.6. Tan, Shaun. 2006. *The Arrival*. Hodder Children's Books. n.p.

buildings. The same animalistic detail is reproduced in the following chapter devoted to the man's first impressions and struggles in the foreign land. Having secured lodging, he opens his suitcase, but instead of portraying the individual items he carried with him, the panel shows the suitcase containing a small, realistic replica of the kitchen table he left behind. His wife and daughter sit at the table, and behind them, framed by the window, is the perplexing dragon tail (figure 5.6).

Larger than the other panels and located in the central row, the panel is set apart from the others making up the page. Eight smaller panels tracing the protagonist's movements in his new home—climbing the stairs to his new bedroom, shooing away his pet, opening the suitcase, taking out the carefully packaged family photograph and nailing it to the wall—encircle the large panel, drawing a contrast that suggests a figurative level of meaning. Readers are thus invited to explore various plausible meanings the panel can have within the narrative universe. Since the panel (and the page) brings the protagonist and the suitcase together, readers are prone to ask what intimate, personal thoughts of the protagonist the suitcase with the familiar table and serpent in it might represent. Does the serpent reflect the character's emotional engagement with the memory of his hometown? Is it indicative of a menace that led him to leave his homeland and family? In other words, is it a metaphor for some kind of oppression he and his family were subjected to? Or does the serpent represent a concrete reality of his homeland, especially given that throughout *The Arrival* readers are often thrust into a highly unfamiliar and somewhat unrealistic universe?

The large panel orchestrates a metaphoric transfer that raises up to consideration not only these questions but also the alternative meanings they obtain for the protagonist. The panel's merging of two scenes, the protagonist's situation in the new world and the scene at the kitchen table in his homeland, cues a blended what it's like that includes experiences in the new world, but tinges them with memories of the old world. Thus, the panel marks a shift in focalization. Its meaning stands in contrast to the panels that frame it, which depict not an imagined because remembered reality, but rather what actually unfolds within the man's apartment and what the suitcase actually holds. The shift in visual vocabulary signals that unlike the mimetic images encircling it, the suitcase panel introduces readers to the protagonist's aspectual window within the diegesis, which here is tinged with memory and nostalgia. In this instance, Jahn's distinction is helpful because focalization is associated with a deictic center situated inside the narrative world.

It is less productive, however, when the ontological and epistemological status of *The Arrival*'s unrealistic elements cannot be determined with certainty, creating ambiguity about the narrative's deictic center, or when the narrative does not so much shift "from one focalization window to another," as Jahn would have it (1996: 257), but rather conflates a narratorial with a character-bound focalization. Several pages after the suitcase panel, the protagonist presents a fellow immigrant with a drawing of his hometown, complete with the serpentine tail towering over the city's rooftops. Upon seeing the drawing, the fellow immigrant recalls the burning of his own hometown. The two-page layout showing the recollected events leading up to his departure depicts the town in flames, being invaded by gigantic one-eyed people that tower over the city buildings, armed with large suction devices that suck up citizens who are running in the street (figure 5.7). Like the serpentine tail, the strangeness of these supersized beings invites a metaphoric interpretation. Yet the overall unfamiliarity of the narrative world may also support a literal understanding. This choice between a metaphoric and a literal reading is crucial for identifying focalization in *The Arrival*. If the images are metaphorical, they indicate a character-bound focalization that adds mental complexity to the narrative by infusing everything that is shown with the immigrant's what it's like. If, how-

FIGURE 5.7. Tan, Shaun. 2006. *The Arrival*.
Hodder Children's Books. n.p.

ever, they participate in a mimetic code, readers would no longer be asked to engage with the what it's like of characters, but rather to take what they see at face value. If the focalization of the scene has its origin in a narratorial deictic center, readers would thus be distanced from the emotional thrust of the telling, imagining the immigrant experience that is at the heart of *The Arrival* more as a historical phenomenon than a personal one. Finally, the images may also represent what the blond man remembers feeling, as imagined by the protagonist who listens to his story, and thus mark a tangled, intersubjective focalization in which the stories and emotions of the protagonist and the blond man mingle.

Each of these readings—in terms of internal focalization, external focalization, or intersubjective focalization—can be supported by arguments. The metaphorical dimension of the blond man's story sticks out from other immigration tales in *The Arrival* and suggests that this story has a special status within the narrative structure. In another embedded story, a young Asian woman relates how she was forced to work behind locked doors in her homeland, feeding coal into smoky ovens and sweeping out chimneys. A series of drawn black-and-white photographs that portray the girl in different weather conditions and laboring among other girls until the day she escapes relate her memory of that time. In these images, nothing is disproportionately strange. People and buildings are normally sized, and the coal-burning ovens appear realistic, as does the train on which the girl escapes. The final immigrant story of *The Arrival*, told by an elderly man whom the protagonist meets while working in a factory, is also free of unrealistic elements. Experiences of war, mutilation, and devastation are presented through straightforward images portraying soldiers running, corpses in the streets, and war-torn towns. As in the Asian woman's tale, drawn photographs collated to worn pages of what appears to be a photo album relate the old man's recollections. The images are based on well-known photographs of World War I, and nothing in them points to the old man's aspectuality. The choice of photography, a medium that is conventionally understood to be more referentially sound than cartooning, further highlights the adherence to a realistic code of expression that characterizes these two immigration narratives.

The visual contrast between these two photographically rendered immigrant stories and the blond man's story, which is related through a series of highly shaded pencil drawings, strongly suggests that the blond man's narrative is filtered through his heightened emotional engagement. The panels of his story are littered with extraordinary elements. Their special status is also announced by a thick black frame. The panel leading into the blond man's tale further suggests that readers are here invited into the blond immigrant's subjective experience (figure 5.8). It contains a close-up view of the man's eye with reflected flames running across his pupil and clearly functions as a point-of-view image, which strongly suggests a character-bound focalization. Other visual features of this sequence, however, suggest a narratorial focalization. The blond immigrant's story is presented in the same realistic pencil drawing style and color scheme that is used in *The Arrival*'s main storyline. The pages are tightly bordered, and large gutters separate panels that have dull borders and are arranged in neat rows. The embedded world includes a recognizable mix of familiar and unfamiliar elements, raising the possibility that perhaps the blond man simply comes from a country that is just as unfamiliar to readers as the new world he migrated to.

FIGURE 5.8. Tan, Shaun. 2006. *The Arrival*.
Hodder Children's Books. n.p.

Finally, the visual similarity of the blond man's story with the main storyline may also suggest that the embedded story is not focalized by the blond man, but by the protagonist: He, and not the story's intradiegetic narrator, provides the window into this narrative world. Several visual features suggest that the protagonist filters the story he hears. The two-page establishing shot technique is used numerous times before and after the blond immigrant's story to mark the protagonist's emotionally charged experiences. Given the similarity of their immigration experience—both men are married, have a young child, and left their cities due to an insurmountable threat—this instance of visual braiding may indicate the protagonist's understanding of his fellow immigrant's story. The oversized one-eyed beings and the large towering blocks may thus reflect the protagonist's choice of symbolism for the fear and hopelessness that made both men feel small and powerless. Other features in the blond man's story also echo the protagonist's experience. The regular-sized panel of the blond immigrant's hand clutched tightly in that of his wife recalls a similar close-up panel of the protagonist holding his wife's hand. In addition, the closing panel of the blond man's story is of the same cloudy sky over a lone boat in a large expanse of water used to portray the protagonist's journey across the ocean.

The context in which the blond man tells his story gives further support to this third reading in terms of an intersubjective focalization. The sharing of their immigration stories is followed by the consolidation of their friendship in the present. Although other immigrants have shown kindness toward the protagonist, the blond man is the first to befriend him, inviting him to his home to share a meal with his family. The size and style of the full-page panel depicting this dinner recall the one at the beginning of *The Arrival* that shows the protagonist taking leave of his wife, their hands intertwined on his suitcase as it rests on the family's dinner table. The table itself and the chairs around it are identical in both scenes. But more than that, the dinner scene with the blond man's family also foreshadows the first dinner in the new world that the protagonist shares with his own wife and daughter, who join him toward the end of *The Arrival*. In both, family members are seated in the same places, and pets play and eat in the same place. This foreshadowing suggests that the blond immigrant's success in integrating into the new world sets the mark for the protagonist's aspirations, which he eventually attains.

In this reading, what is imaged in the blond man's story reflects not what the blond man experienced, but rather what the protagonist felt the man experienced as it intersects with his own past experiences and current desires. This would, in turn, suggest that the protagonist's perspective is at once personal and general, reflecting his private experience and the experience of many immigrants, a point Shaun Tan draws attention to (2010: 10; 2011: 6). Ultimately, the effect is that of two simultaneously subjectivized perspectives that are not entirely subjective. The blond immigrant's story resonates so closely with that of the protagonist, their stories overlap in such significant ways, that a definitive answer to the question of where the deictic center lies is impossible to reach. Together with the ambivalent use of visual metaphor, it is this ambiguity surrounding deixis that pulls readers of *The Arrival* into the personal, shared, and common immigrant experience of confusion, anxiety, and hope.

•

Wordless comics often invoke a fantastic poetics to create disorienting reading effects. Their purely visual aspect can make it difficult or impossible for readers to pinpoint deixis or decide between conflicting readings of the same panels or sequence. The depiction of unstable narrative worlds and the use of unusual visual metaphors and of narrative metalepses systematically blur the boundaries between realistic codes of representation and distorted depictions of the what it's like of characters, between narrative levels and emotional states. An intensification of focalization in *House*, *Flood!*, and *The Arrival* communicates the characters' emotional life and asks readers to engage in story events through this emotional life. At the same time, key passages in these wordless comics also obscure the distinction between character-bound and narratorial focalization. By creating ambiguity about the deictic center, these passages engage readers who have to weigh the plausibility, and the consequences, of different kinds of perspective-taking against each other. They thus invite emotionally rich and cognitively interesting readings. The following, final chapter of our study extends the inquiry into the cognitive challenges of focalization by analyzing two particularly complex metafictional graphic narratives in order to question whether the often playful ambiguity of comics storytelling helps or hinders readerly immersion and empathy.

CHAPTER 6

Metafictionality

Comic critics often draw attention to the comic form's innate self-consciousness.[1] Many of our analyses in this book have explored how narratorial and stylistic choices expose a growing awareness of graphic narrative's potential to grant readers access to different perspectives. As we pointed out in chapter 4, Art Spiegelman's *Maus*, one of the earliest graphic narratives to enter the mainstream book market, builds a reflection on its own mediality into its form by including many scenes in which Artie ponders how to draw a person or scene, while alternative options are introduced and, sometimes, rejected. These instances of hesitation provide readers with crucial access to Artie's mind. They also highlight how comics style is always expressive of a specific viewpoint, and how it is a highly individual way of perceiving, processing, and judging the world.

In this final chapter, we focus on the implications that ambitious self-referential storytelling has for readers' understanding of focalization cues. More than anything, scenes like the cat-mouse hesitation in Spiegelman's *Maus* serve to expose the ambivalence that inheres in the necessary, yet inevitably restricting, world filtering of focalization. They often also contain powerful focalization markers, especially when metafictional scenes and devices draw

---

1. See Chute (2008: 457); Gardner (2008: 6); O'Neill (99); Round; Thon (73); Verano (326); Versaci (12); and Wolk (118). Also see Schmitz-Emans, who argues that the auto-referentiality of comics establishes comics as art.

attention to visual construction or world building. Whereas wordless comics rely on self-reflexive strategies such as metalepses, visual metaphors, and braiding to create ambiguity and engage readers in acts of perspective-taking (chapter 5), graphic memoirs draw notice to the creation process through narrators and graphiators who address subjectivity by reflecting on their own coming into being as artists (chapter 3).[2] In this chapter, we argue that graphic narrative's self-reflexivity needs to be considered in tandem with the increasingly sophisticated forms of postmodern reflexivity that were developing across media during the same time Art Spiegelman was working on *Maus*. As early as 1984, Patricia Waugh posited metafiction or "self-conscious fiction" as an important contemporary trend, while Linda Hutcheon described postmodernism as an explicitly self-reflexive form of cultural practice (1988, 1991, 2002). Since then, Werner Wolf (1992, 2004, 2005) and other narratologists have clarified how forms of metafictional commentary (Scholes), metanarrative self-reference (Kukkonen 2011b), metaleptic transgression (Genette 2004; Kukkonen 2011b; Kukkonen and Klimek; Pier and Schaeffer), intermedial allusion (Elleström), and transmediality (Mittell 294–318) proliferate in postmodernist literature, art, and media. The self-reflexivity of comics storytelling is thus part of a larger, transgeneric and transmedial trend (Wolf 2007).

To account for the variety and complexity of self-referential operations, a detailed vocabulary has developed around the prefix "meta-." In the context of this study, we designate as "metafictional" such comics that reflect back on their own fictionality, as "metanarrative" those that represent the act of verbal or graphic enunciation in a self-aware manner, and as "metaleptic" comics that cross between worlds by translocating or addressing authors, narrators, characters, or readers. These closely related terms sketch out a range of stronger and weaker options for self-reflexive narration that serves as a context to our investigation of focalization markers and the options these offer for involved readings in anti-illusionistic narratives.

The two graphic narratives that we focus on in this chapter—David Mazzucchelli's *Asterios Polyp* (2009) and Craig Thompson's *Habibi* (2011)—fall somewhere between the weaker metafictional and the stronger metaleptic option. Both are self-conscious fictions noteworthy for their detailed and sustained engagement with narrative world making, with the mediation of character experience, and with the potential of graphic narrative to draw readers into these experiences. Considered within the context of an inquiry into focalization in graphic narrative, the metafictional dimension of these books

---

2. Several critics posit self-reflexivity as integral to the graphic memoir genre, including Baetens; Groensteen (1990); and I. Williams (356).

might appear as an anti-illusionistic stratagem that, while highlighting the creation of narrative style and the constructedness of a novel's experientiality, may hinder readerly investment in the storyworld. After all, metafiction and its stronger cousin, metalepsis, are often considered to "[disrupt] the readers' imagining the fictional world and their immersion in it" (Kukkonen 2011c: 10). As we explained in chapter 4, however, distancing devices and the disruption of identification often lead to a detailed engagement in which readers try out different, even contradictory perspectives and position themselves in the face of such contradictions (see Nünning).

In this chapter, we extend our argument by explaining how the self-conscious doubling of a narrative that is its own meta-commentary encourages readers to reflect on their own engagement with graphic narrative, contributing to a cognitively rich reading because it renders comics legible on several levels simultaneously. Thus, *Asterios Polyp* is both a moving story of love and loss and a cunning play with the comic book's potential to evoke what it's like through stylistic choice. And *Habibi*, while abounding in reflection on its own creation and fictionality, is also an engagement with orientalism, a theological commentary on shared religious heritages, and an aesthetic work of eco-criticism. Both comics offer fertile ground for determining how focalization contributes to building narrative worlds, informing readers about them, and guiding the interpretation of those narrative worlds.

World Building and Destruction: David Mazzucchelli, *Asterios Polyp*

A thunderstorm builds over a city. Large purple clouds release a bolt of lightning, which dramatically bisects a blue and purple full-page panel of rain. The lightning hits one specific building, small and insignificant when seen from the panel's extravagantly elevated "eye of God" perspective. A second double page in the same blue and purple color scheme zooms in on a messy apartment full of unwashed laundry, half-empty takeout cartons, and stacked overdraft notices. Readers have no sooner discovered that the bed talk emerging from the back of the apartment actually comes from a video tape that is being watched by an unshaven man opening and shutting a metal lighter than the apartment building is hit by a huge purple "KLAPP!" of lightning. As this portentous event awakens the man from his stupor, the narrative's color scheme changes. The fire that breaks out seems to infect the panels on the next two pages, colored in purple and yellow, while the man races around his apartment, grabbing the Zippo, a wristwatch, and a Swiss army knife. Finally, just as the man escapes from the burning building, the yellow fire devours his entire apartment, including what we now see is an extensive collection of date-labeled VHS cassettes. Thus, the very first chapter of *Asterios Polyp* sees the protagonist Asterios's world and life to date destroyed at the same time as it introduces readers to him.

With this conflation of world creation and destruction, and with the subtle change in color scheme, *Asterios Polyp* reflects from the start on the questions that interest us in this study: the role that a character's perception plays in granting readers access to narrative worlds and the relation between focalization, narration, and authorship. Its playful postmodernist narrative frequently makes explicit reference to the affordances of graphic narrative and to how stylistic choices can cue a particular character's what it's like. Verbally and visually, attention is drawn to how characters experience and configure the narrative world differently, as well as to the way individual experiences may influence each other. The narrative's self-reflexivity forces us to think through how reading is impacted when a character's focalization combines with the mediation of a potentially unreliable narrator. Ignazio, the character narrator of *Asterios Polyp*, died at birth, a narrative detail that prompts us to ask how he can be narrating the events of the story. Ignazio confirms the doubts of readers early in the narrative by admitting, "If it were possible for me to narrate this story, I'd begin here." At the same time that we are led to doubt Ignazio, however, we cannot help but place our trust in him, since, as *Asterios Polyp* repeatedly reminds readers, a fictional world does not exist outside of its presentation. Indeed, Ignazio's radically constructivist thesis—"What if reality (as perceived) were simply an extension of the self?"—makes it questionable whether the novel itself believes in the actuality of its presented world outside of the different perceptual constructions associated with its focal characters and in relation to the narrative mediation that embeds them.

At the same time, different ways of filtering the world may be negotiated both between characters and vis-à-vis a narratorial consciousness. This idea is foregrounded in the final section of *Asterios Polyp*, which marks the possibility of an intersubjectively integrated worldview through a nuanced color scheme. While earlier sections of the book employ distinct color schemes to cue the what it's like of individual characters, the rich color palette at the end highlights the interdependence of characters' experientialities over and against the world filtering of isolated minds. Thus, while making no strong claims about truth and reality, *Asterios Polyp* indicates that a compromise or consensus between different world versions can be reached from which a shared world may be successfully built. As in many postmodernist texts, that shared worldview falls to readers to create.

When describing *Asterios Polyp* as a postmodernist comic, we refer to Linda Hutcheon's definition of postmodernist fiction as an "aesthetic practice" (1988: ix) that takes "the form of self-conscious, self-contradictory, self-undermining statement" (2002: 1). According to Brian McHale (1987), postmodernism is premised on an ontological "dominant," as opposed to the epistemological dominant of modernism. Typically postmodernist questions "bear either on the ontology of the literary text itself or on the ontology of the world it projects, for instance: What is a world?; What kinds of world are there, how are they constituted, and how do they differ?; What happens when different kinds of worlds are placed in confrontation, or when boundaries between worlds are violated?" (10). We argue that the initial and final pages of *Asterios Polyp*, as well as other passages in the comic that play the capacity to create a rounded storyworld and its simultaneous destruction off against each other, accentuate such an ontological dominant. However, we also show that the foregrounding of ontological concerns does not mean that focalization, and thus epistemology, becomes negligible. On the contrary: By tying the exploration of what constitutes *Asterios Polyp*'s fictional world to questions about the narrator's existence and grasp of the world, the narrative frequently engages the possibilities and shortcomings of external and internal modes of focalization.

In our analysis, we explore this connection in three steps. First, we explain how color is used in *Asterios Polyp* to mark the internal focalization of different characters. We then turn our attention to style and its use as a metacommentary on the comics form, which is often associated with the narrator, Ignazio. Given that Ignazio is a dead narrator, it is difficult to categorize his focalization as either internal or external. In the final step of our analysis, we investigate the complications that the use of a dead narrator introduces to the analysis of focalization.

Beyond Pink and Purple

In *Asterios Polyp*, readers are given access to multiple versions of and perspectives on events. The graphic novel is narrated on two temporal levels, one focusing on Asterios's life in Apogee, where he moves after his apartment burned down, the other detailing his former life in New York through a series of extended flashbacks. Readers learn that Asterios was a professor of architecture who met his wife, sculpture artist and art professor Hana Sonnenschein, at a faculty party. The two shared a flashy life among the New York art scene until Asterios's habit of not listening to his wife drove her into a close collabo-

FIGURE 6.1. Mazzucchelli, David. 2009. *Asterios Polyp*. Pantheon. n.p.

ration with the choreographer Willy Ilium who, unlike Asterios, showered her with attention and praise.

Asterios Polyp makes extensive use of internal focalization, contrasting different takes on events by associating individual characters and their what it's like with specific color schemes. Color and style indicate a being-in-the-world that involves a character's entire body, cognition, and perception. But color and style are also used as metanarrative strategies that comment on how characters experience their world and on how the comics form constructs such experiences. By mixing distinct color schemes when characters interact, the graphic novel makes the point that individual ways of being-in-the-world do not exist in isolation from each other (figure 6.1). It is therefore through the reduction of the perspectives of characters and of the narrator to similar building blocks that a balance is finally achieved between the perspectives of Asterios; his wife, Hana; his Apogee landlady, Ursula; and his twin brother, the narrator Ignazio.

Six color schemes can be distinguished in *Asterios Polyp* (see Duncan). (1) The initial blue and purple scheme marks Asterios's internal focalization. It recurs in later parts of the book to highlight Asterios's what it's like, especially whenever he clashes with Hana or feels isolated from her. (2) Pink and magenta constitute Hana's color scheme. That these two central color schemes derive from the "typical" boy and girl colors for Western infant clothing indicates a primordially male and female aspectuality associated with Asterios and Hana. (3) Both schemes combine in a muted blue, purple, and red scheme that indicates Asterios and Hana's shared memories of happy moments, such as their initial romance and their visit to the composer Kalvin Kohoutek. The combination of these colors announces that Asterios and Hana participate equally in this version of events, whereas split panels in bright blue and in magenta, such as those summarizing Asterios's string of short-term relationships prior to meeting Hana, express a disjunction between Asterios's and Hana's what it's like.

(4) The blue/purple and magenta range clashes sharply with a bright yellow and purple scheme that characterizes Asterios's life in Apogee. Here, it seems that Asterios contributes the purple, while the yellow is associated with his landlady, Ursula. Although not a trained artist like Hana or Asterios, Ursula shares their creative passion for arranging spaces—an important theme through which the novel's spatial layout is reflected within the narrative world. That Ursula's overturned chairs and tables are not at all practical points toward the playful autonomous aesthetic upon which the narrative of *Asterios Polyp* is built. (5) A similar yellow and faded purple color scheme is used in the surreal dream episodes that open five of the book's chapters and that tell of a series of imagined encounters between Asterios and his dead twin, Ignazio. In these, Asterios and Ignazio switch roles, and alternative life paths are imagined. The bright yellow that dominates both the Apogee storyline and the dream episodes, as well as the fact that the dream episodes invariably lead into the Apogee narrative, suggest that it is here that the relation between the twins is resolved and different aspects of Asterios's identity are negotiated.

(6) The addition of a yellow color to Asterios's palette enables the rich, varied color scheme of the final section where Asterios returns to Hana. This color scheme includes a warm red, brown, beige, and shades of green, as well as dark purple, which is Asterios's color and the color of the lines on which all drawings and lettering are based across the six color schemes. The varied color scheme suggests that Asterios has finally achieved a more socially committed way of seeing. In the novel's final scene, Asterios and Hana engage in dialogue and in constructing a shared story; rather than constantly interrupting each other, their speech balloons begin to intertwine.

Color serves as the most important and most noticeable focalization marker in *Asterios Polyp*. It exposes, reinforces, and elaborates how characters configure reality, demarcating which character's subjective viewpoint is adopted and distinguishing between a character's processing of present reality and that of a recollected past. Color also expresses changes in perception and the learning process through which Asterios comes to relate to a variety of ways of seeing the world. While the six color schemes serve an important function for orienting readers, they do not constitute static semiotic codes. Rather, they set in motion dynamic interactions between characters. Often, the novel's chapters are organized around shifts in color scheme. In the very first chapter, there is a shift between blue/purple and then purple/yellow (very bright colors), while the sixth chapter, which introduces Hana to readers, switches dramatically from blue/purple to pink/magenta. Finally, it is not surprising that in a book that deals so directly with vision and with Asterios's restricted view of the world, the purple and yellow color scheme is intensified when Asterios's present reality intersects with the clairvoyant Ursula. In the following section, we consider the role of style to further explore the connection between individual and shared forms of focalization.

Style and Rhetoric

"What if reality (as perceived) were simply an extension of the self?" With this loaded question, the narrator opens the fourth chapter of *Asterios Polyp*, continuing: "Wouldn't that color the way each individual experienced the world?" The reference to color is a rhetorical one: As the graphic novel amply shows, the ways in which individuals experience the world are indeed colored. But that does not mean that reality is an extension of the self. An important rhetorical goal of the narrative consists in refuting such a solipsistic worldview and replacing it with a softer version of constructivism by showing how world making always occurs in the context of, and in reference to, the reality versions of others.

The use of color schemes and their successful integration provide important insight into this implicit theory of experience by illustrating how although we live in a shared reality, this reality possesses not only radically different qualia for each one of us, but also varying qualia according to our situation in life and the influence that others have on us. A good life, however, is characterized by intersubjective negotiation—through mutually respectful discussion, shared memories, and emotional closeness—resulting in a shared or at least overlapping set of qualia between loved ones. In terms of focalization, the novel proceeds from a radically individualistic filtering of the world toward a more collective or shared focalization.

The fourth chapter provides an entry point into this process by pairing Ignazio's claims with fifteen characters (including a dog) walking around the campus where Asterios teaches, each drawn according to different degrees

FIGURE 6.2. Mazzucchelli, David. 2009. *Asterios Polyp*. Pantheon. n.p.

of abstraction, angularity, and clarity to indicate the subjective coloring of reality. As Ignazio explains two pages later, this coloring does not occur in isolation from the experiencing of others: "Maybe one person's construction of the world could influence someone else's. You would have to imagine that these constructions, whatever their origins, are not immutable" (figure 6.2).

The page portrays Asterios as an artist's wooden figure lecturing to a group of students. While half of them are depicted in the same wooden-figure style as Asterios, the other half are represented through a mix of graphic styles in varying degrees of abstraction. At this point in the narrative, style evokes the coming together of how each student experiences the world or, as Ignazio describes it, of individual constructions of the world. Since they are visible to others (including the reader), the different styles may also be taken to indicate the effect that someone's what it's like has on how others perceive him or her.

Besides the attention drawn to color, this focus on stylistic choice provides a second metanarrative feature of *Asterios Polyp*. It is already signaled by the fourth chapter's title vignette, which shows an apple drawn in sixteen styles in a four-by-four grid. The use of the grid relates the concern with viewing the world according to different constructive principles—which is a question of focalization—to the book's narrative organization by way of frames and panels. It prompts us to ask how the spatial organization of comics narrative and the stylistic choices underlying this organization impact visions of the world.

Two different approaches to form and space and their relation to subjective experience are vividly expressed through Asterios's and Hana's interior decoration tastes. Hana's studio is littered with huge, irregularly shaped metal sculptures, tools, and cardboard boxes, while Asterios's living room is neatly furnished in a strictly rectangular, minimalist style. The themes of building, living, and the combination of living arrangements that make up a large portion of Asterios and Hana's relationship narrative as well as the narrative present of Asterios's life in Apogee are further explored in a metanarrative sequence in which Asterios, Hana, and Willy Ilium walk through the chaotic "bohegeois" setup of the composer Kalvin Kohoutek. As they do so, a series of interlocking panels provide a focusing device for individual aspectualities and how they may (or may not) combine (figure 6.3). Where previous panels had rendered Kohoutek's apartment in muted blues, pinks, and purples, the interlocking sequence takes these color schemes apart: Asterios's panel has a blue base and pink/purple foreground, while Hana inverts this scheme through a pink background and blue foreground. Both panels interlock with a third one, showing Kalvin Kohoutek, who is at the center of these divergent aspectualities. That both Asterios and Hana are listening to Kohoutek indicates a mode of engagement, as does the complementarity of their color schemes, even though their panels do not intersect with each other directly.

The composer Kohoutek offers a musical metaphor for such a balance between individual and shared forms of perception when he explains that "in a cacophony of information, each listener, by focusing on certain tones and phrases, can become an active participant in creating a unique, unique poly-

FIGURE 6.3. Mazzucchelli, David. 2009. *Asterios Polyp*. Pantheon. n.p.

phonic experience." The ideal of a shared experience is offset by Willy Ilium's aspectuality. Although his panel intersects with Kohoutek's body, it avoids his head to indicate that Willy is not listening, but rather fantasizing about the food that Kohoutek is not offering ("A scone? Some petits fours?"). Willy's grayish-purple color scheme, which does not integrate the kind of contrasts constitutive of Asterios's and Hana's panels, also marks his failure to engage with others. However, that a corner of Asterios's panel intersects with Willy's suggests some reticence on Asterios's part to engage with Hana's qualia, which eventually leads to their separation. Against the narrator's claim that reality is an extension of the self, many sequences in *Asterios Polyp* foreground the need for a socially committed way of seeing the world. The contrast between two distinct drawing styles—illustrating two sets of assumptions about the world filtering of human minds—plays a crucial role in this foregrounding. Regular panels drawn in a *ligne claire* style with strong outlines, simplified physical features, and flat surfaces establish a background of expectation against which drawing styles that emphasize the constructedness of images stand out. Following Thierry Groensteen's terminology, these two styles may be said to set up a "simple" or "elaborated rhetoric," on the one hand, and a "neo-baroque" rhetoric on the other (2013: 46–47). By linking different graphic styles to rhetorical communication, Groensteen draws attention to how style in comics impacts readers' reception of the narrative world by setting the conditions for immersive or for nonimmersive readings. While practiced readers are conditioned to regard simple comics rhetoric as an unobtrusive narrative vehicle that provides easy access to the narrative world and thereby furthers illusionistic readings, the more playful neobaroque rhetoric that accords readers greater liberty breaks with clarity and legibility (46–47).

In *Asterios Polyp*, a simple rhetoric provides the main narrative vehicle for Asterios's and Hana's love story, Asterios's flight to Apogee, and his reunion with Hana. Within that base rhetoric, isolated instances of a neobaroque rhetoric deliver a meta-commentary on how the story is told by reflecting on narratorial mediation and pointing to possible, but discarded, alternative pathways. This deviating style signals how drawings, including those in a "simple" cartooning style, are always constructed and emerge out of a wide choice of how things can be experienced. Together with color, style is used in *Asterios Polyp* to engage in an interplay between individual and shared forms of focalization to signal the mental growth of some of its characters, especially its protagonist Asterios, toward a social engagement with the world. The graphic narrative makes use of different cartooning styles to mark the focalization of its main characters and of the character narrator Ignazio, who often comments on different ways of seeing the world. In the following section, we focus on the role that this unusual dead narrator plays in the creation of the narrative world and in embedding focalization.

An Unnatural Narrator

From the start, there is something unsettling about the narrator of *Asterios Polyp*. An as-yet-nameless voice introduces the protagonist, specifying: "If it were possible for me to narrate this story, I'd begin here. This is Asterios Polyp. Right now, he's watching his home burn up. Today—coincidentally—also happens to be his fiftieth birthday." The hypothetical mode at the narrative's very beginning invites readers to ask who this mysterious narrator is. Read alongside the book's sustained shifts between graphic styles and color schemes, the hypothetical "If it were possible . . ." comments on the artifice of fictional graphic narrative in a playful postmodern fashion by simultaneously claiming and denying that the narrator is indeed telling the tale.

Ignazio is a character narrator whose voice is rich in ironic nuance and emotion, infusing the narrative with a strong sense of his personality. At the same time, he is able to narrate from an exalted, omniscient position that is not commonly available to character narrators, reporting on the thought processes and behavioral patterns of Asterios and Hana without ever occupying the same space as they do. This ambiguous construction exploits the contradictory possibilities offered by the figure of the dead narrator, who is difficult to describe through narrative typologies and who also offers the potential to embed character focalization and thus give access to the thoughts and feelings of others in ways that are not open to living character narrators. Alice Bennett, who has studied dead narrators in literary fiction in detail, calls the dead narrator a loaded narrative technique since it

> has the potential to overturn every category used to talk about the narrator: from the distinction between hetero- and homodiegetic narrators and the concomitant association of extradiegetic-heterodiegetic narrators with an extended knowledge, to any concept that the narrator might be a person, even an imaginary one. Equally, dead narrators make some assault on virtually every critical model of the phenomenon of narratorial omniscience. (117)

In practice, the dead narrator offers a number of possibilities that make him attractive to experimental postmodernist writing. He is an "impossible speaker" who breaks "the 'mimetic contract' that had governed conventional fiction for centuries" (Richardson 5, 1). He can combine otherwise incompatible aspects such as omniscience with a personal voice and history, or possess an "unnatural" power over the narrative act that breaks through logical and ontological boundaries. Writers like the German novelist Georg Klein have employed dead narrators as powerful agents of metaleptic narrative (S. Horstkotte 2018). In *Asterios Polyp,* however, the dead narrator's hold both on the act of narration and on the narrative world that it brings forth is more ambivalent, as is already indicated by the fact that the book ends with a renewed event of possible world destruction when an asteroid races toward the cabin where Asterios and Hana have just reunited.

Just as the world that Ignazio brings into being is limited to the length of the story he tells, his hold over the thoughts and perception of characters is also limited, principally because he is never fully differentiated from his twin brother, Asterios. In fact, Ignazio's independence from Asterios decreases over the course of the novel until his extradiegetic commentary disappears altogether. He never comments on events in the present, but restricts his metanarrative commentary to the flashbacks detailing Asterios's past. Although this may indicate a limited form of narratorial knowledge and a compromised grasp of the thoughts and actions of characters, Ignazio exerts some influence on the narrative world and provides Asterios with crucial information about himself.

This revealing function comes to the fore in the five dream sequences that punctuate Asterios's stay in Apogee and reflect on the relationship between Ignazio and Asterios. Each portrays surprising meetings between the adult brothers in unexpected places—a ruined Greek temple, a roaring river, the Vietnam memorial wall in Washington, a posh architect's office, and a mechanic's shop. Their codependence and limited individuation in relation to each other characterizes these meetings. In the second dream episode, for instance, Asterios and Ignazio are conjoined twins in a rowing boat. As one body with two heads, the brothers are determined to maneuver the boat through rough waters. Their rowing, which requires a left-handed Asterios to relinquish control of the body's right hand to Ignazio so that they can stop going around in circles, seems to parallel Asterios's life trajectory, ending just as the brothers are about to be swallowed by a giant wave. Asterios's journey of self-discovery, too, ends with his car spinning in circles in the snow as he struggles through a snowstorm toward Hana's cabin. But the boat sequence also indicates a way out of this pattern: To regain a sense of balance, Asterios must break the circle of his self-centered, destructive behavior and become attentive to others and their differing worldviews.

While Asterios and Ignazio here appear as two aspects of the same person, other dream sequences indicate that Ignazio serves as a counterfactual imagination of unrealized alternative life paths Asterios could have taken. Thus, the fourth dream sequence portrays Asterios in the casual mechanic attire he wears in Apogee as he visits world-renowned architect Ignazio in his pristine office inside a Guggenheim-style building. After telling Asterios about his upcoming engagements, Ignazio lights a cigarette with the same lighter Asterios was holding at the beginning of the graphic novel, while admitting that he owes all of his success to Asterios. In reply to Asterios's surprise, Ignazio responds, "You made me what I am today," an assertion that echoes back to Asterios's wondering aloud to Hana whether or not he is living his dead twin's life.

The brothers' role-switching continues in the ensuing conversation when Ignazio tells his life story, which readers know to be Asterios's. Ignazio repeats the assertion that "reality as I perceived it was simply an extension of myself," melding that insight into Asterios's voice when Ignazio's speech balloons take on the shape of those used by Asterios throughout the narrative. The scene culminates with Asterios yelling at his brother to "stop it" and, when Ignazio does not listen, picking up a crowbar and bludgeoning his brother. Not only does this mark the last time we see or hear Ignazio, but it also impacts the color scheme, which becomes much more rich and diversified after this point. Taken together, these two changes may suggest the disintegration of Ignazio's overt narrative voice and the adoption of Asterios's perspective by a covert narrator. In light of the dream sequences, however, Ignazio might also be taken as a projection or alter ego of Asterios. His disappearance from the narrative would then signal a reintegration of two sides of Asterios's personality, or else a kind of making peace with the past in order to find a way into the future and a new life with Hana.

After Ignazio's disappearance, the final section of *Asterios Polyp* envisages a shared world that emerges out of mutually embedding acts of focalization—the coming together of pink and purple—with no unified narrative authority to ground it. Just as *Asterios Polyp* can be read as a graphic novel about fiction and its world-building potential, it can also serve as a metafocal book that asks readers to consider how the processing of individual minds colors the world around them, or whether that processing brings into being entirely separate worlds. *Asterios Polyp* concludes that while characters color the fictional world with their own aspectualities, these may be negotiated in a shared world. It shows that a postmodernist plurality of worlds is negotiable, and this may be taken as an invitation to collaborate in the creation of a new world.

While the encoding of world experiencing is a matter of explicit concern in *Asterios Polyp*, it always takes place under the proviso that the world experienced is an artificial one, created by an ambiguous dead narrator with only a tenuous hold on the narrative and a hypothetical voice. This means that focalization, too, occurs under an ontological dominant in *Asterios Polyp*. However, how the narrative confronts the what it's like of Asterios and Hana with each other, with the aspectuality of other characters, and with the narrator's claims about the world is itself a strong statement about the status of focalization within it. While relativizing each individual claim on the world, the narrative leads from a radically fractured narration to a level of stylistic integration that accommodates some, if not all of the versions. In a significant way, then, *Asterios Polyp* uses a self-conscious postmodernist narration to tackle important questions about focalization. It may therefore justifiably be called a metafocal as well as a metanarrative and metafictional graphic narrative.

Writing and Drawing Create the World: Craig Thompson, *Habibi*

Like *Asterios Polyp*, Craig Thompson's *Habibi* marks a high level of aesthetic aspiration in current graphic narrative. The book's hardcover imitation of a leather binding and its many intertextual references to Holy Scripture, Greek philosophy, Middle Eastern ornamental art, and world literature imply value, prestige, and aesthetic standing. Visually, the book is extremely rewarding. Besides conventional three-by-three panel page layouts or variations thereof with one or two larger panels, *Habibi* makes extensive use of original page layouts that break the conventional comics grid pattern. It also includes many metarepresentational reflections on narrative processes and on the comics form. In particular, these concern the semiotic interplay of writing and drawing that characterizes comics narration, with Arabic calligraphy frequently serving as an intermediate mode between writing and drawing or as a way of switching from linguistic to visual representation.

Different backgrounds and frames are used in *Habibi* to mark distinct narrative strands, temporal layers, and levels of reality, fantasy, myth, and dream. Intricately drawn whole-page panels with ornamental frames often explore the meaning of story events through embedded narratives taken from the Qur'an and Bible, setting up typological relations between the experiences of characters and the stories they tell each other. For the most part, these intradiegetic stories are narrated by Dodola, the book's protagonist, who is also the narrator of some (but not all) of the extradiegetic storyline. In a number of key scenes, however, the same mythological motifs and images that illustrate Dodola's storytelling also express the experience, perception, and cognitive processing of Zam, Dodola's foster son and, later, her lover. Thus, while *Habibi* joins other graphic narratives in employing focalization markers such as style, shading, panel size and arrangement, rhythm, and repetition and variation to draw attention to the aspectual orientation of scenes and sequences, it also turns to storytelling itself as a form of understanding and a resource for focalization.

The retelling and remembering of stories throughout *Habibi* illustrate how stories and their perspectivation are often crafted together. Many of these retellings include instances of embedded focalization in which story events become reinterpreted from new perspectives and recurring visual metaphors gain new meaning. In this process, the vantage points of different characters are repeatedly shown to infect each other, often in a hypothetical mode as characters speculate about each other's level of knowledge. These complex, multilayered narrative strategies as well as *Habibi*'s strong emphasis on storytelling as a way of processing difficult and unusual experiences provide new challenges to our question of how a graphic novel's metanarrative and metafictional doubling back on itself may involve readers in its reflection process.

In this chapter section, we detail how *Habibi*'s narrative often self-consciously references writing and drawing as ways of creating entire worlds. Approaching *Habibi* as a metasemiotic as well as a metanarrative, metafictional, and metafocal book, we examine its narrative structure, showing how its proliferation of narrative origins and agents further develops the metafictional theme of comics narrative as world creation. We then delve into worlds of experience in *Habibi*, questioning how the clash of incommensurable fictional worlds such as the modern megacity, the orientalist world of the *Arabian Nights*, and the world of religious myths is used to both help and hinder the emotional and cognitive engagement of readers with the what it's like of the two focal characters.

Habibi, which means "my love" in Arabic, traces the separation, transformation, and reunion of Dodola and Zam, two escaped child slaves. The novel's fantastic tale begins with Dodola's childhood in an impoverished, water-depleted village and traces her forced marriage, the murder of her much older husband, and her abduction by slave traders. Once Dodola escapes from the slave market with Zam, an abandoned baby boy, she makes a home in an ark inexplicably stranded in the desert. From there, she is once more abducted and taken into the sultan's harem in the wealthy megacity Wanatolia, which thrives on controlling the region's water with a reservoir dam. Meanwhile, Zam returns to the village and joins a community of hijras—eunuch prostitutes—before he, too, is kidnapped by the sultan's men. The story closes with Dodola and Sam's romantic reunion, detailing the couple's escape from the sultan's harem, their attempt to live as illegals in Wanatolia, and their ultimate departure from the sultanate.

Habibi is a highly digressive graphic novel. Its main plotline is interspersed with a rich web of embedded stories, dream and fantasy sequences in which focal characters process experiences and memories. It is also dotted with metanarrative and metafictional reflections on writing and drawing, storytelling and image making as ways of creating and interpreting worlds. In particular, *Habibi* exposes (and sometimes contrasts) two frames of understanding that correspond with the two semiotic modes it relies on for its own communication: the line and the square, with the line associated with writing, the progression of time, and moving water and the square with visual art, simultaneity, the formation of patterns, and the comics form. From the novel's very first page, lines and squares intersect and interact in complex ways, often providing opportunities for implicit or explicit metafictional commentary.

Where *Asterios Polyp* introduces its narrative with a sharp bang of simultaneous world creation and destruction, *Habibi* begins with a creation story that self-consciously aligns the creation of a text with the creation of the world: "From the Divine Pen fell the first drop of ink. And from a drop, a river" (9). Much of the novel's plot centers around this river whose sparse water, collected in a gigantic reservoir lake, is kept inaccessible to the rural communities that surround it. At once real and metaphorical, the river frequently stands in for the narrator's voice, for writing, and for narrative in general. Thus, the river is described as looping "like letters, letters extending into stories, until suddenly it stopped—dried up—a muted voice" (31). It is frequently associated with Dodola, such as when its flow visually morphs into the shape of Dodola's body (589) or when it is described as "fragile, vulnerable, and scared" (614). Throughout *Habibi*, the river motif is also used to connect other characters to storytelling activities. When Dodola's husband, a scribe, is murdered, the blood flowing from his throat mirrors the flow of the river, indicating that he, too, is a source of stories that will now dry up (22).

This pervasive imagery of line and flow combines and contrasts with a second way of ordering the world: the square, which underlies both the three-by-three comics grid adopted on many of *Habibi*'s pages and the magic square or "buduh" (129) on which its nine-chapter structure is based. The first chapter, "River Map," explains that like the river, the square is connected to writing and its origin, which a second creation story locates in markings on a turtle's shell (34–35). The square is also related to sacred writing, as its first letter, B, stands for Bismillah, the first word of the Qur'an (37). In a series of intricate page designs (figure 6.4), the turtle shell is overlaid with and transformed first into a budhu, then into Arabic calligraphy, which, as the verbal narrative explains, "can be tangled up in many forms . . . even that of an animal" (39). This is one of many passages in the book in which line and square morph into each other, suggesting that the relation between writing and drawing is not a contrasting but a complementary one. From this intradiegetic story of origins, the buduh then enters the main plotline when Dodola gives a hand-drawn magic square to Zam as protection against evil spirits (40). Suggesting an ancient, mythical origin of the classic comics page, the buduh functions as a metanarrative reflection of *Habibi*'s structure at the same time as it serves to connect disparate parts of its plot. The square directs a focus on structure and the ordering of material, while also introducing a playful element through its

FIGURE 6.4. Thompson, Craig. 2011. *Habibi*. Faber. p. 39.

symbols of varying complexity. This aspect of playful ordering is made explicit when Dodola reads philosophical books—from the teachings of Aristotle to those of Jabir Ibn Hayyan—in the sultan's library and discovers new ways of visually ordering knowledge of the world (249–54).

While the first chapter's creation story highlights the outwardly visible authority of creation, the magic square conceptualizes creation as a quest for a hidden, secret order of things, for symmetry and harmony in a contingent world. Within the diegesis, the magic square, whose letters Dodola traces over and over again as she learns to read and write from her husband (16), is the foundation upon which her understanding and telling of stories are based. Its depiction frequently signals metanarrative reflection as well as metafocal insight into how *Habibi* draws readers into the experience of characters. On the extradiegetic level, moreover, the buduh crystallizes a metasemiotic concern with the elements of comics storytelling: words, letters, images, and panels. In the next section, we trace these different levels of narrative and detail their relation to focalization.

Metanarrative and Metafocalization

Habibi engages in intricate reflections about the stories we tell ourselves and others, and about the effect these stories have on our creative perception of the world and of ourselves. Its first sentence sets in motion a narrative process that closely identifies divine and artistic creation: "From the Divine Pen fell the first drop of ink" (figure 6.5). The first panel shows a black splash against a white background (9). In the second panel—"And from a drop, a river."— that splash has grown into a large body of water moving dramatically against a black background, from which the third panel on this three-by-three panel page zooms out to reveal a dark river flowing down a range of mountains. Subsequent panels in the grid's middle column depict an expanse of dry, cracking earth and a glaring sun, providing a stark contrast to the images accompanying the book's initial verbal statements. Meanwhile, the left and right columns show men and women drawing water from a well, a stick-thin girl in vegetal garb being sadly looked down on by a number of grown-ups, and that same girl gazing up at the sun. These images are not explained until much later in the book, when Dodola tells Zam that "Dodola is the rain goddess from the far northwest" (175), leading into an embedded narrative about the "long drought in the village where [she] was raised" (176).

The first page's enigmatic images illustrate the creation of a narrative through the creation of a landscape, associating narrative creativity with the flow of a river, while simultaneously indicating a drought of creativity—and of water. Throughout the book, creation and discreation, flow and drought provide a pattern of tensions that structures the narrative and its visual language. This close association of creativity and creation puts the book's narrator in a godlike position. At the same time, the enigmatic combination of wordless panels also grants a crucial role to readers, who have to interpret images that seem to be without context and draw connections between fragmentary impressions. Frequent instances of braiding, where images and stories intersect and combine across spatially distant panels and pages, challenge the

FIGURE 6.5. Thompson, Craig. 2011. *Habibi*. Faber. p. 9.

meaning-making processes of readers by demanding that earlier scenes and sequences be reinterpreted in light of later repetitions or variations. In this way, readers are included in the narrative process of creation and discreation.

Identifying the ink dropping from a storyteller's pen with the river that the pen draws, *Habibi* expresses a magical attitude toward narration that ties in with the self-conscious preoccupation of many graphic narratives with the world-building capacity of storytelling. Initially, it is unclear which narrative agent controls that creative power, as the first page does not indicate a source for its first sentences, and the tone is more suggestive of an authorial narrator than of a character narrator. The following page, however, is introduced by what is clearly the voice of a character narrator: "When the land dried up with drought, my parents sold me into marriage" (10). From this point onward, Dodola becomes the novel's main verbal narrator, although she is not present in all parts of the book and Zam, not Dodola, narrates at least one of its chapters ("Orphan's Prayer"). Thus, while Dodola functions as a "particularly overt extradiegetic homodiegetic narrator" in parts of the novel (Thon 76), self-consciously referring to the act of narration, to the manifold functions of narratives, and to narrative absence, silence, and loss of voice, she is not *Habibi*'s only narrator, and she does not appear to be responsible for all that is said and shown.

Beginning with the creation story on its first pages, *Habibi* posits several possible origins of narration, each one inviting readers toward a unique kind of perspective-taking. During those parts of the narrative where Dodola serves as the character narrator, her autobiographical tale of enforced marriage at the age of nine, of being repeatedly raped and sold into slavery, and of extreme poverty encourages readers to empathize with her, as the close combination of voice and vision in internally focalized homodiegetic narratives invites readers to adopt the cognitive, perceptual, emotional, and embodied deixis from which the narrative is experienced. According to Suzanne Keen's model of narrative empathy, which we explored in chapter 3, character identification generally invites empathy (2007: xii). Blakey Vermeule similarly suggests that "people—or stand-ins for people—are the primary vehicle by which we make sense of stories," as readers "adapt their point of view to one or another of a story's characters, usually the protagonist, and make their way through the narrative by tracking that character's actions" (41; see Coplan 142). The strangeness of *Habibi*'s narrative world, which is far removed from the experience of Western readers, may also contribute to a feeling of closeness, as "fictional worlds provide safe zones for readers' feeling empathy without experiencing a resultant demand on real-world action" (Keen 2007: 3).

Although Dodola often serves as a verbal narrator, she is not generally presented as the graphiator of the novel's visuals. Instead, Dodola functions as one of the novel's focal characters on the visual track, with many panels indicating what she is feeling by portraying her expressive face or bodily posture. Thus, two panels in "River Map" show the little girl Dodola crouching naked on a bed (figure 6.6). In the first, Dodola is in the background, her half-dressed husband looming over her; the panel's foreground shows a desk with writing instruments and an open manuscript (13). The second panel zooms in on the girl, who is tightly hugging her legs and looking up at her husband with large tear-filled eyes. At the bottom of the page, a third panel reveals what has

FIGURE 6.6. Thompson, Craig. 2011. *Habibi*. Faber. p. 13.

just happened: It shows the smiling husband holding up a bloodstained sheet. This sequence provokes empathy in readers, who witness Dodola's emotional state and realize that she has just been raped. As Keen explains, the portrayal of bodily postures that convey emotional states is crucial for such a process of identification and empathy, as it may trigger a neural mechanism in readers that enables the mental representation of others' actions (2007: 15).

However, Dodola is not *Habibi*'s only verbal narrator. While she narrates most of "River Map," the first sentence's reference to a "Divine Pen" also points to a higher narrative authority that appears to be charged with the inking of words and pictures and the ordering of the narrative. This authority that brings forth the entire narrative world is placed in a godlike position, evoking the authorship model of Holy Scripture. The first chapter and many later passages of *Habibi* draw a direct connection with the authorship of the Qur'an, which is traditionally assumed to have been revealed to Muhammad by God through the archangel Jibreel.

Habibi's narrative structure is further complicated when, after its first sentences, Dodola's husband is introduced as a scribe who copies sacred texts. Adding his act of narration to the initial authorial voice that brings forth an entire narrative world and to Dodola as a character narrator who voices her life story, the husband functions as a third narratorial agent—one who copies and embellishes texts that have been authored by God. At the same time, he too is put in a godlike position when he teaches Dodola to read and write, since his instruction is compared to God teaching Adam (16–17). From the start, *Habibi*'s complex narrative proliferates authorship and narrative origins in a way that is designed to frustrate attempts to pin narrative agency down to any one character or instance, thus impacting readers' cognitive and emotional involvement in the narrative.

As the agents who narrate in *Habibi* multiply, so too do the stories they tell. The act of storytelling is first introduced through Dodola's husband, who initiates her into the world of religious myths and legends. Toward the beginning of *Habibi*, an ornately framed full-page panel shows the husband standing over a crouching Dodola as she practices her letters (16). The incommensurate scale of the open book behind her with Arabic letters rising from it like mist and the black abyss—also filled with Arabic writing—under the carpet on which both characters are located indicate that this panel is allegorical in nature. It serves as a transition from the real world in which Dodola and her husband live into the world of stories he copies out. In a subsequent full-page panel, a large Dodola lies in a meadow looking at a tree growing in front of a river from which animals are drinking. A small fur-clad male figure, identified as Adam by a text box, stands next to the tree (17). Both the tree branches and the ground under them are filled with Arabic calligraphy, illustrating how myths and legends are made up from words and letters, but also how they are fleshed out into complete worlds by immersive readers and listeners such as Dodola. This is one of several metafocal panels in *Habibi* that bring readers to engage with Dodola's what it's like, while also making us stop and consider how the reading scene within the book that we are reading relates to our own reading experience. Like the previous page, this one too has an ornate frame. These are used throughout *Habibi* to mark off intradiegetic storytelling. Yet the intrusion of Dodola as a listener into the panel also confirms that the separation indicated by the frame is not a complete one, but partial at best.

Although the sources of stories are multiple in *Habibi*, Dodola relates the majority of intradiegetic stories, with Zam as her primary audience. The second chapter, "Veils of Darkness," includes a typology of storytelling functions, all relating to Dodola's developing relationship with Zam. Storytelling soothes (94), nurtures the imagination (96), distracts from problems (97), and teaches moral lessons (99). Unbeknownst to Dodola, the closeness she creates with her stories also raises Zam's sexual interest in her, which drives them apart. Through panels that depict Zam as he spies on Dodola bathing (104, 108), the novel exposes an alternative what it's like of which Dodola's narrative voice does not appear to be aware. By contrasting Dodola's and Zam's focalization, *Habibi* grants readers access to different ways of experiencing the world and to distinct interpretations of events.

That Dodola's and Zam's perception and experience compete for attention is sharpened through the inclusion of sequences and chapters that exclude Dodola and instead focus on Zam. Some of these sequences in which Zam is the focal character (41, 164–69) can be interpreted as retrospective assessments of events from an exterior vantage point, especially when some indications, like the use of past tense, suggest that Dodola's "narrating I" is located outside the first-order storyworld (Thon 76). The assessment of focalization is significantly more complicated in longer passages marked by Dodola's absence, such as the chapter "Hand of Fatimah," which constitutes the center of a narrative gap in which Dodola's voice is silent for almost two hundred pages (285–463). The chapter narrates Zam's experiences following Dodola's abduction to the sultan's harem, when he returned to the village and joined a community of hijras, eventually becoming one himself. Zam never relates this story to Dodola, and the chapter contains no indication of a narrator. However, many focalization markers show that the what it's like in this chapter is Zam's, including close-up portraits of Zam's facial expression and bodily posture that reveal his emotional processing as well as the use of a swirling pattern to frame dream and memory sequences. Repeatedly, these dream sequences reveal thoughts and emotions of which Dodola appears to be unaware at this point in the narrative, especially the erotic dreams about Dodola that torment Zam throughout this chapter and eventually lead to his decision to be castrated and become a hijra.

When Zam's erotic fantasies are considered in the larger context of repeated similar sequences, however, they appear in a different light. Dodola is first shown bathing in the course of her retrospective metanarrative account of telling stories to Zam at different ages in his development. In the bottom row of each three-by-three panel page, the changing relationship between foster mother and son is illustrated with a bathing sequence that indicates Zam's reluctance to bathe, then his growing enthusiasm for bathing with Dodola, and finally Dodola's decision to have separate baths in the future (94–103). Initially, the bathing scenes are introduced in the context of Dodola's homodiegetic verbal narrative, and they appear to visualize her perception of the evolving mother-son relationship.

The first peeping-Tom scene that follows upon the next double page is split into three parts, each marking a different focalization (figure 6.7). In the top half stretching across both pages, a series of four full-body portraits

FIGURE 6.7. Thompson, Craig. 2011. *Habibi*. Faber. pp. 104–5.

depict Dodola's perception of her progressing pregnancy with her second, biological child, conceived in the sultan's harem. The bottom halves of the two pages contain the peeping-Tom scene (104) and a naked, pregnant Dodola standing in front of a mirror (105). While the left bottom panel is set against a black background, used in preceding sequences to indicate Dodola's retrospective narrative, the right bottom panel has a white background, signaling a switch to the present moment in which Dodola is remembering. The top half is bordered by a flaming pattern with tongues connecting to the heads of Zam (left) and Dodola (right), suggesting that while the verbal voice is Dodola's, the focalization in the images is Zam's as well as Dodola's. Compared with *Asterios Polyp*, however, the switches between a male and a female focalization in *Habibi* are less focused on an overlaying of perspectives and more on the possibility to adopt a variety of perspectives on events. Their ambivalence and ambiguity grant an important role to readers, who are invited to similarly embrace different perspectives.

Habibi's strong metanarrative concern and its self-conscious representation of authorship, with many scenes in which characters recall, narrate, write, and draw stories, include readers in a process of ongoing creation. This is not a straightforward process: Different models of narration and authorship are set beside each other, creation is set off against constantly threatening processes of destruction, narrative voices become muted, and panels turn blind. The ambiguity around Dodola's position as narrator and possible authorial figure further adds to this complexity (see Thon 78). Especially suggestive in this context is a passage in *Habibi*'s final chapter, "Start Breathing," which details Dodola's search for Zam in Wanatolia. When she can't find him in the city, she "searched for him on paper . . . in the stories I grew up telling him drawing from the well, filling up the emptiness of our room with writing" (617). The page's bottom panel contains a close-up view of Dodola's hand holding a fountain pen whose tip blends into the arabesque pattern used to frame intradiegetic stories in *Habibi*, which here flows out of the panel's frame and off the page. While this suggests that Dodola may have some responsibility for the novel's visual presentation, that suggestion remains an isolated instance when considered in the context of the entire book, and it is contradicted by many other passages whose visuals are tied to Zam, or else appear to emerge from Dodola's unconscious mind, out of her control. Authorship of and responsibility for *Habibi*'s visuals thus cannot be tied conclusively to any one narrative instance.

Time and again, *Habibi*'s complex narrative structure taxes understanding and slows down the meaning-making processes of readers. At the same time, the many scenes that expose focalization by highlighting the cognitive and emotional processing of characters invite readers into acts of perspective-taking. The book's arabesque structure, with its proliferating and diverging stories, also serves as a means of focalization, as stories and their different interpretations are placed beside each other. Depictions of Dodola reading books in which characters and objects come to life reflect the experience of readers reading the book in which Dodola is reading a book. In the final section of this chapter, we explain how readers can use their own bodily awareness to experience the narrative, and how the exploration of embodiment in *Habibi* may therefore draw readers into the narrative. First, however, we discuss the clash between ontologically distinct worlds and explain how *Habibi*'s postmodernist concern with fictional ontology contributes to this ambiguity of perception.

Multiplying Worlds of Experience

By directing attention to the drawing pen, *Habibi* asks readers from the very start to consider the authorial consciousness behind its storytelling. In unveiling authorship, which is kept hidden by convention, *Habibi* incorporates a narrative metalepsis into its very world building. Therefore, the world that readers come to see and experience through the narrative does not present as a realistic one overall, even though it contains realistic elements such as poverty and child abuse. Instead, a plurality of worlds, some of which are highly artificial, coexist in the graphic novel. What is more, the narration that mediates these worlds frequently makes itself felt as an opaque layer between world and reader by stepping back from its events and characters, and by drawing attention to its structure and style. This self-consciousness particularly affects the relation between words and images, writing and drawing. In *Habibi,* the world is called into being by Arabic script, which presents as more dynamic and fluid than the static, austere characters of the Latin alphabet, and whose rich tradition of calligraphy and arabesque ornamentation undercut rigid distinctions between writing and drawing. Arabic script brings forth elaborate page designs, serving as a visual model for ornamental panel frames and the page layout of all except the first chapter's title pages. It gives birth to trees, angels, birds, and fruit (17, 18, 39) and pours into and out of people (475, 514). With *Habibi*'s subtle interplay between narration and authorship, the fluidity between writing and drawing proves crucial to the book's aesthetics and narrative structure.

In this chapter section, we detail the relation between different worlds and spheres of action in *Habibi,* and we explain what consequences the metafictional multiplication of worlds has for the potential involvement of readers. That *Habibi*'s world is radically multiple is firmly introduced in the novel's first chapter by two means. First, the stories that the little girl Dodola hears and learns to read from her husband—stories that will become the source of all her embedded tales collected throughout *Habibi*—are intimately bound up with the Arabic script that conveys them. As we explained in the previous section, the tales that Dodola reads are shown to come alive for her and the reader in the shape of lush scenery, thus establishing that every narrative opens up a new world.

Second, *Habibi*'s diegetic world itself is also revealed to be multiple. A "map of the region" included in the first chapter is split into three parts: the desert, where Dodola and Zam have made a home in a mysteriously stranded ark ("our home"); "to the north, the prosperous nation of WANATOLIA barring entry"; and "to the southeast, the destitute village we escaped from" (28). While each sphere contains realistic elements, several incongruities indicate that neither should be read as a depiction of a real Middle Eastern location. These include mixing aspects of locations in the Arabic peninsula (a wealthy sultanate in a megacity) with depictions of places associated with the Hindukush region (the tribal village) and the Nile or Jordan Valley (the river dam and disputes over water). Moreover, the narrative contains many fantastical motifs from a Western oriental imagination (the harem and arabesque patterned fabrics and ceramics) that are incongruent with its more realistic aspects. This has consequences for the temporal pinpointing of *Habibi*'s plot in relation to the real world, as the narrative combines elements of modernity, orientalism, colonialism, and myth. Rather than depicting identifiable places, the relation between the three spheres appears to be emblematic of power relations between wealthy and developing regions both within the Middle East and worldwide. This emblematic nature is also indicated by the name "Wanatolia," a pun both on "Anatolia" and "wanna," alluding to the persistent grabbing of resources (water, women, and slaves) that has constituted the city's wealth.

An ontologically distinct world comes into being in the intradiegetic myths and stories that Dodola first hears from her husband and later imparts to Zam. In *Habibi*'s first chapter, the story of the dried-out river leads into this alternative world (31), and both the real river in Dodola's desert environment and the one in the flood myth she narrates at the end of the chapter offer explanations for the origin of writing, drawing, and storytelling. One function of Dodola's intradiegetic storytelling, then, lies in its metanarrative reflection that focuses on sources and origins. It ties narrative mediation and world building to focalization by highlighting how stories are always inflected by the subjectivity of their narrators and by drawing connections between the stories and the present situation in which they gain meaning.

Dodola's stories invite readers to transpose questions of originality and of ethical positioning to their own interpretation of the extradiegetic narrative. By showing readers how the world is and, at the same time, reflecting on how it comes into being through stories that flow out of her, Dodola asks them to engage in the diegetic world and to question their own ideological and ethical positioning in it. Since Dodola's stories are presented as parables, readers are prompted to adopt a similarly allegorical perspective on the novel as a whole in relation to their own reality. However, in assessing such an allegorical reading, readers must come to terms with Dodola's fragile position as a character and as a narrator. Initially, Dodola's stories often seem to imply a quest for origins that may substantiate an absolute claim for truth, but as they develop, they are often elaborated so as to undercut ideas of authority and originality in favor of ambiguity and undecidability. Throughout *Habibi*, slight but significant variations between divergent renderings of the same or similar stories are highlighted, usually in a visually parallel fashion, and left unresolved. This ambiguation concerns religious truth claims as well as the authority of the narrative that embeds them. It therefore opens up a variety of options for readers to position themselves in relation to Dodola as a storyteller, to the main plotline detailing her life story, and to the many stories she relates.

The majority of Dodola's mythological stories derives from the Qur'an. However, as with the multiplication of creation stories, these myths are rarely explored in isolation. Rather, they are frequently set off against alternative versions, often taken from the Hebrew Bible. Three myths in particular are used throughout *Habibi* to reflect on the main plotline and draw readers into the what it's like of Dodola and also Zam: (1) the Paradise story, (2) Moses and the theme of orphanhood, and (3) the sacrifice of Isaac (in the Hebrew Bible) or Ishmael (in the Qur'an). We will now consider each of these myths, reflecting on how the use of mythological material contributes to the tension between authority and playfulness that characterizes *Habibi*'s narrative construction as a whole.

As discussed above, the Paradise story related in Genesis 1 and 2 and referred to in Qur'an 7:19 constitutes the material of Dodola's first contact with books and stories, and introduces her to reading and writing. Throughout Dodola's traumatic childhood, the Paradise story provides an alternative reality in which she immerses herself to escape from her harrowing experiences. But later parts of the novel also explore a darker side of the Paradise myth, drawing parallels between Adam and Eve's expulsion from Paradise and Dodola and Zam's fate when they are forced to leave their desert ark. The third chapter, suggestively titled "Raping Eden," relates the story of Adam and Eve across five arabesque-framed vignettes that interrupt the story of Dodola prostituting herself so that she and Zam can eat, and of Dodola's rape by a sadistic stranger. In this context, the expulsion from Paradise serves as a narrative tool for Dodola's processes of understanding and recovery. While Dodola tells how Adam and Eve had to "toil and sweat over a barren land to provide themselves sustenance" (158–59), the ornately framed visuals give way to an unframed image of Dodola pulling a heavy cart full of the food she has been paid with through the desert sand. Her downward glance and extended legs, the rope she holds on to, and the angle of representation indicate a clear resemblance between Dodola and the donkey that pulls a plough in the final panel of the expulsion myth. Their visual similarities cue readers to Dodola's process of understanding her situation, linking that process to the authority of religious myth. The shift from the diegetic world to the mythical world and back to the diegesis thus marks Dodola's internal focalization.

The story of Moses, narrated in the Biblical book of Exodus and in sura 128 of the Qur'an, is a second myth through which both Dodola and Zam interpret their life in the desert. In chapter 2, "Veils of Darkness," the account of Dodola's harem experience is set off against a series of flashbacks detailing her escape from the slave market with Zam. Clearly marked off from the primary narrative by a black background, the flashbacks blend into the world of myth when Dodola, trying to hush a wailing Zam, exclaims, "Look! We're like baby Moses!" and tells him how Moses was rescued by Pharao's daughter. The parallels between the two stories are visually reinforced with the superimposition of an ornately framed half-page panel of Moses's rescue with two smaller frameless panels of Dodola and Zam, who, like Moses, bob on the water in a basket (77).

As with the Eden story, later chapters address a different portion of the myth, that of Moses's encounter with God in the burning bush (308–9). When Zam enters an ornately framed illustration of the myth, extradiegetic and intradiegetic narrative worlds once again blend into each other, with the Moses myth providing a cognitive and emotional lens through which Zam considers his life. The burning bush sequence is part of the chapter "Hand of Fatimah," which relates Zam's experiences in the village and his decision to become a eunuch. The two-page insert supplants a part of the story when Zam, close to dying of thirst, finally finds a source of water. Two parallels between the two story levels—a miraculous encounter and the depiction of a snake both in the insert (309) and in the diegetic world (310)—and the repeated depiction of Zam in the mythical scenery and in a separate panel at the bottom of the page establish the function of the myth as a focal filter that grants readers access to Zam's what it's like.

The third myth, the sacrifice of Isaac (in the Bible) or of Ishmael (in the Qur'an), is of particular importance to the self-reflexive narrative strategies that are employed throughout *Habibi*. It is referred to repeatedly over the course of the graphic novel, often with the explicit aim of highlighting the inherent ambiguity surrounding mythological stories and storytelling as a whole. Ambiguity is at the heart of this myth insofar as it has two sources that are in direct contradiction to each other: Whereas the Biblical book of Genesis tells of Abraham being tested in his faith when God asks him to sacrifice Isaac, the son by his wife Sarah, the Qur'an presents Ishmael, Abraham's firstborn son by his servant Hagar, as a willing participant in the sacrifice. For modern Biblical exegetes, the sacrifice or binding of Isaac often presents a stumbling block of faith, since it seems to imply a tyrannical God who demands blind obedience and retracts given promises at will. In *Habibi*, Dodola's version of the Isaac story subtly alludes to this discussion with a full-page panel illustrating the diverging paths the myth has taken in the two religious traditions. The panel depicts Abraham on top of a mountain as Ishmael and Isaac each make their way up it on opposite sides (47; figure 6.8).

When the sacrifice of Ishmael/Isaac is first introduced, Dodola's question, "Which son was it?," remains unanswered (48). On the surface, the question refers to the Jewish and Islamic faiths, who base their authority on tracing

FIGURE 6.8. Thompson, Craig. 2011. *Habibi*. Faber. p. 47.

their lineage to each of the two half-brothers. When considered within the richly layered metafictional narrative of *Habibi*, the undecidability of which version is the correct one cautions against an overconfidence in authority and origins in a more general manner. However, the comparison between the two versions also raises the question of the authenticity of descendants. Indeed, Dodola's repeated reliance on the parallel stories of Isaac and Ishmael to explore her ambivalent feelings about her biological son Rajab and her adopted son Zam suggests that it is the function, not the origin, of stories that matters. Although Dodola recognizes that "every story has a source" (615), she comes to be aware that her relationship with Zam is "more than a story" (648). Consequently, when the question "Which one was sacrificed?" is posed again toward the end of the book, the narrative voice responds, "Neither" (646), indicating that love, not violence, is behind all stories in *Habibi*.

Visually, the relationship of the religious stories to the diegesis is further accentuated through the repetition of an arabesque frame that links disparate parts of Biblical and Qur'anic myths but also introduces a repetition that fills in gaps in the main storyline, even across chapters. Through this process, *Habibi* engages in a creative crafting and blending of myths that brings together its multiple worlds and that reflects the diegesis in different ways, for instance paralleling the binding of Isaac with the rape of the Mesopotamian goddess Ishtar and with Dodola's rape (324). Together with the many visual parallels *Habibi* puts into play, ornate frames serve as markers of character focalization, indicating that mythological material is not introduced for its own sake, but to let readers participate in the processing activity of characters.

When Dodola and Zam first escape to the desert, a series of panels draws forth parallels between Hagar and her son Ishmael, on the one hand, and Dodola and Zam, on the other (44–45). Dodola relates the story to Zam to explain how and why she renamed him: Like Ishmael, Zam found a water source in the barren desert. In the Qur'an's account, the water was so abundant that Hagar called out, "Zam! meaning 'calm down'" (45). With this revelation, the intradiegetic story ends and an image of an infant Zam and a young Dodola by a water source is introduced at the bottom of the page, with the top of Dodola's head breaking through the intradiegetic tale's arabesque frame, thus visualizing the overlay of the two realities.

In *Habibi*, the many intradiegetic stories that emerge out of intimate situations give shape to characters' experiences, providing an interpretative framework and a visual vocabulary through which characters process those experiences. The bridging of extradiegetic and intradiegetic worlds, especially when the protagonist is also the narrator of the intradiegetic story or when details from intradiegetic stories are also part of a protagonist's dreams or fantasies, strongly indicates the cognitive processing of characters. In the final section of this chapter, we examine the cross-fertilization of stories across *Habibi*'s narrative and discuss the relation between storytelling and embodiment.

Cross-Fertilization and Embodiment

The repetition and variation of motifs from the same myths in different contexts highlights how stories express different viewpoints and open up an imaginative space in which characters work through real-world problems. In

Habibi, mythological stories are not presented as absolute or immutable content. They are told, remembered, and imagined from one or several subjective points of view, and the focus of their presentation lies on that subjective angle as much as on the myths themselves. Myths thus express a teller's what it's like, provide the means to reflect on that what it's like, and impact on the being-in-the-world of narrator and narratee. The frequent illustration of this process throughout *Habibi* draws on fundamental insights into the orienting function of storytelling. As fiction theorists have pointed out, the potential of narratives to immerse their readers was instrumental to the rise of the novel from the eighteenth century onward. According to Blakey Vermeule, literary fiction is part of a "news/novel matrix" in which "cultural forms . . . fulfill deep psychological imperatives, on the one hand, and changing economic and historical incentives, on the other" (8, 10). Stories help readers orient themselves in a changing world (C. Gallagher 346) by providing a form of second-order observation of the world (Esposito). However, as we have indicated, myths in *Habibi* often fail to orient characters and do not offer answers to the questions that provide a context for their introduction. Habibi's use of mythological stories may thus be read as a critique of overly optimistic expectations regarding stories and storytelling.

In the absence of uncontroversial narrative origins, stories in *Habibi* often appear to have their own life. They cross with other stories, are reframed, expanded upon, and adjusted to reflect the world and those who inhabit it, and they also invite readers to make meaningful links between distinct experiences. Early in "Raping Eden," Zam sets out to find water. When he realizes that his usual source has run dry, he wanders farther into the desert and becomes lost. Hearing the sounds of the desert, Zam imagines that they are produced by jinns, "spirits that live amongst us. Made of smokeless flame, they take many forms. Winged creatures . . . animals—like snakes and dogs . . . . even humans" (134). A large image illustrates Zam's thinking process by showing two jinns, drawn exactly as described, glancing over a mountain ridge at Zam. Also pictured are a number of winged creatures, a dog, a snake, and a human figure foreshadowing the chapter's rape scene. Images from the diegetic world (Zam and the rapist) and from the intradiegetic world of myths (jinns and snakes) combine seamlessly through Zam's understanding of the world, an understanding that is impacted by the stories that Dodola has told him.

That Dodola's stories give meaning to experiences, but also take on a life of their own through Zam's focalization is confirmed on the next page where Dodola figures in the top left corner telling the story of where the jinns live as she looks down at Zam searching for water. Images of a seated Zam interchange with bold framed panels in which he gives water to Dodola as she undresses. The final panel of the page, which spans the length of three panels, portrays a naked Dodola in its center surrounded by jinns in a luscious garden. The text framing this in an arabesque border reads, "Eve—the first woman—possessed an amulet to wield the power of the jinn" (136). The three panels on the next page show Zam in a state of arousal, staring down at his erection. They are vertically framed by two L-shaped panels, the first of a naked Dodola and the second of a large snake descending from the tree of knowledge. On the following page, however, that snake frightens Zam, who, upon seeing it, fears for his life (138). When Zam places his buduh in the pouch around his neck, however, the snake disappears, leaving readers uncertain whether the snake was a figment of Zam's imagination, a fictitious entity from the stories Dodola has told him, or an animal in the diegesis. This episode thus vividly illustrates the cross-fertilization between religious stories, the reality of myth, and the diegesis, between imagined views of the world and real ones, and between the what it's like of Dodola and of Zam.

Although many details of the narrative world have their origin in Dodola's act of narration, other aspects are outside her control. The fifth chapter, "Hand of Fatimah," does not have a narrative voice, and neither does the first half of the sixth chapter, "Drowning." Moreover, the penultimate chapter, "Orphan's Prayer," is composed of nine three-by-three panel pages narrated in Zam's voice with no visuals. In other chapters, the visual track is often, but not consistently, associated with Dodola's perception and imagination. For instance, when she gives birth to Rajab, she figures in the center of a star ornament that includes paradise imagery, rivers, and the magic square in an ornamental frame similar to those used to frame Dodola's intradiegetic stories (111). Although these are formally set off from the primary narrative, their imagery and style often recurs in episodes of thought and perception, not only of Dodola but also of other characters. Zam's fantasies and memories are also arranged in a star ornament on occasion (317), and although the association of Dodola with the mythical buraq originates in a legend she tells Zam, it also infects the tales told about her by the caravans (127) as well as the sultan's perception of her (282). Moreover, the jinn imagery, which is also first introduced in the caravan tales, is taken up in Zam's perception of Dodola being raped (156) and in his confused and guilt-ridden erotic fantasies (165).

Even where the focalization of Dodola's stories is tinged by intersubjectivity, it is rooted in Dodola's body. In chapter 3, we stressed that an embodied sense of self matters in graphic memoir where a character interacts with the body and through the body with the world that body inhabits. In a similar manner, Dodola's position in relation to the narrative is dependent on her body. Her corporeal experiences—abuse, rape, prostitution, pregnancy, starvation, sickness—inflect her storytelling practices and her being in the world. Just as being raped by her husband leads Dodola into the world of stories, the stories the sultan has heard about her motivate her imprisonment in the harem (198). Adapting the storytelling model of the *Arabian Nights* to suit his own purposes, the sultan challenges her "to please [him] for seventy nights in a row" (201). When Dodola prepares to give birth, she is made to focus on the letters of the magic square to ensure good luck (110), and when she falls ill, she is made to "drink each of the letters" so that her "body absorbs the message / the word becomes flesh" (474–75). These and other examples postulate Dodola's body as existing in story and through story, while her storytelling arises in and through her body.

Especially during Dodola's pregnancy, many intricate page designs draw analogies between biological gestation and artistic creativity. At the beginning of chapter 2, "Veils of Darkness," a three-by-three panel page contrasts a column of arabesque vignettes on the left with three different depictions of Dodola's pregnant belly on the right (53). The vignettes quote Qur'an 39:6: "He makes you in the wombs of your mothers in stages one after another in three veils of darkness." The panels in the right-hand column show Dodola's pregnant belly from the outside, an inside view of her uterus, and a close-up view of the fetus. The middle column contains three black panels with different degrees of shading. As we explained in our analysis of *Maus*, shading can serve as a focalization marker. In this instance, the shading reoccurs as background to the right-hand middle panel showing Dodola's "womb (uterine wall)" and also in the top row of panels on the next page showing first the Black slave Nadidah, who states, "You're pregnant," and then a stricken Dodola, who replies, "I can't be . . ." (54). The composition suggests that the shading in the middle column marks Dodola's internal focalization, both concerning the connections that can be made between the Qur'an and the baby growing inside her but also her rejection of her pregnancy and her consequent disassociation from her body, which the chapter will explore at great length.

Later in "Veils of Darkness," a full-page panel combines depictions of Dodola's uterus and the baby growing inside it with symbols, letters, and numbers relating to *Habibi*'s structure. A medical image of a female uterus is arranged in the middle of a nine-point star. The star's tips are connected by a circle surrounded by nine smaller circles, numbered one to nine, each containing a schematic view of a female abdomen in the nine months of pregnancy. The three trimesters of pregnancy alluded to in the Qur'an quotation on the introductory page are here indicated through heart-shaped lines, each combining three of the pregnancy images and numbered ١ (1), ٢ (2), and ٣ (3).

The complex arrangement of images, letters, numbers, and geometric shapes resembles the book's table of contents, binding the book's structure to Dodola's pregnant body.

The analogy between body and book is further explored when Dodola gives birth (110–13). An intricate page design (111) combines a smaller and a larger ninefold star pattern with images of the tree of paradise, two hands of Fatimah, flowing rivers, the waves of the sea, and the buduh that Dodola gave to Zam (40) and on which the chapter structure of the book is based. Inside the central star shape is an image of Dodola in a birth stool, assisted by a midwife and the slave Nadidah, her feet placed on two buduhs that are meant "to ensure a quick and safe delivery" (110). Similar page compositions found throughout Habibi include the arrangement of numbered squares (253) and alchemical imagery (254) when Dodola reads in the sultan's library, the star pattern used when Zam remembers Dodola telling him the story of Moses (317), and Zam's portrait in a pentagram surrounded by calligraphic renditions of the Qur'an's incipit "Bismilahirahmanirahim" ("In the name of God, the most gracious, the most merciful"; 398). Bound up in stories, Dodola is thus frequently presented as the physical mother of the whole graphic novel, whose structure is based on her embodied experience.

Dodola is repeatedly shown drawing the magical squares on which the novel's composition and underlying philosophy about stories are based (40, 298). As the main source of storytelling, moreover, she assumes features of characters that populate her stories. From the tree of knowledge (107, 137) to a winged jinn to a buraq, Dodola embodies the traits of the characters she tells about. She also drives the book's move toward designs of increasing complexity, from squares to the inclusion of triangles that become rings and then a layered pattern underlying the graphic novel's arabesque aesthetic. In chapter 7, "Ring of Solomon," when Dodola and Zam finally kiss, a white triangle symbolizing Dodola and a black triangle symbolizing Zam combine in a six-point star, then a six-triangle form, connected by six squares, forming a ring, interlocking with other rings, and finally providing the matrix on which the arabesque pattern that marks intradiegetic stories is based (562–63).

This sequence once more makes the point that although Dodola is the source of stories, she is not exclusively responsible for them, as other characters, especially Zam, also contribute to their shape and content. Indeed, when Zam and Dodola make love in the final chapter, "Start Breathing," the geometrical shapes on which the narrative's structure is based become visually superimposed upon Dodola's body (641), while Zam's voice, across ten blind panels, supplies the verbal narrative (639–40). The relations between words and images that Zam's voice suggests—"They say a man's inspiration is visual, but for a woman, it's the narrative" (639)—are thus inverted by the representation. That Zam, and not Rajab, becomes not only a true son but also a sexual partner for Dodola despite his castration further divests origins of privilege and authority, while also indicating the degree to which *Habibi* rejects all forms of binary thinking.

•

In chapter 2, we explained that narratives have the potential to change the perceptive, imaginative, and affective environment of their audience by inviting participation and provoking reciprocal acts of imagination (Cave). Narratives involve the whole reader, not only minds but also bodies, when they invite the simulation of the embodied activity represented in the narrative, and when they provoke nonimitative activity, such as when readers use their own bodily processes to enhance the reading experience or when they react viscerally to the narrative (Esrock 2004). An embodied approach to narrative is particularly called for when a narrative self-consciously focuses on bodies as the source of stories and as the medium through which they are experienced, as is the case in *Habibi*. Karin Kukkonen explains that the goal of an embodied approach to comics storytelling lies in considering "how the ways in which [bodies in comics] relate to and interact with each other and the world around them shape readers' perception of time, space, and causality in graphic narratives" (2013b: 49).

As we have seen throughout the six chapters of our study, bodies in comics often represent deictic centers from which the narrative world is experienced and thus cue readers into the what it's like of focal characters. In Kukkonen's words: "Considering the bodily activities of characters, readers can get a sense of how they perceive the storyworld around them, without having to read about their mental states in thought bubbles and without having to see the storyworld from their point of view" (2013b: 51). Readers may run embodied simulations of characters' bodies (Kukkonen 2013b: 54; see Gallese), or experience somatic responses to the experiences and emotions of characters. Although this can occur in metarepresentational narratives as well as in more conventionally representational ones, our analysis of *Asterios Polyp* and *Habibi* suggest that meta-ization may contribute to a particularly rich experientiality because it renders graphic narratives legible on several levels at once. Metafictional graphic narratives involve readers in the experience of characters but also in the processing of that experience and in the narrative and visual rendering of its processing. Readers are engaged through real-world reading activities such as page turning, glancing around the page, or flipping back and forth across the book to make connections; through embodied simulation of characters' movements and emotions; through sensorimotor activity such as fast or shallow breathing or goosebumps; and through imaginative participation (immersion, empathy, or imagining oneself as part of the storyworld).

Our findings that metafictional strategies often help, rather than hinder, readers' understanding of focalization cues and their engagement in the narrative world are supported by studies in cognitive and empirical narratology. For instance, Caroline Kutsch and Sven Strasen suggest that absorption, defined as "a type of story-driven experience," may be caused "by readers' experience of defamiliarization through deviated text features" (72). Even though deviation is often described as foregrounding and contrasted with absorption, empirical studies by Bálint et al. come to the conclusion that foregrounding and absorption often go hand in hand, as readers describe the experience of being absorbed in response to a perceived deviation. Perceived deviation, they theorize, may lead to a "shift of attention from *what* is told to *how* it is told [which] may result in readers' increased awareness of the artifact" (180).

The two graphic novels we analyzed in this chapter approach such narratological questions in a playful manner by building an engagement with narrative into their representation. Where *Asterios Polyp* asks, How does a person perceive their world, and how constructive is that vision?, *Habibi* poses the more radical question: How are entire worlds created? Both insist that experiences and minds are shaped by stories, both the stories that we tell about ourselves and the myth stories that we rely on to make sense of our experience of the world. Through sustained metafictional commentary, *Asterios Polyp* and *Habibi* reflect on how stories bring worlds into being by giving rise to a communal vision. They also show that the stories that create worlds also create minds that cannot be indefinitely contained by those very stories that created them. Stories change through individual experiences of the world, and new stories arise with every telling so that several worlds exist alongside each other. All story is creation, and all creation (and the destruction that it carries) is bound up in telling and experiencing, narration and focalization.

CONCLUSION

Putting Focalization in Perspective

Since Gérard Genette first proposed the focalization concept (1972), many theories of focalization have sought to specify what distinguishes focalization from perspective, from point of view, and from the representation of sense perception. Throughout the six chapters of this study, we have built on these inquiries by developing an encompassing, integrative understanding of focalization, and we have demonstrated the usefulness of a broadly conceived focalization concept to the analysis of graphic narrative. We have shown how the communication of perspectivation, but also of the cognitive functioning, emotional engagement, and ideological stance of characters and of noncharacter narrators engages and activates readers by inviting them into the what it's like of characters and their world. Our examination of focalization in comics extends beyond the representation of perception or consciousness to consider lived experience both within and outside of the narrative world. Adopting a phenomenologically inspired approach to focalization, we have studied a broad spectrum of comics to explore how focalization triggers different kinds of reading practices. In this conclusion, we sum up our most important findings and connect them to ongoing research in comics studies and narratology.

Focalization Is neither the Same as Perspectivation, nor Something Completely Different

Like Mieke Bal, we consider focalization to be narrative's "most important, most penetrating, and most subtle means of manipulation" (1997: 116). Focalization presents readers with one or several experiential angles on story events and regulates what and how much readers get to know and experience about the storyworld. By doing so, it sets the mood and feel of a narrative. Through the perceptual, cognitive, and evaluative angle of a character or noncharacter narrator, focalization guides reader responses to storyworld events and plot developments, creating closeness or distance toward characters and their experiences. Readers are also drawn into characters' reflections about and interpretations of their world and experience.

This readerly engagement can be triggered by a number of markers that have been identified by narrative theorists as indicating focalization in comics. These include the perspectival presentation of panels, the facial expression and bodily posture of characters, spatial articulation, and forms of shot/reverse-shot editing that evoke the "horizon of knowledge and emotional involvement, from which the sequence in the panels is told" (Kukkonen 2013b: 50). Such a focalization grammar of comics models itself on categories from film narratology that mark the subjective perspective of a character, including point-of-view shots, perception or projection shots, and subjective optical effects (Branigan 79; Mikkonen 2013: 102–3).

Our analyses of graphic narratives support the conclusion that these and other perspective markers provide access to the minds and lived experience of characters and can be indicative of focalization. However, other comics storytelling techniques that may cue focalization are less readily tied to optical perspectivation, or not at all. These include color, shading and line work, panel size and framing, layout, ordering, the use of blank or empty panels, the presence or absence of captions, lettering, the inclusion or exclusion of background detail, and the use of visual metaphors, as well as more global aspects such as style and genre that direct the overall mood of a graphic narrative. All of these aspects can operate individually or in conjunction to indicate focalization in a graphic narrative. As comics narrate across words and images but also across multiple levels, including that of the panel, the sequence, the page layout, and the entire book, these aspects need to be considered not as isolated instances, but across an entire narrative and in the context of a particular narrative world expressed through a specific style and genre.

The multileveled narrative structure of comics asks readers to consider several combinations of narrative instances at once. It further pressures linear reading by prompting readers to return to previous moments in the narrative and to reconfigure their understanding of these in relation to newly acquired information. In addition, comics (like all narratives) place certain conditions on their narrative world and on the presentation of its information, much of which is governed by genre conventions and expectations. Comics also frequently reflect on their own mediality and on the close intertwining of optical perspectivation, knowledge, and power as it is expressed through comics storytelling, thereby revealing optical perspectives to be part of a system of visuality.

It follows that a list of perspectival markers that signal consciousness does not exhaust the possibilities of focalization as it manifests in graphic narrative. Indeed, it cannot even serve as a starting point in the formulation of a focalization grammar of comics because the very notion of a focalization grammar of comics is theoretically unsound. Both narration and focalization are embedded within the world building of entire narratives and thus need to be considered within the web of experiences to which a particular narrative gives access. In this way, our work aligns with that of David Herman (2009b), who examines focalization in relation to complete storyworld construals.

Focalization Impacts Readers

The identification of a large range of focalization cues and devices used in comics leads to a clearer understanding of how focalization in comics shapes the emotional and cognitive response of readers. Our study builds on the basic insight from cognitive narratology that all narratives have the potential to change the perceptive, imaginative, and affective environment of their audience by inviting participation and provoking reciprocal acts of imagination (Cave). Throughout *Experiencing Visual Storyworlds: Focalization in Comics,* we approach focalization as linking text-internal modes of experience and information processing to text-external ones that are dependent on the knowledge and experience of readers. In tying focalization strategies and sense-making cues to the domain of reception through close readings, we show how specific structures of focalization guide readers toward a particular reading experience. This effect occurs because focalization manipulates storyworld information, regulating its delivery and presenting it through one or several experiential angles but also by alerting readers as to how to process that information so that it comes into meaning.

Imparting the attitude of characters and narrators, focalization contributes to setting the tone of a narrative. It guides readers in navigating through the narrative world, inviting them to expand upon the information provided through doubt or ambiguity, genre directives, and other participatory enticements. In other words, focalization directs and constrains how a text can be read. As we have shown through our analyses, focalization may highlight as well as obscure certain details or experiences, and often introduces uncertainty and doubt into the narrative, destabilizing knowledge that is central to a solid, unwavering understanding of the narrative world. Indeed, readers of comics are frequently faced with difficult decisions about how to reach an unequivocal meaning from the coming together of verbal and visual cues. Focalization contributes to this richly layered reading experience, often granting readers considerable interpretative leeway. Thus, although focalization guides processes of interpretation by making accessible the experiences and minds of characters, it often incites several interpretative possibilities. It does so in a number of ways that render text-internal experience and its text-external processing ambiguous.

For example, focalization in comics can simultaneously engage multiple sets of experiences, leave the origin of consciousness undetermined or distribute it across several narrative agents, embed and otherwise connect distinct subjective experiences of the same world detail across characters, or not clearly distinguish real narrative world experience from imagined experience. Depending on the type(s) of focalization employed in a given graphic narrative, different roles are made available to readers, implying different degrees of closeness or distance to the world and characters of a narrative. This is a point made also by Kate Polak, who concludes that different focalization types "have an affective context that influences how the reader perceives not only characters but their own position in relation to the narrative" (27).

Narratives in general involve the minds but also the bodies of readers when they invite the simulation of the embodied activity represented in the narrative and when they provoke nonimitative activity, such as when readers use their own bodily processes to enhance the reading experience or when they react viscerally to the narrative (Esrock 2004). In the context of comics storytelling, an embodied approach is particularly called for. Karin Kukkonen details that the goal of such an embodied approach to comics storytelling lies in considering "how the ways in which [bodies in comics] relate to and interact with each other and the world around them shape readers' perception of time, space, and causality in graphic narratives" (2013b: 49). In this context, our analyses conclude that how comics involve their readers depends not so much on individual narrative devices, but rather on the coming together of various strategies, including style, content, choice of symbols, image composition, juxtaposition of panels, and braiding of passages across the length of a comic book. The combination of these strategies creates an atmosphere that evokes the what it's like of characters' experiences that, in turn, solicits and activates the participation of readers whose mind is also embodied.

When comics invite an embodied engagement with the narrative world on the part of the reader, this may produce sympathy (feeling *for* the characters) or even empathy (feeling what the characters feel), as "readers of comics . . . experience bodily echoes of the motions and actions they observe" (Kukkonen 2013b: 53). Particularly self-conscious comics storytelling, however, often invites a less immediate physical engagement. When comics portray disabled or disfigured bodies, for instance, this may lead to a visceral reaction on the part of readers, but it also sets in motion a reflection on corporeality that extends beyond shared experiences. In this context, Eszter Szép draws on the concept of a shared vulnerability rooted in the basic neediness of the human body to describe new, reflexive modes of interaction between a graphic narrative and its readers (8–9). For her, the vulnerability of the portrayed body in comics can be read as an invitation toward an ethical encounter that is "initiated by the drawers of comics autobiography and reportage" by means of the "drawn line, other traces of the drawer, and the actual printed comic" (14). In comics, drawn bodies allow for a multidirectional exchange between a comic and its readers in which all involved parties will be impacted.

Focalization Provides Access to Lived Experience

Focalization in comics puts in motion a felt experience in readers that can produce closeness or distance to the world-experiencing of narrative agents, be they characters or narrators. In order to better account for this specificity of individual or shared experience that focalization in comics evokes, we have brought together two scholarly traditions, narratology and phenomenology, whose connections are only now beginning to be explored. Phenomenology, the philosophical discipline concerned with studying the *what it's like* that structures subjective experiences, describes experience as happening between a subject and its world. In narrative texts, this means that experience is not a static occurrence or an event within a text or within a subject. Rather, it is a continuous, dynamic exchange between a subject and its world.

Phenomenology provides the means to grasp how focalization works alongside other aspects of a text (such as the handling of time, space, and plot) to create the mood and atmosphere through which experiences inside the narrative world become available to readers, and how readers in their turn have experiences of closeness or distance as a response. The emphasis on subjective experience in a lived space, the conceptualization of that experience as relational, and the call for a close description of experiential structures make phenomenology an attractive methodology for the study of focalization. In its accentuation of lived experience, embodiment, and intersubjectivity, phenomenology is particularly suited to the study of the type of embodied, lived consciousness operative in graphic narrative. It also aligns with our understanding of focalization as bridging narrative experience and the experiential knowledge of readers.

Consciousness and its narrative mediation have been crucial issues for narratologists and literary theorists since the 1970s. While early definitions of narrative tended to emphasize the representation of action in time, more recent approaches focus on characters and the representation of their minds. In her seminal study *Transparent Minds,* Dorrit Cohn argues that "the special life-likeness of narrative fiction—as compared to dramatic and cinematic fictions—depends on what writers and readers know least in life: how another mind thinks" (5). Monika Fludernik, who laid the groundwork for much subsequent work in cognitive narratology with her *Towards a "Natural" Narratology,* points to the "anthropomorphic bias of narratives and its correlation with the fundamental story parameters of personhood, identity, actionality, etc.," concluding that "there can . . . be narratives without plot, but there cannot be any narratives without a human (anthropomorphic) experiencer" (1996: 13). Lubomír Doležel, too, stresses that "worlds with persons or, better, persons within worlds . . . generate stories" (33). Following suit, Alan Palmer defines narrative as "the description of fictional mental functioning" (2004: 12). With this widespread critical turn toward character, consciousness, and subjective experience, it is no wonder that focalization has become one of the most important and widely discussed narratological concepts.

In the past decade, cognitive narratologists have directed attention to the subjective quality of narrative experience and mental states, sensorial selectivity and discrimination, and the social aspects of subjectivity (Emmott) and thought (Palmer 2002, 2003, 2004). A host of cognitive work has drawn attention to the manifold ways narratives evoke the experience and the thinking of characters (see Palmer 2010; Zunshine 2006). Scholars have studied the physical and mental experience of characters (Emmott and Sanford) but also the role of the minds of readers in accessing narrative. Thus, Marco Caracciolo points out the "situated, embodied quality of readers' engagement with stories," arguing that "stories offer themselves as imaginative experiences because of the way they draw on and restructure readers' familiarity with experience itself" (2014: 4).

Experiencing Visual Storyworlds: Focalization in Comics builds on this work to detail how focalization is not confined to a narrative text, but rather constitutes a crucial point of access for readers. Comics, due to their bimodality and stylistic versatility, multiply this access in interesting and complex ways, at the same time as they also limit the access of readers by foregrounding their own mediality. As Kate Polak points out, "with comics . . . we are simultaneously presented with images that we have to decode alongside of the text, which on one hand presents a 'window' through which we can 'see' the scene but on the other hand, reminds us—through the frame and our imaginative closure—that we are *not* 'there' in any real sense" (26). Another way comics often complicate readers' access to experience is by providing multiple viewpoints or by combining or else confronting different optical and experiential views of the world. Instances of subjective representation that express character focalization in comics are frequently embedded in intersubjective networks of looking and feeling. Phenomenologically speaking, graphic narratives thus provide the insight that experience is not necessarily individual; indeed, often it is not.

Focalization in Comics Is a Matter of Embodied Cognition

As a multimodal medium that depends heavily on sequential visual images to narrate, graphic narrative places particular demands on the study of focalization. But the analysis of comics also leads to an enriched understanding of how focalization functions in narrative. Comics, as Ramzi Fawaz points out, "exaggerate, or pump up the volume on, formal and narrative tropes that are already widely at play in most literary production" (591). In comics storytelling, focalization, too, is intensified, its manifestation multiplied across words and images, and its impact on both characters and readers amplified. To study focalization strategies in comics through a phenomenologically inspired comics reading practice, as we have done, allows us to learn more about the subtle ways in which focalization is marked within a narrative, as well as about what narrative action it accomplishes both inside and outside of a particular narrative world.

Our analyses take into account findings from cognitive psychology and phenomenology that emphasize the role of the body as a medium and focus of experience. As Peter Stockwell explains, current research in cognitive linguistics and cognitive psychology leads to the conclusion that "all forms of expression and forms of conscious perception are bound, more closely than was previously realized, in our biological circumstances" (2002: 4). Cognition and perception are not immaterial aspects of human existence that occur in an inner realm separate from the human body. On the contrary, "it is certain that our cognitive experience is shaped by an embodied brain and that the brains we have are shaped by the bodies we have, and by our real-world actions. Cognition is not only embodied, it is situated and, of course, it is situated because it is embodied" (S. Gallagher and Zahavi 150). In phenomenology, there cannot be physical or cognitive experience apart from the body, which "is deeply implicated in our relation to the world, in our relation to others, and in our self-relation" (S. Gallagher and Zahavi 153).

Thus, both the cognitive sciences and the tradition of philosophical phenomenology argue against a mind-body split. For the study of focalization, these arguments point to the conclusion that focalization should not be conceptualized as concerning only interior processes of disembodied thought. Rather, focalization encompasses embodied, embedded, and enactive cognitive and perceptual processes, both inside the text as well as concerning a text's readers. As we have shown in our analysis of *Habibi,* the combination and overlaying of perspectives in panels and sequences and, on a larger scale, the complex structure of the entire book with its many flashbacks, fantasy, and dream sequences opens up a variety of options for readers to position themselves in relation to Dodola as a storyteller, to the main plotline detailing her life story, and to the many intradiegetic stories she relates. Such positioning involves the entire body and all the senses, as extended explorations of embodiment invite readers to use their own bodily awareness to experience the narrative.

In an article for the groundbreaking volume *Cognitive Literary Science,* Raymond Gibbs points out that "reading, of all sorts, involves our imaginative, embodied engagement with texts, and that this engagement does not just constitute our reactions to literature, but shapes the very process by which linguistic meanings are interpreted" (221). Comics studies, too, have drawn attention to the centrality of the body in comics, since comics storytelling indexes the drawing hand of the artist through the physicality and materiality of the line and thereby foregrounds an embodied deixis. For Eszter Szép, "activities of the body are crucial to making and reading comics" (2), while Elisabeth El Refaie describes the recurring portrayal of the body in comics as a form of "pictorial embodiment" (2012: 51).

The embodied characters that populate a graphic narrative universe, that move through settings that may or may not reflect their attitude or mood and that interact and are acted upon by other embodied characters, force into play a consideration of focalization that moves away from the study of individual minds. The minds of comics characters do not present as isolated or singular. Instead, engaging in lived experience, they are intersubjective, interrelated minds; embodied minds; entangled minds; ambiguous and multifarious, dynamic and interactive experiencing minds. Our phenomenologically inspired approach to focalization accounts for the lived experiences, embodied minds, and intersubjectivity of characters in graphic narratives. Phenomenology accentuates these very features of existence and, by doing so, prompts the revisiting of descriptions of focalization as "a reflex of the mind . . . conceptualizing scenes within storyworlds" (D. Herman 2009b: 122) or as "the textual representation of specific (pre)existing sensory elements of the text's story world as perceived and registered (recorded, represented, encoded, modeled and stored) by some mind or recording device which is a member of this world" (Margolin 2009: 42) through a lens that critically addresses the sharing of experience between embodied minds within and outside of the narrative world.

Focalization in Graphic Narrative Is Marked through the Particular Style of a Comic

The style of a comic is an important means by which graphic narratives mark focalization. In comics, visual style is much more than a marker of authorial identity (see Gardner 2011; Lefèvre; Wolk) or a visual language of seeing (Mikkonen 2013: 102). It communicates thinking and knowing, motives and intentions, dispositions and beliefs, feelings and emotions—in short, all that Alan Palmer considers under an aspectual "fictional mental functioning" (2004: 15). The style of a comic also communicates the mood, atmosphere, and feel of a narrative world, and it informs readers how events in it are perceived and experienced by specific characters. Expressive of subjectivity and of mood, style is among the most subtle focalization markers used in comics. It is also among the most powerful, inviting readers into the embodied experience of characters or into the take of a noncharacter narrator.

Stylistic expressivity in comics is crucial for identifying focalization. As a global effect, visual style in comics emerges out of a network of visual features (line, color, border, white space, etc.) and strategies (repetition, size, layout, contrast, etc.) that texture an image, the page, and the entire book and communicate "shifts in tone, focus, and implicit meaning" (Fischer and Hatfield 76). The visual presentation, composition, and organization of narrative elements are thus "symbolic forms of meaning making" (Bundgaard 64) and therefore exist in relation to modes of discourse and focalization. Like other focalization markers, style connects the expression of experience within a comic to the experience of readers. Stylistic choices, or the way the text represents its story and the characters that inhabit it, are highly influential for the relation between characters and their world as well as between characters and readers. By implicitly conveying character emotion and attitude, style triggers an affective response in readers.

Comics style is also closely linked to embodiment, as focalization in graphic narrative is marked through embodied practices that are expressed stylistically. At the same time as it makes a graphiator's or character's experience available to readers, however, the frequent foregrounding of style in graphic narrative also encourages critical, reflective readings that bring focalization up to notice, and this foregrounding may produce distance or frustration as a dominant reading experience. For example, instances when a graphiator hesitates about how to draw a scene or character provide readers with crucial access to that graphiator's mind. They highlight how comics style is always expressive of a highly individual way of perceiving, processing, and judging the world. But because these self-reflexive instances refuse to fix one version of events, they also draw readers into the doubt and uncertainty of the graphiator concerning their stylistic choices.

In making a case for how focalization is tied up with style, we draw inspiration from Uri Margolin, who proposes the notion of "cognitive style" to theorize a narrative's shape and mode of presentation (2009). Whereas Margolin sets out to shed light on the transition between actual and fictional world, however, we indicate how style communicates the cognition, personality, and attitudes of world participants, besides those of the discourse shaper. Shifting questions of style from voice to focalization has allowed us to better assess how style in graphic narrative necessarily works to instruct readers about the workings of fictional minds and shared, lived experience.

Focalization in Graphic Narrative Is Bound up with Genre

Besides style, genre is a second global aspect of graphic narrative that regulates how and to what extent experiences inside a comic become available to readers. Genre conventions shape the formal features and situation of address as well as the thematic structure of comics storytelling. They regulate what kind of access an individual comic provides to the experience of its characters and to the mood and atmosphere of its narrative world. Readers, in their turn, draw on familiar genre conventions when they interpret a narrative. For instance, competent readers of a graphic memoir will come to the text with the expectation that its character narrator is an avatar of the comic's author. Their understanding will moreover ideally be based on a familiarity with the conventions of life writing that place a strong emphasis on one subject and on that subject's experience, and on couching that experience in a language of authenticity. In this way, genre shapes the narrative structure of comics while also directing the expectations of readers before they even begin to engage in the narrative world of a particular text.

When genre is approached as "the precondition for the creation and the reading of texts" (Beebee 250), it becomes less a tool for classification and more a critical concept describing the mediation of knowledge about tightly interrelated aspects of the narrative world, including setting, plot, style, composition, and mood. As our analyses show, genre plays a distinctive role in structuring narratives by setting the ground rules according to which focalization is marked, and by which focalization markers are understood. Genre is a crucial element in the production and reception of a text, central to communication and interpretation, and can thus be conceptualized as a dynamic process "created through the interaction of writers, readers, past texts, and contexts" (Devitt 699). Within this dynamic process, the familiar conceptual frameworks and expectations of genre may be confirmed or they may be thwarted, and this impacts reception. Throughout *Experiencing Visual Storyworlds: Focalization in Comics,* we emphasized that when graphic narratives frustrate, change, or break established genre expectations, this also bears on focalization.

Each of the genres analyzed in *Experiencing Visual Storyworlds: Focalization in Comics* builds on combinations of narration and focalization that have become conventionalized in the history of these genres and set up specific expectations regarding the content as well as the form, expression, and mood of a graphic narrative. For instance, graphic memoir typically employs a first-person narrator who is also the intradiegetic artist or graphiator of the visual narrative (Marion) as well as the focal source of perceptions and experiences, thereby enabling readers to closely identify and empathize with the memoirist. Graphic journalism and historiography often rely on a similar combination of character narration and internal focalization, but employ narrators who are impartial witnesses of other people's stories (rather than their own) and whose attempts to understand those stories provide a blueprint for readers who may similarly wish to gain access to experiences that are not their own. Some graphic historiographies eliminate the figure of the character narrator in favor of a non-character-based narrative with no determinate origin. This also makes the deictic center of the narrative difficult if not impossible to determine, resulting in an ambiguous focalization. Such open-endedness is also characteristic of wordless comics, which often tax readers' understanding by deliberately veiling the distinction between character-bound focalization and narratorial focalization or between a character's what it's like and the mood of an entire narrative world. Thus, although we in no way want to confuse focalization with a genre narrative stance that manifests in different varieties (see Faris), we do emphasize that focalization is bound up in genre.

Graphic Narratives Are Often Metafocal Texts

The self-conscious concern with the framing and staging of optical perspective, style, genre, and the processing of experience in many comics makes graphic narrative a powerful metafocal medium. Comics not only rely on a wide range of focalization markers to cue readers into the aspectuality of characters and the mood and atmosphere of entire narrative worlds; they also frequently consider the construction of voice and vision within their narrative. Comics thus reflect on their own mediality as well as on the role that aspectual filtering plays within their medial set-up. In *Berlin: City of Stones,* for example, the staging of different kinds of gazes (that of characters against the omniscient view of the impersonal narrative) serves to investigate the close intertwining of optical perspectivation, knowledge, and power as it is expressed through comics storytelling. In this manner, comics frequently double their narrative into its own commentary.

The frequent introduction of an aesthetic meta-commentary on narration and focalization has important consequences for the extent to which comics storytelling makes experience within the diegesis available to readers. An explicit concern with meta-ization may encourage readers to step back and reflect on their own engagement with graphic narrative, slowing down the reception process and disrupting readerly empathy. In chapter 5, we have shown how wordless comics, which are often set in a surreal world, force readers to interpret images without recourse to any context provided by orienting verbal discourse, asking them to draw their own inferences and make connections between disjointed and fragmentary impressions. Our analysis of Craig Thompson's *Habibi,* in chapter 6, comes to the conclusion that the book's complex narrative structure posits several possible sources of narration, each one inviting readers toward a unique kind of perspective-taking. This is a cognitively challenging task, which is itself the object of metanarrative reflection when several panels show the protagonist Dodola reading a book in the book that we are reading. The Chinese-box structure of representation in *Habibi* invites readers to consider their own reading process. In Art Spiegelman's *Maus*, which we analyze in chapter 4, the repeated hesitation of the graphiator Artie on how to draw a scene involves readers in the comic's representative choices, including different options for perspective-taking. Several of the books analyzed in *Experiencing Visual Storyworlds: Focalization in Comics* introduce unusual page layouts that interrupt habitual reading patterns or metafocal panels that bring readers to engage with a character's aspectuality, while also making them consider how the scene within the book relates to their own experience. The resulting slowing down and emotional distancing may be a desired effect, especially in graphic narratives that represent unusual or traumatic experiences that are not shared by many readers, including atrocity history or crippling disease and disability. Indeed, the representation of atrocity may very well require an ethical positioning on the part of the reader, rather than an affective response (Szép).

However, a metafocal concern in graphic narrative may also contribute to a richer readerly experientiality precisely because it renders the narrative legible on several levels. Thus, when *Asterios Polyp* indicates the world processing of characters through the choice of different color schemes, it invites readers to consider how the processing of individual minds colors the world around them, and it involves readers in the question of whether that processing brings into being entirely separate worlds. When the vantage points of different characters are repeatedly shown to infect each other, often in a hypothetical mode as characters speculate about each other's level of knowledge, this suggests that the graphic novel may function to school readers, urging them to join the protagonist in acquiring social ways of perceiving and interpreting reality.

Comics use many complex, multilayered narrative strategies to address readers on a metafictional, metanarrative, and metafocal level. Multiple and ambiguous focalization strategies in graphic narratives draw readers into the workings of focalization by engaging them in acts of perspective-taking and by asking them to negotiate different takes on events and to consider the relation between storytelling and experiencing. Focalization allows readers to dwell on the rendering of its processing, while offering a higher-level reflection on how the aspectuality of narrative informs readers about narrative worlds and guides interpretation.

Focalization in Comics Is Particularly Powerful When It Is Ambiguous or Multilayered

Ambiguous instances of focalization are powerful stratagems for securing reader engagement. As early as 1994, Patrick O'Neill argued that "the more ambiguous the focalization, the greater the scope for interpretation" (94). Ambiguities of focalization tax readers because they undermine the construction of a stable, unequivocal meaning or point of origin. They force readers to stand on unsteady ground in their quest to reach coherence of meaning and engage intellectually and emotionally with the narrative world. Because it leaves room for interpretation, ambiguous focalization is productively exploited by authors of comics to entangle readers in an intricate web of interpretative possibilities that fosters their subjective engagement with the narrative world. This immersive reading practice is "shot through with sensory images, emotions, evaluations—the stuff our experiences are made of" (Caracciolo 2014: 46)—but also with the physical, emotional, and cognitive experience of characters in that world.

When graphic narratives highlight characters' struggle for understanding, they ask readers to consciously process storyworld information and engage in acts of meaning-making mirroring the ones unfolding within the diegesis. Through this process, readers are drawn into the cognitive functioning of characters as they engage in their own quest for knowledge. While focalization is usually associated with the degree of knowledge or information, it may also activate readers by signaling a lack of knowing or presenting a restricted, incomplete knowledge that requires readers to fill in.

In addition, although graphic narratives affect readers because they offer access to the experience, perception, and cognition of possible or imagined others, this experience need not be bound to any one character. As a multimodal medium, comics have a high potential for embedding numerous layers of focalization, and this may also produce ambiguity. *Black Hole,* for instance, contains several mutually embedded focalizations with no clear source or origin. While its verbal narrative generally offers an internal focalization bound to its character narrators, the visual images accompanying that verbal narrative often reveal more than the characters know, suggesting an omniscient narration that communicates with readers without the awareness of the narratorial voice. Although unable to determine a single source or origin of focalization in these instances, readers nonetheless experience the narrative world through a particular experiential angle, which guides their understanding and experience of that narrative world. In other graphic narratives, intersubjective networks of experience evoke deliberate ambiguity about the narrative's deictic center, making readers consider the depicted scenes and events from multiple perspectives. Often, repeated depictions of the same scene expose different aspects or moods under which the same or similar events can be experienced. Taken together, the examples of ambiguous focalization analyzed in our book serve to show that readers react not so much to isolated instances of focalization as to the overall effect of focalization.

Ambiguity can be tied up with genre. In chapter 5, we argued that wordless comics are particularly apt at creating ambiguity, indeterminacy, and confusion around focalization. Because wordless comics lack orienting verbal detail, readers often cannot distinguish between visual details associated with a natural, exterior world and those associated with the surreal depiction of dreams, visions, and imagination. In terms of focalization, this means that some panels and sequences can be read as narratorially focalized statements or else as the internal focalization of one or several characters' mental and emotional experience. Eric Drooker's *Flood!* and Shaun Tan's *The Arrival* deliberately exploit the resulting narrative ambiguity between an authoritative, narratorial origin and a more indirect, character-bound understanding of panels and sequences, ultimately collapsing the boundary between a realistic external world and an internal dream world. This makes for a highly disorienting reading experience.

Focalization in Graphic Narrative Exposes Noncanonical Forms of Subjectivity

When focalization is understood as an "expression of subjectivity" (Köppe), that subjectivity is often implicitly or explicitly associated with the idea of the individual, autonomous self. Thus, many narrative theories describe focalization in terms of the activity of an individual "focalizing agent" (Margolin 2009: 42) or "focalizor" (Bal 2009: 149), who is referred to in the singular and more often than not gendered through masculine pronouns (e.g., "the identity of the focalizer and his location in the narrated and/or narrating system"; Margolin 2009: 53). Internal focalization, in particular, is thought to lie "with one character which participates in the fabula as an actor" (Bal 2009: 152). That character is the locus of mental processes such as "perception, thought, recollection, and knowledge," which are "considered to be criterial features of focalization" (Jahn 1996: 243) and marked by narrative techniques for mind representation, such as reported thought, psycho-narration, and free indirect discourse.

Many graphic narratives challenge these associations of focalization with a single agent, with individuality, with disembodied thought, and with an autonomous self that is in full command of itself and its circumstances. Graphic memoir, in particular, is notorious for bending the rules of autobiographical storytelling to trouble understandings of the self as stable, unified, and knowable. Not only narrating but also portraying the self, graphic memoirs provide a complex presentation of selfhood that puts the self's body into focus through repetition (El Refaie 2012). The repeated visual presentation of the body that accompanies and offsets the narrativization of the self on the verbal track provides many opportunities for exposing a multifaceted, changing self.

With this multilayered presentation of self across two semiotic tracks, graphic memoir also challenges the art historical tradition of self-portraiture. In her study *Portrayal and the Search for Identity*, art historian Marcia Pointon describes the portrait as an active agent in constructing identity. However, in graphic memoir as in other comics genres, not one, but many portraits stand side by side, creating a self that is always in process, changing and multiplying, moving in and out of different configurations. The rhythm of repetition and variation of this typical portrayal practice creates many "possibilities for interpreting experience, reworking memory, and staging self-reflection," as Julia Watson points out (124–25). The visual representation of self thus becomes amplified, expounded, and complicated through "variation, embellishment and interpretation" (Mitchell 257). Besides realistic portrayals, the act of interpretation may also result in distorted or surreal self-images or in the portrayal of the self through visual metaphors.

By repeatedly drawing the body, graphic artists reflect the physical as well as mental nature of experience, and they fashion embodiment on their own terms. While the represented body draws attention to a memoirist's shifting self-image, the act of portraiture as a trace of the memoirist's drawing hand marks the production of these images as an embodied practice. Embodiment is marked stylistically when portraits in graphic memoir are rendered in a subjective style that is tied to the artist's body. Representations of the body in graphic memoir are often less concerned with physical appearances than with how the body is seen and experienced from the inside. The engagement with the body extends beyond visual portrayal in other ways, too, especially when it touches on questions of one's personal understandings and imaginings of the self, thereby dismantling distinctions between the cartoonist's interior and exterior realities.

In comics, body as well as mind are sites of subjectivity, and exterior as well as interior conceptions of the self are explored across the body. Embodiment entails not only how the body looks or should look but also how the self feels and thinks about, experiences, and interacts with its body and the world that body inhabits. In graphic memoir, the frequent highlighting of a shifting, multifaceted, or split self, often imagined through distorted body images, exposes a second crucial insight: The embodied self is a social self. Many graphic memoirs debunk the myth of solitary perception by creating patterns of intersubjectively tangled perception. The tangling of subjectivities, highlighted in such titles as Marjane Satrapi's *Embroideries*, Sarah Leavitt's *Tangles*, and David Small's *Stitches*, shows subjectivity not as isolated, but rather as part of a social web that includes minds, senses, and bodies. To account for an entangled subjectivity, the focalization through which experience becomes available in these graphic narratives is multiple, layered, or mutually embedded. Visually, it can be marked through spliced portraits combining two halves of different characters as these perceive each other or through shot/counter-shot sequences, reversals, or stylistic variation, as when the sparse style in *Tangles* is used to express how Sarah imagines her mother's what it's like, thus merging two distinct sets of qualia. Employing forms of communal, intersubjective, spliced, or sutured focalization that challenge narratological systems that narrowly tie focalization to an individual narrative agent, graphic memoir foregrounds the crucial phenomenological insight that the phenomenological world is intersubjective (Merleau-Ponty 2012: 8).

Graphic memoir can therefore be described as a meta-phenomenological genre that represents experience but simultaneously also reflects on the nature of experience, on the self having experiences, and on the relation between subject, object, and other subjects in experience. This tendency toward self-reflexivity once again supports the conclusion that focalization in comics is tied to the body and its experiences and should not be narrowly identified with mental activity. It also shows that focalization is often social and intersubjective, not restricted to a single agent in the narrative, and should be conceptualized as such.

Focalization in Graphic Narrative Structures Historical Experience Differently

Focalization in comics is innovative not only in relation to ideas of the self and its representation that underlie it and to the variety of focalization markers that cue comics readers into the what it's like of characters and worlds but also regarding the stories it filters. Graphic historiography, a popular comics genre whose narrative structure is closely related to graphic memoir, presents historical events of global importance that are often little known outside of the regions where they occurred and that are suppressed from official commemoration. Previous research on atrocity comics has stopped on the formal qualities of graphic narrative, "including the gutter, the staging of point of view, and the textual-imagistic hybridity" (Polak 2), fragmentary narration, and in-built metanarrative reflection to propose that atrocity comics introduce a "metacognitive aspect of representation, emotion, and personal ethical positioning" to the reading process that may be lacking in other forms of atrocity representation (20). Atrocity comics' strategies of narrative metaization grant readers the unique opportunity to "reflect on the representation itself, our imaginative engagement with that representation, and our relationship to the content" (20).

We have built on these insights by arguing that graphic historiography challenges thinking about the writing of history, especially atrocity history, in similar ways to the challenge that graphic memoirs pose to ideas about subjectivity. Where historian Hayden White suggests that imaginative literature is uniquely able to communicate a phenomenologically inspired perspective on history (1992), we extend that idea toward comics. Following Hilary Chute (2016), we emphasize that the variety of styles in comics drawing and the bimodality of the comics form may be exploited to structure history differently. The telling of history always carries a perspectival index, and styles of representation express perspectival ownership on historical events. But the comics medium's bimodal narrative allows for the simultaneous adoption of different perspectives on the same events. For instance, the double-layered narrative of *Maus* filters the Holocaust survival story of Vladek Spiegelman through Vladek's own words as well as through the drawings of his son, Artie. Their dialogic communication, presented across text and images, highlights not so much the historical facts of Vladek's experience as the personal understanding of those facts formed by father and son. The tentative presentation of alternative versions of events and the explicit assertion that the telling of history is always tinged with doubt invite competing counter-narratives from readers who are drawn into the work of interpretation and, at the same time, are made aware of the role interpretation and imagination play in the creation of historical narratives.

Graphic historiographies represent historical experience at the same time as they offer a meta-commentary on how these experiences can be represented and understood. Despite offering insight into historical experiences that are not usually available to Western readers by presenting what it's like to live through extreme experiences, the graphic historiographies we studied do not invite simple identification. Instead, their self-reflexive narrative strategies draw attention to the angle or agent through which historical events are focalized. Moreover, they often visualize historical events in nonrealistic ways through the use of visual metaphors as well as juxtaposing competing versions of events by exploiting the co-presence of panels and the interaction of text and image on the comics page. They also build the difficulties of historical understanding into their narratives by using narrators who are uninvolved bystanders, members of a second generation, or foreigners. It is this belated and secondary processing of history, and not the experiencing of history firsthand, that provides a position in relation to history into which readers may step.

In these ways, graphic historiographies set in motion a process of transmission in which understanding, achieved by accessing historical experience through acts of focalization and counter-focalization, becomes a task for readers. By drawing on conflicting visual and verbal focalization sources that inscribe doubt and indeterminacy into the story, they call forth a layered reality that includes multiple, sometimes contradictory experiences. The subjective experiential engagement of individual characters is frequently shown to be part of an intersubjective or social web of experiences, perceptions, memories, and retrospective appraisals, which are in turn embedded in the mood and atmosphere of a narrative world. Readers are invited into a complex network of attitudes, postures, and perspectives that bear on each other, and they are made to assess the plausibility of one version of events against another version. When they foreground a character narrator who is in an outsider role in relation to the narrated events, graphic historiographies create a situated perspective that, as Hilary Chute points out, is specifically geared toward readers who are also outsiders (2016: 252). In this context, focalization does not necessarily mark a fixed position into which readers can step. Rather, it often functions as a generator of perspective-taking in readers, who can adopt different or multiple perspectives on events and characters as well as on the representation of those events and characters. As *Experiencing Visual Storyworlds: Focalization in Comics* shows, focalization in graphic narrative is a powerful tool for involving readers in a number of ways and on several levels simultaneously. Focalization grants readers access to the experience and to the aspectual what it's like of characters, and involves them in the perceptual and cognitive processing of that experience.

BIBLIOGRAPHY

Acheson, Charles. 2015. "Expanding the Role of the Gutter in Nonfiction Comics: Forged Memories in Joe Sacco's *Safe Area Goražde*." *Studies in the Novel*, vol. 47, no. 3, pp. 291–307.

Adams, Jeff. 2008. *Documentary Graphic Novels and Social Realism*. Peter Lang.

Aldama, Frederick Luis, editor. 2010. *Toward a Cognitive Theory of Narrative Acts*. University of Texas Press.

———. 2013. "Mood, Mystery, and Demystification in Gilbert Hernandez's Twenty-First Century NeoNoir Stand-Alones." *ImageTexT: Interdisciplinary Comics Studies*, vol. 7, no. 1. http://imagetext.english.ufl.edu/archives/v7_1/aldama/. Accessed March 25, 2021.

Altman, Rick. 2008. *A Theory of Narrative*. Columbia University Press.

Atwood, Margaret. 1986. *The Handmaid's Tale*. McClelland and Stewart.

B., David. 2005. *Epileptic*. Translated by Kim Thompson. Pantheon Books.

Badman, Derik A. 2010. "Talking, Thinking, and Seeing in Pictures: Narration, Focalization, and Ocularization in Comics Narratives." *International Journal of Comics Art*, vol. 12, no. 2/3, pp. 91–111.

Baetens, Jan. 1991. "Pour une poétique de la gouttière." *Word and Image*, vol. 7, no. 4, pp. 365–76.

Bal, Mieke. 1977. *Narratologie. Essais sur la signification narrative dans quatre romans modernes*. Klincksieck.

———. 1991. *Reading "Rembrandt": Beyond the Word-Image Opposition*. Cambridge University Press.

———. 1997. *Narratology: Introduction to the Theory of Narrative*. 2nd ed. University of Toronto Press.

———. 1999. *Quoting Caravaggio: Contemporary Art, Preposterous History*. University of Chicago Press.

———. 2009. *Narratology: Introduction to the Theory of Narrative*. 3rd ed. University of Toronto Press.

Bálint, Katalin, Frank Hakemulder, Moniek M. Kuijpers, Miruna M. Doicaru, and Ed S. Tan. 2016. "Reconceptualizing Foregrounding: Identifying Response Strategies to Deviation in Absorbing Narratives." *Scientific Study of Literature*, vol. 6, no. 2, pp. 176–207.

Banfield, Ann. 1987. "Describing the Unobserved: Events Grouped around an Empty Centre." In *The Linguistics of Writing*, edited by Nigel Fabb, pp. 265–85. Methuen.

Barry, Lynda. 2002. *One! Hundred! Demons!* Sasquatch Books.

Beaty, Bart, and Benjamin Woo. 2016. *The Greatest Comic Book of All Time: Symbolic Capital and the Field of American Comic Books*. Palgrave.

Bechdel, Alison. 2006. *Fun Home: A Family Tragicomic*. Mariner.

———. 2007. "The Alison Bechdel Interview." *The Comics Journal*, vol. 282. http://www.tcj.com/the-alison-bechdel-interview/. Accessed May 25, 2021.

Beebee, Thomas O. 1994. *The Ideology of Genre: A Comparative Study of Generic Instability*. Pennsylvania State University Press.

Bekhta, Natalya. 2017. "We-Narratives: The Distinctiveness of Collective Narration." *Narrative*, vol. 25, no. 2, pp. 164–81.

———. 2020. *We-Narratives: Collective Storytelling in Contemporary Fiction*. The Ohio State University Press.

Bell, Susan Groag, and Marilyn Yalom. 1990. *Revealing Lives: Autobiography, Biography, and Gender*. SUNY Press.

Bennett, Alice. 2012. *Afterlife and Narrative in Contemporary Fiction*. Palgrave Macmillan.

Bennett, Jill. 2005. *Empathic Vision*. Stanford University Press.

Benstock, Shari. 1991. "The Female Self Engendered: Autobiographical Writing and Theories of Selfhood." *Women's Studies*, vol. 20, no. 1, pp. 5–14.

Beronä, David A. 2001. "Pictures Speak in Comics without Words: Pictorial Principles in the Work of Milt Gross, Hendrik Dorgarthen, Eric Drooker, and Peter Kuper." In *The Language of Comics: Word and Image*, edited by Robin Varnum and Christine T. Gibbons, pp. 19–39. University Press of Mississippi.

———. 2008. *Wordless Books: The Original Graphic Novels*. Abrams.

Bortolussi, Marisa, and Peter Dixon. 2003. *Psychonarratology: Foundations for the Empirical Study of Literary Response*. Cambridge University Press.

Branigan, Edward. 1984. *Point of View in the Cinema: A Theory of Narration and Subjectivity in Classical Film*. Mouton.

Bredehoft, Thomas A. 2006. "Comics Architecture, Multidimensionality, and Time: Chris Ware's *Jimmy Corrigan: The Smartest Kid on Earth*." *Modern Fiction Studies*, vol. 52, no. 4, pp. 869–90.

Breithaupt, Fritz. 2009. *Kulturen der Empathie*. Suhrkamp.

Brosch, Renate. 2007. "The Curious Eye of the Reader: Perspective as Interaction with Narrative." In *Seeing Perception*, edited by Silke Horstkotte and Karin Leonhard, pp. 143–65. Cambridge Scholars.

———. 2008. "Weltweite Bilder, lokale Lesarten: Visualisierungen der Literatur." In *Visual Culture: Beiträge zur XIII. Tagung der Deutschen Gesellschaft für Allgemeine und Vergleichende Literaturwissenschaft*, edited by Monika Schmitz-Emans and Gertrud Lehnert, pp. 61–82. Synchron.

Bumatay, Michelle, and Hannah Warman. 2012. "Illustrating Genocidaires, Orphans, and Child Soldiers in Central Africa." *Peace Review: A Journal of Social Justice*, vol. 24, no. 3, pp. 332–39.

Bundgaard, Peer F. 2010. "Means of Meaning Making in Literary Art: Focalization, Mode of Narration, and Granularity." *Acta Linguistica Hafniensia*, vol. 42, no. 1, pp. 64–84.

Burns, Charles. 2005. *Black Hole*. Pantheon.

Caracciolo, Marco. 2012. "Notes for A(nother) Theory of Experientiality." *Journal of Literary Theory*, vol. 6, no. 1, pp. 177–94.

———. 2014. *The Experientiality of Narrative: An Enactivist Approach*. de Gruyter.

Cave, Terence. 2016. *Thinking with Literature: Towards a Cognitive Criticism*. Oxford University Press.

Chaney, Michael A. 2011. *Graphic Subjects: Critical Essays on Autobiography and Graphic Novels*. University of Wisconsin Press.

———. 2016. *Reading Lessons in Seeing: Mirrors, Masks, and Mazes in the Autobiographical Graphic Novel*. University Press of Mississippi.

Chatman, Seymour. 1990. *Coming to Terms: The Rhetoric of Narrative in Fiction and Film*. Cornell University Press.

Chute, Hillary. 2008. "Comics as Literature? Reading Graphic Narrative." *PMLA*, vol. 132, no. 2, pp. 452–65.

———. 2010. *Graphic Women: Life Narrative and Contemporary Comics*. Columbia University Press.

———. 2016. *Disaster Drawn: Visual Witness, Comics, and Documentary Form*. Belknap.

Ciment, Gilles, and Thierry Groensteen. 2002. "Itinéraire: Entretien avec Jean-Philippe Staassen." *9e Art: Les Cahiers du Musée de la Bande Dessinée* (January), p. 7.

Cohn, Dorrit. 1978. *Transparent Minds: Narrative Modes for Presenting Consciousness in Fiction*. Princeton University Press.

Coplan, Amy. 2004. "Empathic Engagement with Narrative Fictions." *Journal of Aesthetics and Art Criticism*, vol. 62, no. 2, pp. 141–52.

Couser, G. Thomas. 1997. *Recovering Bodies: Illness, Disability, and Life Writing*. University of Wisconsin Press.

———. 1999. "Autopathography: Women, Illness, and Lifewriting." In *Women and Autobiography*, edited by Martine Watson Brownley and Allison B. Kimmich, pp. 163–75. Scholarly Resources.

———. 2009. *Signifying Bodies: Disability in Contemporary Life Writing*. The University of Michigan Press. https://www.sas.upenn.edu/~cavitch/pdf-library/Couser_Signifying_Bodies.pdf. Accessed May 31, 2021.

———. 2013. "Disability, Life Narrative, and Representation." In *The Disability Studies Reader*, edited by Lennard J. Davis, pp. 456–59. Routledge.

Davis, Whitney. 2011. *A General Theory of Visual Culture*. Princeton University Press.

Devitt, Amy J. 2000. "Integrating Rhetorical and Literary Theories of Genre." *College English*, vol. 62, no. 6, pp. 696–718.

Doležel, Lubomír. 1998. *Heterocosmica: Fiction and Possible Worlds*. Johns Hopkins University Press.

Dong, Lan. 2015. "Inside and Outside the Frame: Joe Sacco's *Safe Area Goražde*." In *The Comics of Joe Sacco: Journalism in a Visual World*, edited by Daniel Worden, pp. 39–53. University Press of Mississippi.

Doubrovsky, Serge. 1977. *Fils*. Édition Galilée.

Drooker, Eric. 2007a. *Flood! A Novel in Pictures*. Dark Horse.

———. 2007b. "An Interview with Eric Drooker." In *Flood! A Novel in Pictures*. Dark Horse.

Duncan, Randy. 2012. "Image Functions: Shape and Color as Hermeneutic Images in *Asterios Polyp*." In *Critical Approaches to Comics: Theories and Methods*, edited by Matthew J. Smith and Randy Duncan, pp. 43–54. Routledge.

Duncan, Randy, and Matthew J. Smith. 2009. *The Power of Comics: History, Form, and Culture*. Continuum.

Durst, Uwe. 2001. *Theorie der phantastischen Literatur*. Francke.

Eakin, Paul John. 1999. *How Our Lives Become Stories: Making Selves*. Cornell University Press.

Eisner, Will. 2008a. *Comics and Sequential Art: Principles and Practices from the Legendary Cartoonist*. Norton. Original edition, 1985.

———. 2008b. *Graphic Storytelling and Visual Narrative*. Norton. Original edition, 1996.

Elleström, Lars, editor. 2021. *Beyond Media Borders, Volume 2: Intermedial Relations among Multimodal Media*. Springer International Publishing, Palgrave Macmillan.

El Refaie, Elisabeth. 2012. *Autobiographical Comics: Life Writing in Pictures*. University Press of Mississippi.

———. 2019. *Visual Metaphor and Embodiment in Graphic Illness Narratives*. Oxford University Press.

Emmott, Catherine. 2003. "Constructing Social Space: Sociocognitive Factors in the Interpretation of Character Relations." In *Narrative Theory and Cognitive Sciences*, edited by David Herman, 295–321. Center for the Study of Language and Information.

Emmott, Catherine, and Anthony J. Sanford. 2012. *Mind, Brain and Narrative*. Cambridge University Press.

Esposito, Elena. 2007. *Die Fiktion der wahrscheinlichen Realität*. Suhrkamp.

Esrock, Ellen J. 2004. "Embodying Literature." *Journal of Consciousness Studies*, vol. 11, no. 5/6, pp. 79–89.

———. 2010. "Embodying Art: The Spectator and the Inner Body." *Poetics Today*, vol. 31, no. 2, pp. 217–50.

Etter, Lukas. 2017. "Visible Hand? Subjectivity and Its Stylistic Markers in Graphic Narratives." In *Subjectivity across Media: Interdisciplinary and Transmedial Perspectives*, edited by Maike Sarah Reinerth and Jan-Noël Thon, pp. 92–110. Routledge.

Ewert, Jeanne. 2004. "Art Spiegelman's *Maus* and the Graphic Narrative." In *Narrative across Media: The Languages of Storytelling*, edited by Marie-Laure Ryan, pp. 178–93. University of Nebraska Press.

Faris, Wendy B. 2004. *Ordinary Enchantments: Magic Realism and the Remystification of Narrative*. Vanderbilt University Press.

Farrell, Maureen, Evelyn Arizpe, and Julie McAdam. 2010. "Journeys across Visual Borders: Annotated Spreads of *The Arrival* by Shaun Tan as a Method for Understanding Pupils' Creation of Meaning through Visual Images." *Australian Journal of Language and Literacy*, vol. 33, no. 3, pp. 198–210.

Fawaz, Ramzi. 2019. "A Queer Sequence: Comics as a Disruptive Medium." *PMLA*, vol. 134, no. 3, pp. 588–94.

Fischer, Craig, and Charles Hatfield. 2011. "Teeth, Sticks, and Bricks: Calligraphy, Graphic Focalization, and Narrative Braiding in Eddie Cambell's *Alec*." *SubStance*, vol. 40, no. 1, pp. 70–93.

Fludernik, Monika. 1996. *Towards a "Natural" Narratology*. Routledge.

———. 2001. "New Wine in Old Bottles? Voice, Focalization, and New Writing." *New Literary History*, vol. 32, no. 3, pp. 619–38.

———. 2009. *An Introduction to Narratology*. Routledge.

Flueckiger, Barbara. 2017. "Color and Subjectivity in Film." In *Subjectivity across Media: Interdisciplinary and Transmedial Perspectives*, edited by Maike Sarah Reinerth and Jan-Noël Thon, pp. 145–61. Routledge.

Forney, Ellen. 2012. *Marbles: Mania, Depression, Michelangelo, and Me*. Gotham.

Frahm, Ole. 2006. *Genealogie des Holocaust: Art Spiegelmans* Maus—a Survivor's Tale. Fink.

Frow, John. 2015. *Genre*. 2nd ed. Routledge.

Gallagher, Catherine. 2006. "The Rise of Fictionality." In *The Novel*, edited by Franco Moretti, pp. 336–63. Princeton University Press.

Gallagher, Shaun, and Dan Zahavi. 2012. *The Phenomenological Mind*. 2nd ed. Routledge.

Gallese, Vittorio. 2011. "Embodied Simulation Theory: Imagination and Narrative." *Neuropsychoanalysis*, vol. 13, no. 2, pp. 196–200.

García, Patricia. 2015. *Space and the Postmodern Fantastic in Contemporary Literature: The Architectural Void*. Routledge.

Gardner, Jared. 2008. "Autography's Biography, 1972–2007." *Biography: An Interdisciplinary Quarterly*, vol. 31, no. 1, pp. 1–26.

———. 2011. "Storylines." *SubStance*, vol. 40, no. 1, pp. 53–69.

Genette, Gérard. 1972. *Figures III*. Éditions du seuil.

———. 1980. *Narrative Discourse: An Essay in Method*. Translated by Jane E. Lewin. Cornell University Press.

———. 1983. *Nouveau discours du récit*. Éditions du Seuil.

———. 1988. *Narrative Discourse Revisited*. Translated by Jane E. Lewin. Cornell University Press.

———. 2004. *Métalepse: De la figure à la fiction*. Seuil.

Gerrig, Richard J. 1993. *Experiencing Narrative Worlds: On the Psychological Activities of Reading*. Yale University Press.

Gibbs, Raymond W. 2017. "Embodied Dynamics in Literary Experience." In *Cognitive Literary Science: Dialogues between Literature and Cognition*, edited by Michael Burke and Emily T. Troscianko, pp. 219–38. Oxford University Press.

Gilmore, Leigh. 1994. *Autobiographics: A Feminist Theory of Women's Autobiography*. Cornell University Press.

Goldberg, Myla. 2004. "The Exquisite Strangeness and Estrangement of Renée French and Chris Ware." In *Give Our Regards to the Atom Smashers! Writers on Comics*, edited by Sean Howe, pp. 204–7. Pantheon.

Gorman, Michelle. 2007. *Getting Graphic: Comics for Kids*. Linworth Publishing.

Groensteen, Thierry. 1990. "Bandes designées (De la réflexivité dans les bandes dessinées)." *Conséquences*, vol. 13/14 (Contrebandes), pp. 132–65.

———. 1997. "Histoire de la bande dessinée muette (première partie)." *Neuvième Art*, vol. 2, pp. 60–75.

———. 1998. "Histoire de la bande dessinée muette (deuxième partie)." *Neuvième Art*, vol. 3, pp. 92–105.

———. 2007. *The System of Comics*. Translated by Bart Beaty and Nick Nguyen. University Press of Mississippi. Original edition, 1999.

———. 2013. *Comics and Narration*. Translated by Ann Miller. University Press of Mississippi.

Hagelstein, Maud. 2010. "La bande dessinée est-elle un art mineur? La laboratoire expérimental de Chris Ware." *Flux New*s, vol. 15, p. 15. https://orbi.uliege.be/bitstream/2268/29480/1/Maud%20Hagelstein%2c%20La%20bande%20dessin%c3%a9e%20est-elle%20un%20art%20mineur%20%3f.pdf. Accessed March 25, 2021.

Hall, James. 2014. *The Self-Portrait: A Cultural History*. Thames and Hudson.

Hartman, Geoffrey H. 1996. *The Longest Shadow: In the Aftermath of the Holocaust*. Indiana University Press.

Hatfield, Charles. 2005. *Alternative Comics: An Emerging Literature*. University Press of Mississippi.

———. 2009. "An Art of Tensions." In *A Comics Studies Reader*, edited by Jeet Heer and Kent Worcester, pp. 132–48. University Press of Mississippi.

Hathaway, Rosemary V. 2011. "Reading Art Spiegelman's *Maus* as Postmodern Ethnography." *Journal of Folklore Research*, vol. 18, no. 3, pp. 149–267.

Herman, David. 2002. *Story Logic: Problems and Possibilities of Narrative*. University of Nebraska Press.

———. 2009a. *Basic Elements of Narrative*. John Wiley.

———. 2009b. "Beyond Voice and Vision: Cognitive Grammar and Focalization Theory." In *Point of View, Perspective, and Focalization: Modeling Mediation in Narrative*, edited by Peter Hühn, Wolf Schmid, and Jörg Schönert, pp. 119–42. de Gruyter.

Herman, Luc, and Bart Vervaeck. 2004. "Focalization between Classical and Postclassical Narratology." In *The Dynamics of Narrative Form: Studies in Anglo-American Narratology*, edited by John Pier, pp. 115–38. de Gruyter.

Hirsch, Marianne. 1993. "Family Pictures: *Maus*, Mourning, and Post-Memory." *Discourse*, vol. 15, no. 2, pp. 3–29.

———. 1997. *Family Frames: Photography, Narrative and Postmemory*. Harvard University Press.

———. 2001. "Surviving Images: Holocaust Photographs and the Work of Postmemory." *The Yale Journal of Criticism*, vol. 14, no. 1, pp. 5–37.

———. 2008. "The Generation of Postmemory." *Poetics Today*, vol. 29, no. 1, pp. 103–28.

———. 2012. *The Generation of Postmemory: Writing and Visual Culture after the Holocaust*. Columbia University Press.

Horstkotte, Martin. 2004. *The Postmodern Fantastic in Contemporary British Fiction*. WVT.

Horstkotte, Silke. 2013. "Zooming In and Out: Panels, Frames, Sequences and the Building of Graphic Storyworlds." In *From Comic Strips to Graphic Novels: Contributions to the Theory and History of Graphic Narrative*, edited by Daniel Stein and Jan-Noël Thon, pp. 27–48. de Gruyter.

———. 2018. "Der Tod des Erzählers: Thomas Hettches *Nox*, Thomas Lehrs *Frühling* und Georg Kleins *Roman unserer Kindheit*." In *Jenseitserzählungen in der Gegenwartsliteratur*, edited by Isabelle Stauffer, pp. 61–98. Winter.

Horstkotte, Silke, and Nancy Pedri. 2011. "Focalization in Graphic Narrative." *Narrative*, vol. 19, no. 3, pp. 330–57.

———. 2017. "The Body at Work: Subjectivity in Graphic Memoir." In *Subjectivity across Media: Interdisciplinary and Transmedial Perspectives*, edited by Maike Sarah Reinerth and Jan-Noël Thon, pp. 77–91. Routledge.

Hühn, Peter, Wolf Schmid, and Jörg Schönert, editors. 2009. *Point of View, Perspective, and Focalization: Modeling Mediation in Narrative*. de Gruyter.

Hutcheon, Linda. 1988. *A Poetics of Postmodernism: History, Theory, Fiction*. Routledge.

———. 1991. *Narcissistic Narrative: The Metafictional Paradox.* Routledge.

———. 2002. *The Politics of Postmodernism.* 2nd ed. Routledge. Original edition, 1989.

Huyssen, Andreas. 2000. "Of Mice and Mimesis: Reading Spiegelman with Adorno." *New German Critique,* vol. 81, no. 3, pp. 65–81.

———. 2003. *Present Pasts: Urban Palimpsests and the Politics of Memory.* Stanford University Press.

Irwin, Ken. 2014. "Graphic Nonfiction: A Survey of Nonfiction Comics." *Collection Building,* vol. 33, no. 4, pp. 106–20.

Iser, Wolfgang. 1978. *The Act of Reading: A Theory of Aesthetic Response.* Johns Hopkins University Press.

Jahn, Manfred. 1996. "Windows of Focalization: Deconstructing and Reconstructing a Narratological Concept." *Style,* vol. 30, no. 2, pp. 241–67.

———. 1997. "Frames, Preferences, and the Reading of Third-Person Narratives: Towards a Cognitive Narratology." *Poetics Today,* vol. 18, no. 4, pp. 441–68.

———. 1999. "The Mechanics of Focalization: Extending the Narratological Toolbox." *GRAAT,* vol. 21, pp. 85–110.

———. 2005. "Focalization." In *The Routledge Encyclopedia of Narrative Theory,* edited by David Herman, Manfred Jahn, and Marie-Laure Ryan, pp. 173–77. Routledge.

Jost, François. 1983. "Narration(s): En deçà et au-delà." *Communications,* vol. 38, pp. 192–212.

Joyce, James. 1992. "The Dead." In *Dubliners,* pp. 175–225. Penguin. Original edition, 1914.

Kafalenos, Emma. 1996. "Implications of Narrative in Painting and Photography." *New Novel Review,* vol. 3, no. 2, pp. 53–66.

———. 2001. "Reading Visual Art, Making, and Forgetting, Fabulas." *Narrative,* vol. 9, no. 2, pp. 138–45.

Kafka, Franz. 1984. *The Trial.* Translated by Willa and Edwin Muir. Knopf. Original edition, 1956.

———. 1990. *Der Process. Roman, in der Fassung der Handschrift.* Edited by Malcolm Pasley, *Kritische Franz-Kafka-Ausgabe (FKA).* Fischer. Original edition, 1925.

Kannenberg, Gene, Jr. 2001. "The Comics of Chris Ware: Text, Image, and Visual Narrative Strategies." In *The Language of Comics: Word and Image,* edited by Robin Varnum and Christine T. Gibbons, pp. 174–97. University Press of Mississippi.

Kaplan, Caren. 1992. "Resisting Autobiography: Out-Law Genres and Transnational Feminist Subjects." In *De/Colonizing the Subject,* edited by Sidonie Smith and Julia Watson, pp. 115–38. University of Minnesota Press.

Keen, Suzanne. 2007. *Empathy and the Novel.* Oxford University Press.

———. 2008. "Strategic Empathizing: Techniques of Bounded, Ambassadorial, and Broadcast Narrative Empathy." *Deutsche Vierteljahresschrift,* vol. 82, no. 3, pp. 477–93.

———. 2011. "Fast Tracks to Narrative Empathy: Anthropomorphism and Dehumanization in Graphic Narratives." *SubStance,* vol. 40, no. 1, pp. 135–55.

Köppe, Tilmann. 2017. "The Expression of Subjectivity in Fiction: The Case of Internal Focalization." In *Subjectivity across Media: Interdisciplinary and Transmedial Perspectives,* edited by Maike Sarah Reinerth and Jan-Noël Thon, pp. 29–44. Routledge.

Køhlert, Frederik Byrn. 2019. *Serial Selves: Identity and Representation in Autobiographical Comics.* Rutgers University Press.

Kozloff, Sarah. 1988. *Invisible Storytellers: Voice-Over Narration in American Fiction Film.* University of California Press.

Kuhn, Markus. 2009. "Film Narratology: Who Tells? Who Shows? Who Focalizes? Narrative Mediation in Self-Reflexive Fiction Films." In *Point of View, Perspective, and Focalization: Modeling Mediation in Narrative*, edited by Peter Hühn, Wolf Schmid, and Jörg Schönert, pp. 259–78. de Gruyter.

———. 2011. *Filmnarratologie: Ein erzähltheoretisches Analysemodell*. de Gruyter.

Kukkonen, Karin. 2011a. "Comics as a Test Case for Transmedial Narratology." *SubStance*, vol. 40, no. 1, pp. 35–52.

———. 2011b. "Metalepsis in Comics and Graphic Novels." In *Metalepsis in Popular Culture*, edited by Karin Kukkonen and Sonja Klimek, pp. 213–31. de Gruyter.

———. 2011c. "Metalepsis in Popular Culture: An Introduction." In *Metalepsis in Popular Culture*, edited by Karin Kukkonen and Sonja Klimek, pp. 1–21. de Gruyter.

———. 2013a. *Contemporary Comics Storytelling*. University of Nebraska Press.

———. 2013b. "Space, Time, and Causality in Graphic Narratives: An Embodied Approach." In *From Comic Strips to Graphic Novels: Contributions to the Theory and History of Graphic Narrative*, edited by Daniel Stein and Jan-Noël Thon, pp. 49–66. de Gruyter.

Kukkonen, Karin, and Sonja Klimek, editors. 2011. *Metalepsis in Popular Culture*. de Gruyter.

Kunka, Andrew. 2018. *Autobiographical Comics*. Bloomsbury.

Kunwu, Li, and Philippe Ôtié. 2012. *A Chinese Life*. Translated by Edward Gauvin. Original edition, 2009.

Kutsch, Caroline, and Sven Strasen. 2019. "Models of Experientiality: Or, When Russian Formalism Meets Embodied Cognition and Empirical Literary Studies." In *Modelle in der Literatur- und Sprachwissenschaft sowie ihrer Didaktik / Models in Literary Studies and Linguistics. Festschrift für Peter Wenzel*, edited by Sven Strasen and Julia Vaeßen, pp. 55–80. WVT.

Lakoff, George, and Mark Johnson. 2003. *Metaphors We Live By*. University of Chicago Press. Original edition, 1980.

Leavitt, Sarah. 2010. *Tangles: A Story about Alzheimer's, My Mother and Me*. Broadview.

Leder, Drew. 1990. *The Absent Body*. University of Chicago Press.

Lee, Ching Kwan, and Guobin Yang. 2007. "Introduction: Memory, Power, and Culture." In *Re-Envisioning the Chinese Revolution: The Politics and Poetics of Collective Memories in Reform China*, edited by Ching Kwan Lee and Guobin Yang, pp. 1–20. Woodrow Wilson Center Press/Stanford University Press.

Lefèvre, Pascal. 2011. "Some Medium-Specific Qualities of Graphic Sequences." *SubStance*, vol. 40, no. 1, pp. 14–33.

Lejeune, Philippe. 1988. *On Autobiography*. Translated by Katherine Leary. Edited by Paul John Eakin. University of Minnesota Press.

Liss, Andrea. 1991. "Trespassing through Shadows: History, Mourning and Photography in Representations of Holocaust Memory." *Framework*, vol. 4, no. 1, pp. 30–39.

———. 1998. *Trespassing through Shadows: Memory, Photography and the Holocaust*. University of Minnesota Press.

Lubin, David M. 1985. *Act of Portrayal: Eakins, Sargent, James*. Yale University Press.

Lutes, Jason. 2001. *Berlin: City of Stones. Book One*. Drawn and Quarterly.

———. 2008. *Berlin: City of Smoke. Book Two*. Drawn and Quarterly.

———. 2018. *Berlin: City of Light. Book Three*. Drawn and Quarterly.

Marchetto, Marisa Acocella. 2006. *Cancer Vixen: A True Story*. Alfred A. Knopf.

Marcus, Leonard S. 1983. "Picture Book Animals: How Natural a History?" *The Lion and the Unicorn*, vol. 7, no. 1, pp. 127–39.

Margolin, Uri. 2000. "Telling in the Plural: From Grammar to Ideology." *Poetics Today,* vol. 21, no. 3, pp. 591–618.

———. 2009. "Focalization: Where Do We Go from Here?" In *Point of View, Perspective, and Focalization: Modeling Mediation in Narrative,* edited by Peter Hühn, Wolf Schmid, and Jörg Schönert, pp. 41–57. de Gruyter.

Marion, Philippe. 1993. *Traces en cases. Travail graphique, figuration narrative et participation du lecture: Essai sur la bande dessinée.* Academia.

Martin, Robert Stanley. 2010. "Comics Review: Josh Simmons, *Jessica Farm,* Volume One." *Pol Culture.* http://polculture.blogspot.de/2010/02/comics-review-josh-simmons-jessica-farm.html. Accessed September 10, 2019.

Mauro, Aaron. 2010. "'Mosaic Thresholds': Manifesting the Collection and Production of Comics in the Works of Chris Ware." *ImageText: Interdisciplinary Comics Studies,* vol. 5, no. 1. http://imagetext.english.ufl.edu/archives/v5_1/mauro/. Accessed May 28, 2021.

Mazzucchelli, David. 2009. *Asterios Polyp.* Pantheon.

McCloud, Scott. 1993. *Understanding Comics: The Invisible Art.* Harper Collins.

McHale, Brian. 1978. "Free Indirect Discourse: A Survey of Recent Accounts." *Poetics and the Theory of Literature,* vol. 3, no. 2, pp. 249–87.

———. 1987. *Postmodernist Fiction.* Routledge.

McKean, Dave. 2016. *Cages.* 25th anniversary ed. Dark Horse.

Mendlesohn, Farah. 2008. *Rhetorics of Fantasy.* Wesleyan University Press.

Merleau-Ponty, Maurice. 1963. *The Primacy of Perception.* Translated by William Cobb. Northwestern University Press.

———. 2004. *Basic Writings.* Edited by Thomas Baldwin. Routledge.

———. 2012. *Phenomenology of Perception.* Translated by Colin Smith. Routledge. Original edition, 1959.

Metz, Christian. 1974. *Film Language: A Semiotics of the Cinema.* Translated by Michael Taylor. Oxford University Press.

Mikkonen, Kai. 2008. "Presenting Minds in Graphic Narratives." *Partial Answers,* vol. 6, no. 2, pp. 301–21.

———. 2011. "Graphic Narratives as a Challenge to Transmedial Narratology: The Question of Focalization." *Amerikastudien,* vol. 56, no. 4, pp. 637–52.

———. 2013. "Subjectivity and Style in Graphic Narratives." In *From Comic Strips to Graphic Novels: Contributions to the Theory and History of Graphic Narrative,* edited by Daniel Stein and Jan-Noël Thon, pp. 101–23. de Gruyter.

———. 2017. *The Narratology of Comic Art.* Routledge.

Miller, Ann, and Bart Beaty, editors. 2014. *The French Comics Theory Reader.* Leuven University Press.

Miller, Ann, and Murray Pratt. 2012. "Transgressive Bodies in the Work of Julie Doucet, Fabrice Neaud and Jean-Christophe Menu: Towards a Theory of the AutobioBD." http://etc.dal.ca/belphegor/vol4_no1/articles/04_01_Miller_trnsgr_fr.html. Accessed August 22, 2018.

Mitchell, Adrielle Anna. 2010. "Distributed Identity: Networking Image Fragments in Graphic Memoirs." *Studies in Comics,* vol. 1, no. 2, pp. 257–79.

Mittell, Jason. 2016. *Complex TV: The Poetics of Contemporary Television Storytelling.* New York University Press.

Nagel, Thomas. 1974. "What Is It Like to Be a Bat?" *The Philosophical Review,* vol. 83, no. 4, pp. 435–50.

Niederhoff, Burkhard. 2009. "Focalization." In *Handbook of Narratology*, edited by Peter Hühn, John Pier, Wolf Schmid, and Jörg Schönert, pp. 115–23. de Gruyter.

Nières-Chevrel, Isabelle. 2010. "The Narrative Power of Pictures: *L'Orage* (The Thunderstorm) by Anne Brouillard." In *New Directions in Picturebook Research*, edited by Teresa Colomer, Bettina Kümmerling-Meibauer, and Cecilia Silva Díaz, pp. 129–38. Routledge.

Noë, Alva. 2004. *Action in Perception*. The MIT Press.

———. 2012. *Varieties of Presence*. Harvard University Press.

Nünning, Vera. 2015. "The Ethics of (Fictional) Form: Persuasiveness and Perspective Taking from the Point of View of Cognitive Literary Studies." *Arcadia*, vol. 50, no. 1, pp. 37–56.

O'Neill, Patrick. 1994. *Fictions of Discourse: Reading Narrative Theory*. University of Toronto Press.

O'Regan, J. Kevin, Erik Myin, and Alva Noë. 2005. "Sensory Consciousness Explained (Better) in Terms of 'Corporality' and 'Alerting Capacity.'" *Phenomenology and the Cognitive Sciences*, vol. 4, no. 4, pp. 369–87.

Oatley, Keith. 1999a. "Meetings of Minds: Dialogue, Sympathy, and Identification in Reading Fiction." *Poetics*, vol. 26, no. 5/6, pp. 439–54.

———. 1999b. "Why Fiction May Be Twice as True as Fact: Fiction as Cognitive and Emotional Simulation." *Review of General Psychology*, vol. 3, no. 2, pp. 101–17.

Palmer, Alan. 2002. "The Construction of Fictional Minds." *Narrative*, vol. 10, no. 1, pp. 28–46.

———. 2003. "The Mind beyond the Skin." In *Narrative Theory and the Cognitive Sciences*, edited by David Herman, pp. 322–48. Center for the Study of Language and Information.

———. 2004. *Fictional Minds*. University of Nebraska Press.

———. 2010. *Social Minds in the Novel*. The Ohio State University Press.

Parry, Joseph D., and Mark Wrathall. 2011. "Introduction." In *Art and Phenomenology*, edited by Joseph D. Parry and Mark Wrathall, pp. 1–8. Routledge.

Pedri, Nancy. 2015. "What's the Matter of Seeing in Graphic Memoir?" *South Central Review*, special issue *Graphic Representation: Contemporary Graphic Narrative*, edited by Nicole Stamant, vol. 32, no. 3, pp. 8–29.

Pedri, Nancy, and Helene Staveley. 2018. "Not Playing Around: Games in Graphic Illness Narratives." *Literature and Medicine*, vol. 36, no. 1, pp. 230–56.

Peeters, Benoît. 2003. *Lire la bande dessinée*. 2nd ed. Flammarion. Original edition, 1998.

Perna, Laura. 2009. "'There was something screwy going on . . .': The Uncanny in Charles Burns' Graphic Novel *Black Hole*." *The Birmingham Journal of Literature and Language*, vol. 2, pp. 7–15. http://ejournals.org.uk/bjll/[z7-15]_ARTICLE_1_PERNA.pdf. Accessed May 25, 2021.

Phelan, James. 2001. "Why Narrators Can Be Focalizers—and Why It Matters." In *New Perspectives on Narrative Perspective*, edited by Willie Van Peer and Seymour Chatman, pp. 51–64. SUNY Press.

Pier, John, and Jean-Marie Schaeffer, editors. 2005. *Métalepses: Entorses au pacte de la représentation*. Éditions de l'EHESS.

Pointon, Marcia. 2012. *Portrayal and the Search for Identity*. Reaktion.

Polak, Kate. 2017. *Ethics in the Gutter: Empathy and Historical Fiction in Comics*. The Ohio State University Press.

Postema, Barbara. 2014. "Following the Pictures: Wordless Comics for Children." *Journal of Graphic Novels and Comics*, vol. 5, no. 3, pp. 311–22.

———. 2015. "Establishing Relations: Photography in Wordless Comics." *Image & Narrative*, vol. 16, no. 2, pp. 84–95.

———. 2017. "Silent Comics." In *The Routledge Companion to Comics,* edited by Frank Bramlett, Roy T. Cook, and Aaron Meskin, pp. 201–8. Routledge.

———. 2018. "Long-Length Wordless Books: Frans Masereel, Milt Gross, Lynd Ward, and Beyond." In *The Cambridge History of the Graphic Novel,* edited by Jan Baetens, Hugo Frey, and Stephen E. Tabachnick, pp. 59–71. Cambridge University Press.

Purcell, Kurt. 2009. "The Groovy Age of Horror: *House* by Josh Simmons." http://groovyageofhorror.blogspot.com/2009/01/house-by-josh-simmons-fantagraphics.html. Accessed May 25, 2021.

Raeburn, Daniel. 2004. *Chris Ware.* Yale University Press.

Reinerth, Maike Sarah, and Jan-Noël Thon. 2018. "Introduction: Subjectivity across Media." In *Subjectivity across Media: Interdisciplinary and Transmedial Perspectives,* edited by Maike Sarah Reinerth and Jan-Noël Thon, pp. 1–25. Routledge.

Richardson, Brian. 2006. *Unnatural Voices: Extreme Narration in Modern and Contemporary Fiction.* The Ohio State University Press.

Ricoeur, Paul. 2003. *The Rule of Metaphor: The Creation of Meaning in Language.* Translated by Robert Czerny, Kathleen McLaughlin, and John Costello, SJ. Routledge.

Rimmon-Kenan, Shlomith. 2002. *Narrative Fiction: Contemporary Poetics.* Routledge. Original edition, 1983.

Round, Julia. 2010. "'Be Vewy, Vewy Quiet. We're Hunting Wippers': A Barthesian Analysis of the Construction of Fact and Fiction in Alan Moore and Eddie Campbell's *From Hell.*" In *The Rise and Reason of Comics and Graphic Literature: Critical Essays on the Form,* edited by Joyce Goggin and Dan Hassler-Forest, pp. 188–201. McFarland.

Ruthner, Clemens. 2012. "Fantastic Liminality: A Theory Sketch." In *Collision of Realities: Establishing Research on the Fantastic in Europe,* edited by Lars Schmeink and Astrid Böger, pp. 49–63. de Gruyter.

Ryan, Marie-Laure. 2001. *Narrative as Virtual Reality: Immersion and Interactivity in Literature and Electronic Media.* Johns Hopkins University Press.

———. 2004. *Narrative across Media: The Languages of Storytelling.* University of Nebraska Press.

Ryan, Marie-Laure, and Jan-Noël Thon. 2014. *Storyworlds across Media: Toward a Media-Conscious Narratology.* University of Nebraska Press.

Sacco, Joe. 2002. *Safe Area Goražde: The War in Eastern Bosnia 1992–1995.* Fantagraphics.

———. 2003. *Palestine.* Jonathan Cape.

———. 2009. *Footnotes in Gaza.* Jonathan Cape.

Satrapi, Marjane. 2003. *Persepolis: The Story of a Childhood.* Translated by Mattias Ripa. Pantheon.

———. 2004. *Persepolis: The Story of a Return.* Translated by Blake Ferris. Pantheon.

———. 2005. *Embroideries.* Translated by Richard McGill Murphy. Pantheon.

Sattler, Peter R. 2010. "Past Imperfect: *Building Stories* and the Art of Memory." In *The Comics of Chris Ware: Drawing Is a Way of Thinking,* edited by David M. Ball and Martha B. Kuhlman, pp. 206–22. University Press of Mississippi.

Schack, Todd. 2014. "'A Failure of Language': Achieving Layers of Meaning in Graphic Journalism." *Journalism,* vol. 15, no. 1, pp. 109–27.

Schlichting, Laura. 2016. "Interactive Graphic Journalism." *VIEW Journal,* vol. 5, no. 10, pp. 22–39.

Schlickers, Sabine. 2009. "Focalization, Ocularization and Auricularization in Film and Literature." In *Point of View, Perspective, and Focalization: Modeling Mediation in Narrative,* edited by Peter Hühn, Wolf Schmid, and Jörg Schönert, pp. 243–58. de Gruyter.

Schmeink, Lars, and Astrid Böger, editors. 2012. *Collision of Realities: Establishing Research on the Fantastic in Europe.* de Gruyter.

Schmid, Wolf. 2005. *Elemente der Narratologie.* de Gruyter.

———. 2010. *Narratology: An Introduction.* Translated by Alexander Starritt. de Gruyter.

Schmitz-Emans, Monika. 2013. "Graphic Narrative as World Literature." In *From Comic Strips to Graphic Novels: Contributions to the Theory and History of Graphic Narrative,* edited by Daniel Stein and Jan-Noël Thon, pp. 385–406. de Gruyter.

Scholes, Robert. 1979. *Fabulation and Metafiction.* University of Illinois Press.

Segal, Erwin. 1995. "Narrative Comprehension and the Role of Deictic Shift Theory." In *Deixis in Narrative: A Cognitive Science Perspective,* edited by Judith Felson Duchan, Gail A. Bruder, and Lynne E. Hewitt, pp. 3–17. Lawrence Erlbaum.

Siegel, Alexis. 2006. Preface. In *Deogratias: A Tale of Rwanda,* by Jean-Philippe Stassen, First Second Books. Original edition, 2000.

Simmons, Josh. 2007. *House.* Fantagraphics.

———. 2008. *Jessica Farm: Volume 1.* Fantagraphics.

———. 2012. "'Sometimes, You Get Your Throat Cut while a Clown Is Pulling Your Pants Down': An Interview with Josh Simmons." *The Comics Journal.* http://www.tcj.com/sometimes-you-get-your-throat-cut-while-a-clown-is-pulling-your-pants-down-an-interview-with-josh-simmons/. Accessed May 25, 2021.

Simonis, Annette. 2005. *Grenzüberschreitungen in der phantastischen Literatur.* Winter.

Singer, Marc. 2015. "Views from Nowhere: Journalistic Detachment in Palestine." In *The Comics of Joe Sacco: Journalism in a Visual World,* edited by Daniel Worden, pp. 68–81. University Press of Mississippi.

Small, David. 2009. *Stitches: A Memoir.* McClelland and Stewart.

Smith, Sidonie. 1987. *A Poetics of Women's Autobiography: Marginality and the Fictions of Self-Representation.* Indiana University Press.

Spiegelman, Art. 1986. *Maus: A Survivor's Tale. Part I: My Father Bleeds History.* Pantheon.

———. 1991. *Maus: A Survivor's Tale. Part II: And Here My Troubles Began.* Pantheon.

———. 2011. *MetaMaus: A Look inside a Modern Classic.* Pantheon.

Stassen, Jean-Philippe. 2006. *Deogratias: A Tale of Rwanda.* Translated by Alexis Siegel. First Second Books. Original edition, 2000.

Stein, Daniel. 2013. "Superhero Comics and the Authorizing Functions of the Comic Book Paratext." In *From Comic Strips to Graphic Novels: Contributions to the Theory and History of Graphic Narrative,* edited by Daniel Stein and Jan-Noël Thon, pp. 155–89. de Gruyter.

Stockwell, Peter. 2002. *Cognitive Poetics: An Introduction.* Routledge.

———. 2009. *Texture: A Cognitive Aesthetics of Reading.* Edinburgh University Press.

Stone, Ellen Elizabeth. 2013. "We All Fear the Lizard Queen: Affect in Charles Burns' *Black Hole.*" *Looking at Contemporary Art.* https://ellenelizabethstone.wordpress.com/2013/03/09/we-all-fear-the-lizard-queen-affect-in-charles-burns-black-hole/. Accessed May 25, 2021.

Swales, John M. 1990. *Genre Analysis.* Cambridge University Press.

Szép, Eszter. 2020. *Comics and the Body: Drawing, Reading, and Vulnerability.* The Ohio State University Press.

Tan, Shaun. 2006. *The Arrival.* Hodder Children's Books.

———. 2010. *Sketches from a Nameless Land: The Art of* The Arrival. Lothian.

———. 2011. "The Accidental Graphic Journalist." *Bookbird,* vol. 49, no. 4, pp. 1–9.

Thaxton, Ralph A. 2016. *Force and Contention in Contemporary China: Memory and Resistance in the Long Shadow of the Catastrophic Past*. Cambridge University Press.

Thompson, Craig. 2011. *Habibi*. Faber.

Thon, Jan-Noël. 2013. "Who's Telling the Tale? Authors and Narrators in Graphic Narrative." In *From Comic Strips to Graphic Novels: Contributions to the Theory and History of Graphic Narrative*, edited by Daniel Stein and Jan-Noël Thon, pp. 67–99. de Gruyter.

Todorov, Tzvetan. 1973. *The Fantastic: A Structural Approach to a Literary Genre*. Translated by Richard Howard. Case Western Reserve University Press.

Verano, Frank. 2006. "Invisible Spectacles, Invisible Limits: Grant Morrison, Situationist Theory, and Real Unrealities." *International Journal of Comic Art*, vol. 8, no. 2, pp. 319–29.

Vermeule, Blakey. 2010. *Why Do We Care about Literary Characters?* Johns Hopkins University Press.

Versaci, Rocco. 2007. *This Book Contains Graphic Language: Comics as Literature*. Continuum.

Verstraeten, Peter. 2009. *Film Narratology*. Translated by Stefan van der Lecq. University of Toronto Press.

Walker, George A. 2007. "Introduction." In *Graphic Witness: Four Wordless Graphic Novels by Frans Masereel, Lynd Ward, Giacomo Patri and Laurence Hyde*, edited by George A. Walker, pp. 15–31. Firefly.

———. 2010. *Book of Hours: A Wordless Novel Told in 99 Wood Engravings*. The Porcupine's Quill.

Ware, Chris. 2000. *Jimmy Corrigan: The Smartest Kid on Earth*. Pantheon.

Warhol, Robyn. 2011. "The Space Between: A Narrative Approach to Alison Bechdel's *Fun Home*." *College Literature*, vol. 38, no. 3, pp. 1–20.

Warner, Chantelle. 2012. *The Literary Pragmatics of Autobiography: Authenticity in German Social Autobiographies*. Routledge.

Watson, Julia. 2011. "Autographic Disclosures and Genealogies of Desire in Alison Bechdel's *Fun Home*." In *Graphic Subjects: Critical Essays on Autobiography and Graphic Novels*, edited by Michael A. Chaney, pp. 123–56. University of Wisconsin Press.

Watson, Julia, and Sidonie Smith. 1992. *De/Colonizing the Subject: The Politics of Gender in Women's Autobiography*. University of Minnesota Press.

———. 2002. *Interfaces: Women, Autobiography, Image, Performance*. University of Minnesota Press.

Waugh, Patricia. 1984. *Metafiction: The Theory and Practice of Self-Conscious Fiction*. Routledge.

White, Hayden V. 1978. *Tropics of Discourse: Essays in Cultural Criticism*. Johns Hopkins University Press.

———. 1992. "Historical Emplotment and the Problem of Truth." In *Probing the Limits of Representation: Nazism and the "Final Solution,"* edited by Saul Friedlander, pp. 37–53. Harvard University Press.

Whitlock, Gillian. 2006. "Autographics: The Seeing 'I' of the Comics." *Modern Fiction Studies*, vol. 52, no. 4, pp. 965–79.

Wildfeuer, Janina. 2019. "The Inferential Semantics of Comics: Panels and Their Meanings." *Poetics Today*, vol. 40, no. 2, pp. 215–34.

Williams, Ian. 2011. "Autography as Auto-Therapy: Psychic Pain and the Graphic Memoir." *Journal of Medical Humanities*, vol. 32, no. 4, pp. 353–66.

Williams, Kristian. 2005. "The Case for Comics Journalism: Artist-Reporters Leap Tall Conventions in a Single Bound." *Columbia Journalism Review*, vol. 43, no. 6, pp. 51–55.

Wolf, Werner. 1992. "Spiel im Spiel und Politik: Zum Spannungsfeld literarischer Selbst- und Fremdbezüglichkeit im zeitgenössischen englischen Drama." *Poetica*, vol. 24, no. 1/2, pp. 163–94.

———. 2004. "Metafiktion." In *Metzler Lexikon Literatur- und Kulturtheorie. Ansätze—Personen—Grundbegriffe*, edited by Ansgar Nünning, pp. 447–48. Metzler.

———. 2005. "Metalepsis as a Transgeneric and Transmedial Phenomenon: A Case Study of the Possibilities of 'Exporting' Narratological Concepts." In *Narratology beyond Literary Criticism: Mediality, Disciplinarity*, edited by Jan Christoph Meister, pp. 83–107. de Gruyter.

———. 2007. "Metaisierung als transgenerisches und transmediales Phänomen: Ein Systematisierungsversuch metareferentieller Formen und Begriffe in Literatur und anderen Medien." In *Metaisierung in Literatur und anderen Medien: Theoretische Grundlagen—Historische Perspektiven—Metagattungen—Funktionen*, edited by Janine Hauthal, Julijana Nadj, Ansgar Nünning, and Henning Peters, pp. 25–64. de Gruyter.

Wölfflin, Heinrich. 1915. *Kunstgeschichtliche Grundbegriffe: Das Problem der Stilentwicklung in der neueren Kunst*. Bruckmann.

———. 1932. *Principles of Art History: The Problem of the Development of Style in Later Art*. Translated by M. D. Hottinger. Dover.

Wolk, Douglas. 2007. *Reading Comics: How Graphic Novels Work*. Da Capo Press.

Worden, Daniel. 2015. "Introduction: Drawing Conflicts." In *The Comics of Joe Sacco: Journalism in a Visual World*, edited by Daniel Worden, pp. 3–18. University Press of Mississippi.

Yagoda, Ben. 2009. *Memoir: A History*. Riverhead.

Yus, Francisco. 2010. "Visual Metaphor versus Verbal Metaphor: A Unified Account." In *Multimodal Metaphor*, edited by Charles Forceville and Eduardo Urios-Aparisi, pp. 147–72. Mouton de Gruyter.

Zubin, D. A., and Lynne E. Hewitt. 1995. "The Deictic Center: A Theory of Deixis in Narrative." In *Deixis in Narrative: A Cognitive Science Perspective*, edited by Judith Felson Duchan, Gail A. Bruder, and Lynne E. Hewitt, pp. 129–55. Lawrence Erlbaum.

Zunshine, Lisa. 2006. *Why We Read Fiction: Theory of Mind and the Novel*. The Ohio State University Press.

———. 2010. *Introduction to Cognitive Cultural Studies*. Johns Hopkins University Press.

INDEX

action, xix, 6–8, 13, 20, 65, 125, 130, 151–152, 159, 199–200, 222–224; action kernels, 17; spheres of, 205

aesthetics, xx, 7, 14, 18, 31, 50, 59, 62, 92, 94, 105, 146, 148, 180, 182, 184, 193, 205, 214, 228

affect, xvii, xviii, 1, 31, 48, 57, 65, 101, 106, 114, 145, 149, 215, 219, 220, 226, 229

Altman, Rick, 155

ambiguity, xxiv, 26, 51, 147–150, 160, 167, 172, 176–177, 179, 203, 204, 206, 208, 220, 230–231; of comics, 177; of wordless comics, 167. *See also* focalization, ambiguous

ambivalence, 49, 88, 104–105, 109, 167, 178, 203

angle, xxiii, 24, 57, 62, 103, 148, 207, 234; emotional, 124; evaluative, 218; experiential, 218; of focalization, 168; subjective, 2, 6, 14, 29, 211; of vision, xix, 62, 123

Arrival, The (Tan), 149, 167–177, 231

aspectuality, 29, 32, 35, 38, 44, 52, 91–92, 103, 111, 115, 116, 122, 146, 162, 169, 174, 184, 187, 188, 192, 228–229; intersubjective, 115

Asterios Polyp (Mazzucchelli), 179–193, 215, 216, 229

atmosphere, xvii, xviii, 32, 36, 38, 60, 93, 146, 147, 152, 159, 168, 221, 225, 226, 228, 235

atrocity, 102, 103, 106, 108, 124–125, 127, 229, 233–234

authenticity, 60, 65–66, 69, 70, 76, 77, 99, 101, 126, 132, 209, 227

authority, 16, 77, 93, 125, 132, 134, 140, 159, 192, 196, 200, 206–209, 215

authorship, 5, 65, 73, 76–77, 125–126, 130, 134, 181, 200, 201, 203–205; collaborative, 33, 107, 125

autobiography, 59–60, 63–66, 69, 70, 99, 221; autobiographical pact, 65

autofiction, 70

avatar, 66, 78, 135, 227

background, xxi, 27, 35–36, 45, 50, 73, 84, 116, 120, 123, 187, 189, 193, 197, 199, 203, 207, 213, 218

Bal, Mieke, 5, 29, 149, 150–151, 168, 218

Bennett, Alice, 190

Berlin: City of Stones (Lutes), 3, 16–27, 28–29, 65, 168, 223, 228

bimodality, xviii, 2–4, 16, 105, 147, 152, 234. *See also* narration, bimodal

251

Black Hole (Burns), 38–48, 57, 58, 230

body, xxiii, xxiv, 31, 33, 39, 51, 52, 57, 60, 62, 63, 66–70, 72, 73, 76–82, 88, 90, 93, 96, 97–100, 110, 120, 121, 135, 152, 162, 169, 183, 188, 191, 195, 197, 202, 212–215, 220, 221, 223, 224, 232, 233. See also corporeality; embodiment

Book of Hours: A Wordless Novel Told in 99 Wood Engravings (Walker), 148

Booth, Wayne C., 64

braiding, 11, 23, 24, 34, 179, 220; in *The Arrival*, 175; in *Berlin: City of Stones*, 24–25; in *Black Hole*, 47–48; in *A Chinese Life*, 134; in *Habibi*, 197–198; in *Jimmy Corrigan*, 52; in *Stitches*, 93

Breithaupt, Fritz, 65

Brosch, Renate, xx, 113

Cages (McKean), xxi–xxiii

Cancer Vixen (Marchetto), 68

captions, 12, 13, 27, 35, 39, 40, 113, 122, 136, 140, 142, 218

Caracciolo, Marco, 222

cartooning, 13, 34, 50, 63, 64, 73, 80, 86, 87, 88, 174, 189

character identification, 64, 199

Chinese Life, A (Kunwu and Ôtié), 103, 107, 125–134

Chute, Hilary, 135, 234–235

closeness, xvii, 2, 30, 101, 106, 145, 185, 199, 201, 218, 220, 221

cognition, 1, 31, 65, 67, 183, 223, 224, 226, 230; cognitive literary studies, 31, 168, 224; cognitive narratology, xx, 216, 219, 222; cognitive poetics, xx

Cohn, Dorrit, xvii, 64, 150, 222

color, xviii, xx, 12, 14, 18, 50, 52, 57, 158, 161, 165, 174, 180–190, 192, 218, 225, 229

composition, xx, 11, 20, 24, 25, 26, 50, 77, 90, 92, 93, 213, 214, 220, 225, 227

consciousness, xvii, xix, 1, 4, 9, 14, 15, 17, 21, 22, 29, 32, 34, 38, 64, 72, 116, 125, 128, 130, 132, 144, 147, 158, 167, 178, 181, 204, 205, 217, 219, 220, 222; representation of, 9, 14, 72. See also mind

corporeality, xviii, xxiv, 16, 33, 60, 221. See also body; embodiment

Couser, Thomas, 69

creation, 74, 103, 106, 126, 150, 179–181, 189, 192, 194–199, 203, 207, 216, 227. See also world, creation

Davis, Whitney, 76–77

deixis, 8, 12, 25, 148, 167–170, 176, 199, 224; ambiguous, 148, 170; embodied, 25, 199, 224; narratorial, 173; deictic center, xxiv, 7–9, 26, 34, 52, 148, 168–169, 172, 173, 176–177, 215, 227, 230; deictic shift, 7, 168

Deogratias (Stassen), 103, 107, 115–125, 126, 168–169

design, xx, xxiii, 38, 49, 50, 53, 73, 91, 92, 101, 103, 126, 130, 179, 195, 201, 205, 213, 214

diegesis, 2, 34, 58, 93, 100, 106, 134, 147, 148, 159, 167, 168, 172, 196, 207, 210, 212, 228, 230

disability, 15, 69, 70, 72, 221, 229

disease, 15, 69, 70, 72, 82, 83, 86, 91, 94–96, 229

distance, xvii, 2, 24, 30, 53, 57, 59, 64, 101–107, 114, 134, 145, 173, 218, 220, 221, 226; distancing, 50, 56, 58, 106, 180, 229

documentary comics, 101–102

Doležel, Lubomír, 222

doubt, 103, 104, 109, 112, 115, 145, 160, 181, 220, 226, 234, 235

drawing, 12, 14, 16, 17, 19, 25, 26, 36, 47, 62, 68, 71, 73, 80, 81, 86, 87, 88, 100, 103, 105, 109, 113, 126, 135, 137, 140, 165–167, 169, 172, 174, 184, 189, 193–195, 205, 206, 214, 232, 234; and the body, 66, 224, 232; as a focalization marker, 74–75; drawing hand, 15, 25, 66, 224, 232; drawing self, 67; drawing style, 34, 49–50, 60, 61, 73, 126, 140, 165, 174, 189

Eakin, John Paul, 63, 69

Eisner, Will, 151

El Refaie, Elisabeth, 92, 224

embedding, xxiv, xx, 20, 26, 111, 140, 142, 144. See also focalization, embedded

embodiment, xxiv, 15, 32–34, 57, 61, 62, 63, 66, 67, 69, 72, 77, 90, 107, 204, 210, 215–216, 220, 221, 222, 224, 225, 226, 232. See also body; corporeality; focalization, embodied

Embroideries (Satrapi), 82, 233

INDEX • 253

emotion, xviii, xix, xxi–xxiv, 2, 5, 12–14, 16, 18, 20, 23, 27, 28, 31, 38, 39, 53, 58, 62, 64, 66, 68, 69, 80, 82, 84–86, 91–93, 96, 105–107, 115, 124, 127, 132, 135, 138, 142, 147, 148, 149, 152, 154, 158–160, 162, 164, 167, 170, 173–177, 185, 190, 194, 199, 200, 201, 202, 204, 208, 215–219, 225, 226, 229–231, 234; emotional engagement, 2, 148, 172, 174, 194, 217; emotional experience, xxiv, xix, 16, 62, 96, 158, 160, 164, 167, 170, 175, 231; emotional investment, xxiii, 92; emotional involvement, 12, 14, 201, 218; emotional response, 92, 219. *See also* feeling

empathy, 2, 31, 33, 38, 48, 53, 57, 64–65, 113, 124, 145, 177, 199–200, 216, 221, 227, 228; shifts in, 113

Epileptic (B.), 94–99

epistemology, 128, 147, 148, 169, 172, 182

ethics, 70, 105–106, 108, 115, 117, 134, 221; narrative ethics, 104–107; ethical positioning, 105, 146, 206, 229; ethics of representation, 125

Etter, Lukas, 61

evaluation, xvii, 4, 10, 81, 92, 93, 115, 136, 230

experience, 28–58; collective, xxiv, 128, 130, 142; embodied, 9, 34, 62, 99, 214, 225; intersubjective, 26, 29, 82–83, 115, 235; subjective, 2, 15, 18–20, 26, 28, 30, 33, 35, 36, 39, 60, 66, 69, 81, 82, 124, 147, 157, 159, 174, 187, 220, 222. *See also* what it's like

experiencing-I, xxi, 10, 63, 66, 67, 96, 99

experientiality, xx, 2, 6, 7, 15, 30, 39, 81, 83, 146, 168, 180, 229

expression, xxiii, 13, 69, 86, 88, 94, 146, 160, 162, 174, 223, 227; authenticity of, 76, 101; communal, 107; of experience, 4, 226; of focalization, 3, 60; metaphorical, 159; of subjectivity, 3, 8, 77, 231; visual, 3, 158, 170

fantastic, 35, 147–149, 152–154, 159–161, 164, 167, 176, 194

Fawaz, Ramzi, 223

feeling, xvii, xix, xxii, 4, 8, 9, 18, 22, 26, 29, 31, 33, 36–38, 50, 57, 60, 64, 78, 80, 81, 90, 106, 108, 112, 117, 122, 127, 130, 137, 138, 142, 155, 157, 161, 162, 173, 190, 199, 209, 221, 223, 225. *See also* emotion

filtering, xvii, xix, 1, 6, 29, 81, 83, 92, 102, 178, 181, 185, 189, 228

flashback, 39, 107, 116, 117, 119, 120, 123, 182, 191, 207, 224

Flood! (Drooker), 148, 160–167, 231

Fludernik, Monika, xx, 6, 29, 222

focalization, xvii–xxv, 1–27, 34, 57, 60, 72, 76, 112–113, 180, 217–235; ambient, 10; ambiguous, xix, xxiv, 6, 48, 66, 104, 115, 116, 124, 160, 167, 203, 227, 229–231; and phenomenology, 28–30, 33, 221–223; character-bound (internal), xix, xxiv, 2, 4, 5, 6, 9, 17–23, 26, 28, 30, 35, 40, 47, 49, 53, 60, 61, 66, 81, 91–93, 101, 104, 117, 122, 135, 142, 145, 150, 161, 165, 172, 174, 183, 199, 207, 223, 231; collective, xxiv, 26, 185; in comics, 11–16, 57, 217–235; communal, 83, 126, 134, 223; counter-focalization, 113, 145, 235; cues, xxi, xxii, xxv, 2, 93, 94, 165, 167, 178, 216, 219; dual, 112; embedded, xxiv, 6, 9, 26, 47, 49, 53, 57, 60, 83, 92, 93, 96, 111–112, 140, 144, 189, 192, 193, 230; embodied, 9, 62, 212; fallible, 132; in *The Arrival*, 170, 174; in *Asterios Polyp*, 182–185, 190; in *Berlin: City of Stones*, 17–20, 22; in *Black Hole*, 40, 47–48; in *A Chinese Life*, 126, 127, 132, 134; in *Deogratias*, 116–117, 122–125; in film, xvii, 13, 18, 36; in *Flood!*, 161–167; in *Footnotes in Gaza*, 142–144; in *Habibi*, 207, 210–213; in *House*, 154–159; in *Jessica Farm*, 36–38; in *Jimmy Corrigan*, 49–53, 57, 58; in *Marbles*, 73, 76, 81; in *Maus*, 104, 108–112; in *Palestine*, 135–137; in *Stitches*, 91–92; intensification of, 148, 176; intersubjective, xxiv, 26, 83, 103, 111–112, 128, 173, 176, 181, 212, 223, 233; in literature, xvii, 7–11; markers, xvii, xviii, xxv, 2, 3, 6, 12–14, 18, 27, 28, 33, 36, 41, 49, 57, 66, 72, 95, 99, 102, 111, 116, 119, 135, 149, 152, 178, 179, 184, 193, 202, 210, 213, 218, 219, 225–228; multilayered, xix, 142, 146, 229–231; multiple, 48, 104, 229, 233; narratorial (external), xxiv, 2, 4, 5, 6, 9, 22, 35, 47, 49, 52, 53, 57, 58, 66, 123, 144, 159, 164, 172, 174, 177, 228; optical aspects, xviii, xx, xxii, 3, 5, 14, 15, 18, 20, 22, 26, 27, 36, 218–219; plural, 134, 141; refocalization, 29, 88, 103, 169; relational, 83, 100; shared, 185, 189; shift in, 141, 160, 172, 203; spliced, 83, 233; variable, 125; zero, 4, 167

focalizer, 108, 124, 134, 153, 156, 160, 165, 167, 231

focalizor, 5, 150, 168, 231

following-unit, 20, 22, 23, 24, 155

font, xx, 49
Footnotes in Gaza (Sacco), 107, 141–144
frame, xx, 12, 17, 25, 41, 45, 47, 48, 50, 86, 91, 97, 110, 117, 135, 137, 140, 151, 165, 174, 187, 193, 201, 202, 204, 205, 207, 208, 210, 212, 223. *See also* panel, frame
framing, xvii, xviii, xx, xxiii, 12, 57, 93, 102, 103, 146, 218
free indirect discourse, xvii, 8, 9
Frow, John, 59–60
Fun Home: A Family Tragicomic (Bechdel), 61–63, 82

gap, 11, 17, 151
Gardner, Jared, 17
gender theory, 70
Genette, Gérard, 1, 4–5, 66, 167, 217
genre, xviii, xix, xxiii–xxv, 6, 12, 39, 58–61, 64–67, 69, 70, 72, 77, 90, 99–102, 108, 125, 136, 140, 146–148, 151, 153, 218–220, 226–228, 231–233
Gibbs, Raymond, 224
granularity, 38
graphiator, 65, 101, 113, 115, 160, 165, 179, 199, 226, 227, 229
graphic historiography, xix, xxiv, 101–145, 227, 233–235
graphic journalism, xix, xxiv, 101, 103, 135, 227. *See also* documentary comics
graphic memoir, xix, xxiv, 33, 59–100, 102, 103, 108, 136, 145, 179, 212, 226–227, 231–234. *See also* autobiography
gridding, 11
Groensteen, Thierry, 11, 23, 61, 159, 189

Habibi (Thompson), 179, 193–216, 224, 228
Hartman, Geoffrey, 104
Hatfield, Charles, 17, 64
Herman, David, xx, xxiii, 6, 14, 29, 31, 219
Hirsch, Marianne, 105, 112
House (Simmons), 152–160
Hutcheon, Linda, 179, 182
hybridity, 66, 114, 126, 233

identity, 39, 59, 67–70, 76, 82, 90, 94, 100, 111, 112, 114, 128, 147, 152, 154, 169, 184, 222, 225, 231, 232

imagination, 18, 22, 31, 32, 33, 36, 49, 90, 91, 96, 103, 151, 159, 191, 201, 206, 212, 215, 219, 231, 234
immersion, 7, 34, 112, 153, 162, 177, 180, 216
immersive reading, 2, 31, 112, 189, 201, 230
indeterminacy, 7, 147, 169, 231, 235
intensity, 28, 117, 148, 161
intersubjectivity, xxiv, 26, 29, 38–39, 57, 65, 77, 82, 90, 93, 94, 99, 103, 105, 108, 112, 115, 169, 181, 185, 212, 222, 223, 225, 233. *See also* focalization, intersubjective
intimacy, 28, 65, 69, 103
irony, xvii, 2, 9, 25, 40, 49, 53, 56–58, 190

Jahn, Manfred, xx, 5, 7, 8, 167–168, 172
Jessica Farm (Simmons), 35–38, 51, 58, 147, 154
Jimmy Corrigan: The Smartest Kid on Earth (Ware), 30, 48–57
judgment, 4, 9, 29, 49, 93, 96, 111, 116, 153
juxtaposition, 17, 76, 81, 90, 93, 97, 111, 112, 145, 169, 220

Kafalenos, Emma, 150–151
Keen, Suzanne, 64, 123, 199–200
knowing, 4, 22, 24, 32, 40, 47, 71, 103, 120, 126, 130, 132, 143, 145, 225, 230
knowledge, xviii, xix, 1, 4, 5, 6, 8, 12, 14, 21, 24–26, 33, 40, 44, 45, 50, 60, 71, 96, 108, 115, 116, 119, 123, 128, 137, 145, 148, 159, 167, 190, 191, 194, 196, 212, 214, 218–220, 222, 227–231
Kuhn, Markus, 13
Kukkonen, Karin, xx, 11–12, 215, 220
Kutsch, Caroline, 216

language, 7, 8, 10, 53, 60, 88, 94, 99, 116, 168, 170, 197, 225, 227
layout, xxvii, xx, xxiii, 3, 11–13, 25, 45, 50, 57, 85, 96, 103, 146, 158, 172, 184, 193, 205, 218, 225, 229
Leder, Drew, 72
Lejeune, Philippe, 65, 69
lettering, xviii, 12, 184, 218. *See also* font
line, xviii, 12, 25, 41, 73, 74, 77, 85, 103, 117, 146, 158, 175, 184, 194, 195, 213, 218, 221, 224, 225
loading, 38

looking, xxiv, 18, 22, 26, 36, 67, 88, 90, 97, 135, 137, 145, 199, 201, 223. *See also* vision

Marbles (Forney), 72–81
Margolin, Uri, 128, 226
Masereel, Frans, 149, 161
Maus (Spiegelman), 102, 103, 104–115, 116, 126, 169, 178–179, 213, 229, 234
McCloud, Scott, 151
McHale, Brian, 182
meaning-making, 12, 115, 168, 198, 204, 230
mediation, xx, 2, 7, 14, 38, 103, 127, 165, 179, 181, 189, 206, 222, 227
medium, xviii, xx, xxi, 2–4, 11, 13–16, 51, 53, 93, 108, 126, 146, 174, 215, 223, 228, 230, 234
memory, 47, 52, 67, 68, 83, 104–109, 112–114, 117, 124, 127, 134, 143–145, 172, 174, 202, 232. *See also* postmemory
Mendlesohn, Farah, 153
Merleau-Ponty, Maurice, 81–82
metafiction, 14, 161, 178–180, 194–195, 205, 209, 216, 229
metafictional comics, xxiv, xxv, 178–216
metafocal, 192–194, 197–204, 228–229
metalepsis, 160–162, 179–180, 190, 204
metanarrative, 17, 53, 99, 103, 115, 132, 179, 183, 187, 191, 193–204, 206, 228, 229, 233
metaphor, 12, 20, 21, 27, 82, 83, 85, 86, 94–95, 116, 148, 151, 160, 172; animal, 33, 94, 105, 108–109, 111–120; visual, xviii, 27, 67–68, 94, 103, 116, 145, 146, 152, 167, 169, 170, 176, 179, 193, 218, 232, 234. *See also* symbolism
Metz, Christian, 151
Mikkonen, Kai, xx, 12, 14, 66
mind, xx, xxii, 4, 9–10, 12, 15, 16, 28, 30, 31, 32, 35, 40, 65, 68, 70, 71, 73, 81, 83, 84, 85, 92–94, 96, 99, 100, 117, 132, 140, 152, 158, 160, 164, 178, 181, 189, 192, 204, 215, 216, 218, 220–226, 229, 231–233; social, 82. *See also* consciousness
mood, xvii, xviii, xix, xxiii, 1, 4–6, 12, 16, 20, 37, 60, 77, 78, 80, 146, 147, 157, 158, 160, 161, 168, 218, 221, 224–228, 230, 235
multimodality, 11, 12, 51, 57

Nagel, Thomas, 32

narrating-I, 10, 63, 66, 90, 96, 99
narration, xviii, 1–11, 203, 205; autobiographical, 60, 64, 69, 70; bimodal, 17, 65, 106, 108, 115, 234; comics, xx, 3, 12, 13, 17, 23, 51, 56, 65, 66, 100, 106, 150, 179, 193, 219, 227, 228, 234; embodied, 90; extradiegetic, 108, 109, 111, 140, 190, 191, 193, 199; film, 13, 20, 122; homodiegetic, xix, 190, 199; heterodiegetic, 8, 17, 116, 190; impersonal, 8, 13, 17, 107, 116, 124, 154, 168; intradiegetic, 3, 108, 134, 193, 212, 227; ironic, 2; self-reflexive, 68, 104, 108, 161, 178, 179, 192, 198, 199, 203, 205, 208, 221, 228, 234; verbal, 3, 12, 13, 108, 109, 126, 150, 199, 200, 203, 230; visual, 150–151; we, 107, 126, 128
narrative: agency, 8, 201; extradiegetic, 108, 161, 165, 166, 193, 197, 206; layers, 52, 57, 107, 117, 122; levels, 48, 51, 165, 166, 176, 208; structure, 40, 48, 99, 104, 105, 107, 108, 113, 115–117, 125, 161, 174, 194, 200, 204, 227; world, xviii, xix–xxi, xxiii, xxiv, 2–8, 11, 15, 20, 22, 26, 29, 31–40, 58, 60, 93, 111, 112, 146, 150–153, 160, 168, 172, 175, 180–185, 187, 189–192, 200, 206, 208, 210, 211, 212, 215, 220, 221, 225, 227, 228
narrativity: 6, 150; of images, 149, 150
narratology, xxv, 6, 29, 150, 217, 221; cognitive, xx, 216, 219, 222; comics, xix, 26; film, 218; post-classical, xx; visual, xiv, 149
narrator: 1, 2, 4, 7, 8, 10, 18, 29, 53, 103, 167, 168, 169, 182, 183, 185, 190, 192, 197, 198, 211; character, 1, 40, 60, 100–103, 113, 115, 122, 128, 130, 135, 181, 189, 190, 193, 201, 204, 210, 227, 235; comics, 13, 17, 113; cinematic, 13; extradiegtic, 169, 190, 199; impersonal, 53, 117; literary, 13; we, 128
nonfictional comics, xxiv, 60
Nünning, Vera, 105–106

Oatley, Keith, 65
ocularization, 3, 18, 26
One! Hundred! Demons! (Barry), 71
O'Neill, Patrick, 229–230

page: composition, xx, xxi, 214; layout, xviii, xxiii, 11, 13, 25, 50, 96, 193, 218, 229; title, 47, 56, 85, 86, 128, 129, 135, 205. *See also* layout
Palestine (Sacco), 107, 135–140
Palmer, Alan, 29, 82, 222, 225

256 • INDEX

panel: border, 40–41, 45, 50, 51, 86, 140, 141, 148, 154, 174, 203, 212, 226; composite, 13, 20, 45, 47, 88–89, 169; distribution, xxiii; frame, xx, 12, 17, 25, 41, 47, 48, 50, 51, 86, 91, 97, 110, 117, 165, 174, 201, 204, 205, 207, 208, 212; frameless, 25, 91, 117, 207, 208; repetition, xviii, 11, 19, 23, 47, 52, 57, 90, 98, 99, 123, 146, 159, 165, 193, 210; shape, xxiii, 26, 212; size, xviii, xxiii, 12, 14, 50, 57, 103, 146, 160, 162, 164, 167, 175, 176, 218; split, 40–45, 48, 184, 202; variation, xxiii, 11, 19, 23, 26, 52, 90, 97–99, 123

pattern, 6, 11, 18, 20, 22, 25, 34, 45, 46, 50, 52, 57, 73, 77, 78, 80, 86, 94, 99, 123, 128, 155, 161, 169, 190, 191, 193, 195, 197, 202, 203, 204, 206, 214, 229, 232

Peeters, Benoît, 149–150

perception, 4, 8, 9, 10, 20–24, 26, 28–41, 49, 53, 58, 60, 65, 68, 70, 72, 76, 77, 80, 83, 84, 88, 92, 93, 96, 99, 108, 111, 113, 116, 136, 146, 153, 162, 170, 181, 183, 185, 187, 191, 193, 197, 202–204, 212, 215, 217, 218, 220, 223, 224, 227, 230–233, 235; distribution of, xviii; and focalization, 1, 2, 5; optical, 17; perception shots, xvii; self-perception, 60, 72, 80, 88, 113, 116, 119, 120; subjective, xviii, 91, 100; visual, 16, 18, 19, 27, 91

perspectivation, xx, 11, 12, 16, 24, 25, 26, 193, 217, 218, 219; optical, xx, xxii, 3, 17,18, 20, 22, 25–27, 218, 219, 228

perspective, 1, 4, 5, 10, 12, 14, 16, 18–27, 35, 38, 39, 57, 66, 72, 92, 99, 100, 104–106, 112, 115, 124, 125, 137, 139–141, 153, 167, 168, 169, 176, 178, 180, 183, 192, 193, 203, 217–219, 224, 234; communal, 82; imagining-other, 106, 145; multiple, 26, 113, 140, 230, 235; narratorial, 35; optical, 18, 20, 22, 26, 36, 156, 167, 219, 228; perspectival index, 102, 234; perspectival ownership, 102, 234; situated, 102, 107, 135, 145; subjective, 61, 64, 76, 101, 135, 218; perspective-taking, 34, 113, 177, 179, 199, 204, 228, 229, 235

phenomenology, xix, xxiii, 6, 29–34, 57, 69, 72, 81, 217, 221–225; meta-phenomenology, 34, 61, 100, 102, 146, 233

photography, 52, 62, 73, 109, 128, 135, 140, 169–171, 174

place, 8, 10, 13, 17, 137, 170, 176, 191, 205, 206

plot, 3, 16, 17, 24, 29, 35, 40, 42, 48, 104, 116, 118, 125, 147, 148, 150, 194, 195, 206, 207, 218, 221, 222, 224, 227

point of view, xxiii, 1, 4, 5, 31, 32, 33, 47, 48, 61, 72, 102, 106, 113, 125, 199, 211, 215, 217; character, 142, 153; image, xviii, 20, 36, 40, 135, 146; panel, 28; sequence, 18; shot, xvii, 18, 62, 218

Pointon, Marcia, 232

Polak, Kate, 106–107, 125, 220, 223

portraiture, 15, 66, 82, 88–90, 110, 135, 137, 142, 154, 155, 202, 214, 232; composite, 88, 233; self-portraiture, 15, 61, 63, 66–68, 71, 73, 80, 81, 82, 99, 100, 135, 146, 232; tentative, 92, 111, 169

Postema, Barbara, 147, 150

postmemory, 104–107, 112–114; affiliative, 107

postmodernism, 152, 179, 181, 182, 190, 192, 204

processing, xx, 14, 15, 18, 26, 27, 65, 66, 68, 72, 92, 99, 103, 108, 111, 137, 144, 145, 147, 167, 178, 184, 192–194, 202, 204, 210, 215, 219, 220, 226, 228, 229, 235

psycho-narration, xvii, 150, 231

qualia, 28, 30, 32, 33, 35, 36, 38, 39, 53, 57, 59, 81, 93, 185, 188, 233

queerness, 15

queer theory, 70

reader: xviii–xxi, xxiii–xxv, 2, 4, 7, 9, 11, 13, 14, 17, 20, 22, 31, 33, 39, 47, 51, 52, 57, 58, 62, 65, 73, 95, 107, 113, 115, 125, 140, 146, 148, 155, 168, 170, 178, 181, 189, 199–200, 204, 206, 211, 224; engagement, xx, 2, 30, 34, 38, 57, 64, 93, 106, 134, 137, 151, 177, 179, 180, 194, 201, 215–218, 221, 222, 223, 229, 230, 234; expectation, 21, 35; experience, 3, 33, 35, 37, 64, 93, 124, 151, 205, 220, 221, 224, 228; implication, 81, 93, 145, 153, 198, 223, 229; involvement, 12, 23, 31, 38, 50, 56, 61, 144, 201, 205, 218; response, xviii, xx, 6, 48, 92, 112, 153, 216, 218, 219, 220, 226–227, 229, 235

realism, xxiv, 18, 28, 35–37, 52, 61, 65, 66, 68, 95, 104, 106, 111, 119, 125, 144, 160, 164, 167, 170, 172, 174, 176, 205, 206, 231–234

reception, 57, 59, 77, 150, 189, 219, 227, 228; theory, 6

referentiality, 68, 77, 174, 178, 179

reflexivity, 63, 179

Reinerth, Maike, 14–15

INDEX • 257

reliability, 70, 102, 125, 130, 132, 144
repetition, xviii, 11, 19, 23, 26, 47, 50, 52, 57, 67, 76, 81, 90, 94, 95, 98, 99, 123, 146, 159, 165, 193, 198, 210, 225, 232. *See also* panel, repetition
reported thought, xvii, 9, 231
representation, xx, 7, 8, 13, 58, 66, 67, 70, 76, 81, 92, 94, 102, 104, 111–115, 128, 130, 132, 160, 168, 203, 207, 215, 216, 222, 225, 228, 229, 231, 233–235; authentic, 64; of the body, 12, 70, 80, 232; of consciousness, 9, 14, 64, 72; ethics of, 106, 125; of experience, 2, 6, 11, 16; of interiority, 18, 150; media representation, 15; mental, 2, 6, 200, 222, 231; narrative, 31, 34, 103; of self, 63, 70, 233; realistic, 18, 25, 28, 164, 167, 176; self-representation, 61, 67, 68, 69; of sense perception, 217; subjective, 8, 9, 14–16, 26, 100, 223; of subjectivity, 9, 14–16, 100; verbal, 193; visual, 72, 193, 232
resonance, 32, 38, 48, 86
rhythm, xxiii, 19, 22, 23, 25, 26, 29, 153, 154, 193, 232
Richardson, Brian, 128
Ricoeur, Paul, 94
Rimmon-Kenan, Shlomith, 5
Ruthner, Clemens, 148
Ryan, Marie-Laure, 150

Safe Area Goražde (Sacco), 107, 140–141
sans paroles, xix, xxiv, 146–177. *See also* wordless comics
selfhood, 15, 60, 61, 64, 66, 67, 76, 84–86, 88, 99–100, 232; collective, 67; embodied, 15, 61, 66, 70, 99, 212, 232; social, 61, 69, 70, 71, 232; split, 15, 64, 100, 232; phenomenological view of, 70. *See also* subjectivity
self-reflexivity, xxv, 13, 15, 53, 62, 88, 99, 105, 140, 178–179, 181, 198, 205, 208, 226, 233, 234; visual, 61, 66–68, 226; unreliability, 13, 134
semiotic, channels, 12, 150; codes, 185; interplay, 193, modes, 3, 17, 194; resources, 36, 169; structure, 16, 147; tracks, 232
senses, 31, 33, 34, 57, 60, 68, 80, 81, 149, 224, 233
sequence, xviii, xxiii, 11, 12, 18, 20–25, 28, 29, 34, 39–41, 45, 47, 48, 52, 58, 86, 88, 90–92, 109–117, 119–124, 132, 147, 151, 155, 157, 159, 164, 165, 169, 174, 176, 187, 188, 191–194, 198, 200, 202, 203, 208, 214, 218, 224, 231, 233
setting, 7, 8, 18, 19, 25, 36, 40, 45, 148, 154, 164, 170, 189, 193, 219, 224, 227
shading, xviii, 12, 103, 109, 110, 111, 146, 148, 157, 158, 174, 193, 213, 218
space, 10, 11, 30, 36, 52, 53, 67, 117, 135, 151, 154, 155, 157, 158, 165, 184, 187, 190, 210, 215, 220–222, 225
speech balloon, xxi, 52, 111, 120, 122, 123, 130, 137, 140, 184, 192
Stanzel, Franz, 64
stereotypes, 108, 115, 116, 119, 123, 124, 151
Stitches (Small), 86–93, 169, 233
Stockwell, Peter, 34, 38, 50, 223–224
storyline, 11, 23, 34, 39, 49, 113, 116, 125, 155, 161, 174, 175, 184, 193, 210
storytelling, 23, 82, 111, 146, 153, 178, 193–195, 198, 201, 204, 206, 208, 210–215, 229; autobiographical, 61, 66, 231; comics, xviii, xix, 3, 27, 147, 152, 177, 179, 197, 215, 218–231; medium, 13; visual, xxiv, 16, 149
storyworld, xvii, xix, 1, 2, 6, 7, 29, 33, 35, 38, 57, 148, 152, 159, 160, 180, 182, 202, 215, 216, 218, 219, 225, 230. *See also* narrative, world; world, building
Strasen, Sven, 216
style, xviii, xx, xxi, xxiii, xxiv, 3, 6, 8, 10–12, 14–16, 31, 34, 50, 56, 57, 60–66, 72–81, 83, 84, 92, 93, 95, 99, 102, 111, 116, 126, 130, 140, 146, 149, 151, 161, 162, 165, 169, 174, 178, 180, 182–193, 205, 212, 218, 220, 225–228, 232–234; and aspectuality, 92, 116; and body, xxiv, 60, 66, 73, 76, 77, 80, 81, 183; cartoon style, 50, 62, 73, 66, 80, 140, 176, 189; choice, xx, 83, 86, 107, 180, 181, 187, 226; drawing style, 34, 50, 60, 61, 126, 140, 165, 189; and subjectivity, 63, 77–81, 93, 178, 232; visual, xx, 11, 76, 225
subjectivity, xx, xxiv, 2, 3, 8, 10, 14–16, 26, 32, 33, 36, 38, 39, 52, 57, 61, 63, 66–73, 76, 77, 79, 81–83, 86, 88, 90, 92–94, 98–100, 101, 112, 125–128, 132, 134, 135, 179, 206, 212, 222, 225, 231–234; collective, 83, 125–128, 134; communication of, 99; exploration of, xxiv, 94; expression of, 3, 8, 61, 63, 77, 231; representation of, 9, 14–16, 100; tangled, 81–93, 233. *See also* selfhood
symbolism, 39–40, 45, 48, 68, 94, 95, 116, 152, 175; animal, 68. *See also* metaphor

258 • INDEX

sympathy, 31, 38, 50, 57, 221
Szép, Eszter, 221, 224

Tangles: A Story about Alzheimer's, My Mother, and Me (Leavitt), 83–86, 90, 93, 233
text box, 12, 13, 20, 45, 62, 73, 93, 120, 137, 201
texture, 11, 31, 34, 38, 142, 225
theory of mind, 31
thinking, xix, 8, 12, 16, 60, 83, 100, 102, 120, 211, 215, 222, 225, 234
Thon, Jan-Noël, 14–15
time, 8, 10, 11, 24, 40, 44, 47, 48, 51, 52, 57, 62, 66, 67, 82, 92, 94, 96, 108, 112, 113, 115, 116, 117, 118, 124, 147, 148, 150, 151, 159, 168, 169, 182, 193, 195, 206, 221, 222
Todorov, Tzvetan, 147–148, 159
tone, 6, 16, 32, 38, 117, 146, 155, 159, 169, 198, 219, 225
truthfulness, xxiv, 65, 66, 69, 71, 93, 99, 101

uncertainty, 48, 67, 109, 115, 117, 159, 170, 220, 226
unnatural narrative, 189–193
unreliable narrative, 20, 117, 181

variation, xxiii, 11, 19, 22, 26, 52, 57, 61, 67, 76, 81, 90, 95, 97–99, 123, 193, 198, 206, 210, 232, 233. *See also* panel, variation
verbal track, xviii, xx, 13, 27, 40, 66, 95, 96, 133, 199, 232
Vermeule, Blakey, 199, 211
Versaci, Rocco, 92–93
vision, xix, 21, 25, 62, 99, 123, 185, 199, 228; communal, 216
visual track, xviii, xx, 15, 27, 40, 64, 66, 133, 199, 212
visuality, xx, 11, 219

voice, xvii, 1, 4, 5, 7–10, 13, 17, 20, 39, 41, 49, 64, 70, 86, 88, 97–99, 103, 104, 108, 109, 116, 122, 126, 128, 130, 134, 137–140, 142, 189, 190, 192, 195, 199–204, 210, 212, 214, 226, 228, 230
vulnerability, 162, 195, 221

Watson, Julia, 67, 232
Waugh, Patricia, 179
we narration, 126, 128, 134
what it's like, xix, xx, xxiii, xxiv, 2, 12, 28–58, 60, 62, 69, 72, 75, 81, 83, 93, 103, 108, 115, 117, 120, 124, 125, 139, 142, 145, 146, 147, 154, 159, 165, 172, 173, 176, 180, 181, 183, 184, 187, 192, 194, 201, 202, 207, 208, 211, 212, 215, 217, 221, 228, 233, 234, 235. *See also* qualia
White, Hayden, 104, 234
Wildfeuer, Janine, 12
witnessing, 105, 108, 111, 132
Wolf, Werner, 179
Wölfflin, Heinrich, 76
wordless: comics, xxiv, 146–177, 179, 228, 231; panels, 24, 35, 86, 197. *See also* sans paroles
world, xviii, xix, xxiii, xxiv, 2, 7, 15, 17, 25, 26, 28–30, 31–34, 39, 43, 48, 49, 52, 57, 60, 66, 70, 72, 76, 77, 80, 88, 91–92, 108, 117, 147, 148, 152, 159–162, 164, 165, 167, 170, 172, 178, 180, 183, 185, 187, 189, 191, 192, 201, 204–213, 216, 220, 221, 222, 223, 224, 226, 229, 231, 233; building, 6, 11, 14, 35, 38, 148, 179–182, 192, 198, 204, 206, 219; creation, 150, 181, 186, 194–199, 216. *See also* narrative world, storyworld
writing, 14, 17, 193–197, 199, 201, 204, 205–207; history writing, 103, 104, 144, 234; life writing, 64, 65, 69, 70, 227

Yagoda, Ben, 69

THEORY AND INTERPRETATION OF NARRATIVE
JAMES PHELAN, KATRA BYRAM, AND FAYE HALPERN, SERIES EDITORS
ROBYN WARHOL AND PETER RABINOWITZ, FOUNDING EDITORS EMERITI

Because the series editors believe that the most significant work in narrative studies today contributes both to our knowledge of specific narratives and to our understanding of narrative in general, studies in the series typically offer interpretations of individual narratives and address significant theoretical issues underlying those interpretations. The series does not privilege one critical perspective but is open to work from any strong theoretical position.

Experiencing Visual Storyworlds: Focalization in Comics by Silke Horstkotte and Nancy Pedri

With Bodies: Narrative Theory and Embodied Cognition by Marco Caracciolo and Karin Kukkonen

Digital Fiction and the Unnatural: Transmedial Narrative Theory, Method, and Analysis by Astrid Ensslin and Alice Bell

Narrative Bonds: Multiple Narrators in the Victorian Novel by Alexandra Valint

Contemporary French and Francophone Narratology edited by John Pier

We-Narratives: Collective Storytelling in Contemporary Fiction by Natalya Bekhta

Debating Rhetorical Narratology: On the Synthetic, Mimetic, and Thematic Aspects of Narrative by Matthew Clark and James Phelan

Environment and Narrative: New Directions in Econarratology edited by Erin James and Eric Morel

Unnatural Narratology: Extensions, Revisions, and Challenges edited by Jan Alber and Brian Richardson

A Poetics of Plot for the Twenty-First Century: Theorizing Unruly Narratives by Brian Richardson

Playing at Narratology: Digital Media as Narrative Theory by Daniel Punday

Making Conversation in Modernist Fiction by Elizabeth Alsop

Narratology and Ideology: Negotiating Context, Form, and Theory in Postcolonial Narratives edited by Divya Dwivedi, Henrik Skov Nielsen, and Richard Walsh

Novelization: From Film to Novel by Jan Baetens

Reading Conrad by J. Hillis Miller, Edited by John G. Peters and Jakob Lothe

Narrative, Race, and Ethnicity in the United States edited by James J. Donahue, Jennifer Ann Ho, and Shaun Morgan

Somebody Telling Somebody Else: A Rhetorical Poetics of Narrative by James Phelan

Media of Serial Narrative edited by Frank Kelleter

Suture and Narrative: Deep Intersubjectivity in Fiction and Film by George Butte

The Writer in the Well: On Misreading and Rewriting Literature by Gary Weissman

Narrating Space / Spatializing Narrative: Where Narrative Theory and Geography Meet by Marie-Laure Ryan, Kenneth Foote, and Maoz Azaryahu

Narrative Sequence in Contemporary Narratology edited by Raphaël Baroni and Françoise Revaz

The Submerged Plot and the Mother's Pleasure from Jane Austen to Arundhati Roy by Kelly A. Marsh

Narrative Theory Unbound: Queer and Feminist Interventions edited by Robyn Warhol and Susan S. Lanser

Unnatural Narrative: Theory, History, and Practice by Brian Richardson

Ethics and the Dynamic Observer Narrator: Reckoning with Past and Present in German Literature by Katra A. Byram

Narrative Paths: African Travel in Modern Fiction and Nonfiction by Kai Mikkonen

The Reader as Peeping Tom: Nonreciprocal Gazing in Narrative Fiction and Film by Jeremy Hawthorn

Thomas Hardy's Brains: Psychology, Neurology, and Hardy's Imagination by Suzanne Keen

The Return of the Omniscient Narrator: Authorship and Authority in Twenty-First Century Fiction by Paul Dawson

Feminist Narrative Ethics: Tacit Persuasion in Modernist Form by Katherine Saunders Nash

Real Mysteries: Narrative and the Unknowable by H. Porter Abbott

A Poetics of Unnatural Narrative edited by Jan Alber, Henrik Skov Nielsen, and Brian Richardson

Narrative Discourse: Authors and Narrators in Literature, Film, and Art by Patrick Colm Hogan

An Aesthetics of Narrative Performance: Transnational Theater, Literature, and Film in Contemporary Germany by Claudia Breger

Literary Identification from Charlotte Brontë to Tsitsi Dangarembga by Laura Green

Narrative Theory: Core Concepts and Critical Debates by David Herman, James Phelan and Peter J. Rabinowitz, Brian Richardson, and Robyn Warhol

After Testimony: The Ethics and Aesthetics of Holocaust Narrative for the Future edited by Jakob Lothe, Susan Rubin Suleiman, and James Phelan

The Vitality of Allegory: Figural Narrative in Modern and Contemporary Fiction by Gary Johnson

Narrative Middles: Navigating the Nineteenth-Century British Novel edited by Caroline Levine and Mario Ortiz-Robles

Fact, Fiction, and Form: Selected Essays by Ralph W. Rader edited by James Phelan and David H. Richter

The Real, the True, and the Told: Postmodern Historical Narrative and the Ethics of Representation by Eric L. Berlatsky

Franz Kafka: Narration, Rhetoric, and Reading edited by Jakob Lothe, Beatrice Sandberg, and Ronald Speirs

Social Minds in the Novel by Alan Palmer

Narrative Structures and the Language of the Self by Matthew Clark

Imagining Minds: The Neuro-Aesthetics of Austen, Eliot, and Hardy by Kay Young

Postclassical Narratology: Approaches and Analyses edited by Jan Alber and Monika Fludernik

Techniques for Living: Fiction and Theory in the Work of Christine Brooke-Rose by Karen R. Lawrence

Towards the Ethics of Form in Fiction: Narratives of Cultural Remission by Leona Toker

Tabloid, Inc.: Crimes, Newspapers, Narratives by V. Penelope Pelizzon and Nancy M. West

Narrative Means, Lyric Ends: Temporality in the Nineteenth-Century British Long Poem by Monique R. Morgan

Understanding Nationalism: On Narrative, Cognitive Science, and Identity by Patrick Colm Hogan

Joseph Conrad: Voice, Sequence, History, Genre edited by Jakob Lothe, Jeremy Hawthorn, James Phelan

The Rhetoric of Fictionality: Narrative Theory and the Idea of Fiction by Richard Walsh

Experiencing Fiction: Judgments, Progressions, and the Rhetorical Theory of Narrative by James Phelan

Unnatural Voices: Extreme Narration in Modern and Contemporary Fiction by Brian Richardson

Narrative Causalities by Emma Kafalenos

Why We Read Fiction: Theory of Mind and the Novel by Lisa Zunshine

I Know That You Know That I Know: Narrating Subjects from Moll Flanders *to* Marnie by George Butte

Bloodscripts: Writing the Violent Subject by Elana Gomel

Surprised by Shame: Dostoevsky's Liars and Narrative Exposure by Deborah A. Martinsen

Having a Good Cry: Effeminate Feelings and Pop-Culture Forms by Robyn R. Warhol

Politics, Persuasion, and Pragmatism: A Rhetoric of Feminist Utopian Fiction by Ellen Peel

Telling Tales: Gender and Narrative Form in Victorian Literature and Culture by Elizabeth Langland

Narrative Dynamics: Essays on Time, Plot, Closure, and Frames edited by Brian Richardson

Breaking the Frame: Metalepsis and the Construction of the Subject by Debra Malina

Invisible Author: Last Essays by Christine Brooke-Rose

Ordinary Pleasures: Couples, Conversation, and Comedy by Kay Young

Narratologies: New Perspectives on Narrative Analysis edited by David Herman

Before Reading: Narrative Conventions and the Politics of Interpretation by Peter J. Rabinowitz

Matters of Fact: Reading Nonfiction over the Edge by Daniel W. Lehman

The Progress of Romance: Literary Historiography and the Gothic Novel by David H. Richter

A Glance Beyond Doubt: Narration, Representation, Subjectivity by Shlomith Rimmon-Kenan

Narrative as Rhetoric: Technique, Audiences, Ethics, Ideology by James Phelan

Misreading Jane Eyre: *A Postformalist Paradigm* by Jerome Beaty

Psychological Politics of the American Dream: The Commodification of Subjectivity in Twentieth-Century American Literature by Lois Tyson

Understanding Narrative edited by James Phelan and Peter J. Rabinowitz

Framing Anna Karenina: Tolstoy, the Woman Question, and the Victorian Novel by Amy Mandelker

Gendered Interventions: Narrative Discourse in the Victorian Novel by Robyn R. Warhol

Reading People, Reading Plots: Character, Progression, and the Interpretation of Narrative by James Phelan

www.ingramcontent.com/pod-product-compliance
Lightning Source LLC
Chambersburg PA
CBHW030108010526
44116CB00005B/158